Bartending FOR DUMMIES®

4TH EDITION

by Ray Foley

WILEY

Wiley Publishing, Inc.

Bartending For Dummies® 4th Edition

Published by
Wiley Publishing, Inc.
111 River St.
Hoboken, NJ 07030-5774
www.wiley.com

Copyright © 2010 by Wiley Publishing, Inc., Indianapolis, Indiana

Published by Wiley Publishing, Inc., Indianapolis, Indiana

Published simultaneously in Canada

For general information on our other products and services, please contact our Customer Care Department within the U.S. at 877-762-2974, outside the U.S. at 317-572-3993, or fax 317-572-4002.

For technical support, please visit www.wiley.com/techsupport.

Wiley also publishes its books in a variety of electronic formats. Some content that appears in print may not be available in electronic books.

Library of Congress Control Number: 2010930965

ISBN: 978-0-470-63312-0

Manufactured in the United States of America

10 9 8 7 6 5 4 3

WILEY

About the Author

Ray Foley, a former Marine with over 30 years of bartending and restaurant experience, is the founder and publisher of *BARTENDER* Magazine, the only magazine in the world specifically geared toward bartenders and one of the very few primarily designed for servers of alcohol. *BARTENDER* Magazine is enjoying its 31st year and currently has a growing circulation of over 150,000.

Ray has been published in numerous articles throughout the country and has appeared on many TV and radio shows, including David Susskind, ABC-TV News, CBS News, NBC News, *Good Morning America,* Patricia McCann, and WOR-TV. Ray has also been featured in major magazines, including *Forbes* and *Playboy.*

Ray is the founder of the Bartender Hall of Fame™, which honors the best bartenders throughout the United States not only for their abilities as bartenders but for involvement in their communities as well.

Ray serves as a consultant to some of the United States' foremost distillers and importers. He is also responsible for naming and inventing new drinks for the liquor industry, the most popular being the Fuzzy Navel.

Ray has the largest collection of cocktail recipe books in the world, dating back to the 1800s, and is one of the foremost collectors of cocktail shakers, with 400 shakers in his collection.

He is the author of *Running a Bar For Dummies, The Ultimate Cocktail Book, The Ultimate Little Shooter Book, The Ultimate Little Martini Book, The Irish Drink Book, Jokes, Quotes, and Bartoons, The Ultimate Little Blender Book, The Best Irish Drinks, Vodka 1000, Rum 1000, Tequila 1000,* and his non-cocktail book, *God Loves Golfers Best.*

Ray has four children: Ray, William, Amy, and Ryan, and lives in New Jersey with his wife, Jaclyn.

For more information about *BARTENDER* Magazine, please contact Jackie Foley at P.O. Box 158, Liberty Corner, NJ 07938; phone 908-766-6006; fax 908-766-6607; e-mail barmag@aol.com; Web site www.bartender.com.

Dedication

This book is dedicated to all who serve the public with long hours, tired bodies, and great patience (and still have fun): bartenders.

And, of course, to Jaclyn Marie, whom I love the best, and Ryan Peter, who loves me the best.

This 4th edition of *Bartending For Dummies* is dedicated to my very good friend Hans "Peter" Nelson, 1948–2010

Author's Acknowledgments

I would like to pour out my gratitude to Tracy Boggier and the overflowing enthusiasm at John Wiley & Sons.

For mixing all the ingredients properly and adding just the right amount of garnish, Mr. Tim Gallan, the project editor of *Bartending For Dummies*.

I humbly acknowledge those at *BARTENDER* Magazine for serving this up at record speed, especially Lauren Saccone.

And for supplying all the ingredients in this mixture and their tremendous support and help, Greg Cohen at Patron Tequila, Chester Brandes, Timo Sutinen, Carolina Marino and Michael Brandes from Sobieski Vodka and Imperial Brands, Vic Morrison at McCormick Distilling, Michel Roux and Jim Nikola at Crillon Importers, the great folks at Bacardi, Jose Cuervo, Diageo, Tabasco, The Food Group, SKYY Spirits, Cointreau, Pusser's Rum, Niche Imports, Joel Fishman from Tree Ripe, Alan Lewis at C&C International, William Grant and Sons, Norton Cooper at Charles Jacquin et Cie, Bill Anderson at Infinium Spirits, all the great people at Brown-Forman, Max Shapira, Parker Beam, and Edward DiMuro from Heaven Hill Distilleries, Jose Suarez and Jake Jacobsen at Coco Lopez, the good people at Pernod Ricard, David Rotunno from Mizkan Americas, and the great people from Angostura bitters.

To Jimmy Zazzali for being a great bartender and friend, Matt Wojciak, John Cowan, Mike Cammarano, Marvin Solomon, Annelies Brandes, Jack Foley, Jr., and of course the great Hymie Lipshitz.

And the best general manager and boss, U.S. Marine, and friend, the late great William Boggier.

And a special tip to LeRoy Neiman and Lynn Quayle, George Delgado, Foster Tennant, Dave Conroy, Rene Bardel, James Howard Wilson, Aurelien de Seze, and Ryan Peter Foley.

Publisher's Acknowledgments

We're proud of this book; please send us your comments through our Dummies online registration form located at http://dummies.custhelp.com. For other comments, please contact our Customer Care Department within the U.S. at 877-762-2974, outside the U.S. at 317-572-3993, or fax 317-572-4002.

Some of the people who helped bring this book to market include the following:

Acquisitions, Editorial, and Media Development

Senior Project Editor: Tim Gallan

Acquisitions Editor: Tracy Boggier

Copy Editor: Todd Lothery

Senior Editorial Assistant: David Lutton

Technical Editor: Mike Tully

Editorial Manager: Michelle Hacker

Editorial Assistants: Rachelle S. Amick, Jennette ElNaggar

Art Coordinator: Alicia B. South

Cover Photos: © iStockphoto.com / John Burwell

Cartoons: Rich Tennant (www.the5thwave.com)

Composition Services

Project Coordinator: Patrick Redmond

Layout and Graphics: Claudia Bell, Carrie A. Cesavice, Joyce Haughey, Jennifer Mayberry, Christin Swinford, Erin Zeltner

Proofreaders: Melissa D. Buddendeck, John Greenough

Indexer: Johnna VanHoose Dinse

Publishing and Editorial for Consumer Dummies

    Diane Graves Steele, Vice President and Publisher, Consumer Dummies

    Kristin Ferguson-Wagstaffe, Product Development Director, Consumer Dummies

    Ensley Eikenburg, Associate Publisher, Travel

    Kelly Regan, Editorial Director, Travel

Publishing for Technology Dummies

    Andy Cummings, Vice President and Publisher, Dummies Technology/General User

Composition Services

    Debbie Stailey, Director of Composition Services

Contents at a Glance

Contents

Introduction

● ●

*W*hen you hear the words "Set 'em up, Joe," you better have at least a basic knowledge of more than 200 of the most called-for cocktails in your head. I say *cocktails* because a cocktail is, according to Webster, "any of various alcoholic drinks made of a distilled liquor mixed with a wine, fruit juice, etc., and usually iced."

In this book, I show you how to prepare and serve cocktails. You find all the recipes you need to mix cocktails for your guests. I show you the correct equipment to use and help you set up for parties. What's more, I also provide an excellent background on liquors, wine, and beer.

About This Book

This book is a reference that you can read now and refer to many years from now. Don't feel at all compelled to read the thing from cover to cover. I would guess that you'll mostly use this book for recipes, and the best place to find them is the A to Z recipe section (Chapter 17), which is by far the largest section of the book. Drinks are also listed by their ingredients in the index.

This book has a complete table of contents and another index of topics. Feel free to use both to find whatever information you need.

Foolish Assumptions

You don't need any special knowledge of liquor or mixology to understand this book. Having an interest in creating crowd-pleasing cocktails is definitely a plus, and having the patience to get recipes just right doesn't hurt either. Good bartenders are always trying new things in the interest of serving the tastiest beverages.

A bartender can't be made overnight, though, and a head full of recipes and facts will get you only so far. You need experience, and you must respect and like people. If you aren't a people person, all the great information in this book won't make you a bartender.

As a bartender for more than 20 years, I always enjoyed the atmosphere and people in bars and restaurants. They are there to relax and have fun. My job was to serve and be a part of the entertainment, to make the guests feel at home and relaxed, and never to be overbearing or intrusive. So a good attitude and a lot of experience are key. From here on in, I'm going to assume that you have the former and are working on the latter. You're a good person, especially because you bought this book.

How This Book Is Organized

Like all *For Dummies* books, this book is organized into parts and chapters. Each chapter is self-contained so that you don't have to read them in order. Feel free to skip around. Here's what's in each of the book's four parts:

Part 1: The Basics

In this part, I describe the bartending tools and glasses you need. I also cover some simple bartending techniques that will help you look like a pro. I tell you what you need to buy to prepare for a party, and I conclude this part with all kinds of interesting alcohol- and bartending-related tables and charts.

Part II: Short Shots from American Whiskey to Wine

I devote each chapter in this part to one of the major kinds of liquor. I tell you where they come from, how they're made, and how to store and serve them. If you wonder what gin is made of, see Chapter 10. Why does Scotch whisky have that smoky flavor? Check out Chapter 13.

Part III: The Recipes

The first chapter in this part, Chapter 17, contains more than a thousand cocktail recipes listed in alphabetical order. This chapter contains classic cocktails from years past, plus the hot cocktails of today and the future. Chapter 18 presents a few dozen trendy and interesting "martinis," and if that weren't enough, the remaining chapters in this part show you how to make punches, a few holiday cocktails, and some non-alcoholic drinks.

Part IV: The Part of Tens

Every *For Dummies* book ends with lists of ten-plus items, and this book is no exception. Chapter 21 lists ten great drinks worth trying and ten drinks I think you should avoid. Chapter 22 contains roughly ten cures for hiccups and hangovers.

The Indexes

This book has two indexes: an index of cocktails by their main ingredient and an index of topics. The cocktail index is simply another way of finding a drink in this book if you don't know its name. The topics index can help you find information in chapters other than the ones in Part III.

Icons Used in This Book

Scattered throughout the book are little pictures, which my publisher calls *icons,* in the margins next to certain blocks of text. Here's what they mean:

This icon lets you know that I'm presenting a neat hint or trick that can make your life easier.

This icon flags information that will keep you out of trouble.

This icon indicates that I'm about to tell a story or provide a little interesting background information.

I use this symbol in Part III to indicate classic drinks that every bartender should know.

Where to Go from Here

Look up some recipes. Read about Irish whiskey. Check out one of my hangover cures. This book was designed so that you can jump around.

When it comes to the recipes, I do have this bit of advice: I recommend that you use only the best ingredients when making cocktails. They represent your opinion of your guests, and you want them to have the best. In some drinks, you can get by with the cheap stuff, but in this day and age, people are drinking less and demanding higher quality. You can't go wrong when you serve the good stuff, so why serve anything else?

That said, get reading and start pouring.

Part I
The Basics

"All right, let's try this one more time. It's not that difficult — you just wiggle the cork with your thumbs until it slips gently from the bottle."

In this part . . .

*F*irst, I show you what tools and glassware you need to be a successful bartender. I then cover some basic bartending techniques. Next, I tell you what you need to buy to prepare for a party, and I conclude this part with all kinds of interesting alcohol- and bartending-related tables and charts.

Chapter 1

Just for Openers: The Right Tools and Glasses

· ·

In This Chapter

▶ Assembling the tools of the bartending trade

▶ Collecting more glasses than you can shake a drink at

· ·

*T*o bartend, you need a few essentials: good people skills, knowledge about the products you're pouring, a collection of cocktail recipes, and the proper equipment. This chapter covers equipment. (Part II can help you with product knowledge, and Part III gives you the recipes. As for people skills, you're on your own.)

The Basic Tools

The most important assets for any profession are the right tools. You need basic bar tools to mix, serve, and store your drinks. Whether you're stocking a home bar or working as a professional, your basic tools are a wine opener, cocktail shaker, and strainer.

Wine opener

The best wine opener is a *waiter's wine opener* (shown in Figure 1-1). It has a sharp blade, a corkscrew (also known as a worm), and a bottle opener. You can find this opener in most liquor stores and bar supply houses.

Another nifty wine opener is called a *Rabbit*. It's also shown in Figure 1-1.

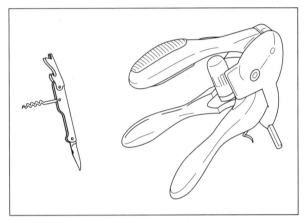

Figure 1-1: A waiter's wine opener (left) and a Rabbit.

Cocktail shaker

Figure 1-2 shows two types of shakers. The *Boston shaker* is the one that most professional bartenders use. It consists of a mixing glass and a stainless steel core that overlaps the glass. The *Standard shaker* usually consists of two or more stainless steel or glass parts and can be found in department stores or antiques stores. Many of these shakers come in different shapes and designs.

Strainer

A couple of different types of strainers are available, but the most popular is the *Hawthorn,* shown in Figure 1-3. The Hawthorn is a flat, spoon-shaped utensil with a spring coil around its head. You can use it on top of a steel shaker or a bar glass to strain cocktails.

Figure 1-2: A Boston shaker and a Standard shaker.

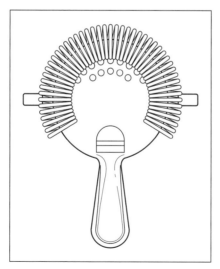

Figure 1-3: The Hawthorn strainer.

Other tools

Many of the following tools are shown in Figure 1-4:

- **Bar spoon:** A long spoon for stirring cocktails.

- **Blender:** Many types of commercial or home blenders with various speeds are available. When making a drink, always put liquid in the blender before switching it on. This will save your blade. Some blenders (but not all) can be used to make crushed ice. Check with the manufacturer or buy an ice crusher.

- **Coasters or bar napkins:** Coasters prevent rings from developing on your bar and tables. Napkins also help your guests hold their drinks.

- **Grater:** For dusting drinks with grated nutmeg, chocolate, and so forth.

- **Ice bucket:** Pick one that's large enough to hold at least three trays of ice.

- **Ice scoop or tongs:** A must for every bar. Never use your hands to scoop ice.

- **Jigger or measuring glass:** A small glass or metal measuring container that usually has a ½-oz. measurer on one side and a 2-oz. measurer on the other.

- **Knife and cutting board:** You need a small, sharp paring knife to cut fruit.

- **Large cups or bowls:** Used to hold garnishes like cherries, olives, onions, and so on.

- **Large water pitcher:** Someone always wants water.

- **Muddler:** A small wooden bat or pestle used to crush fruit or herbs.

- **Pourer:** This device gives greater control to your pouring. Many different types are available, including some with a lidded spout, which prevents insects and undesirables from entering the pourer.

- **Stirrers and straws:** Used for stirring and sipping drinks.

Figure 1-4: A collection of bar tools: (1) bar spoon, (2) blender, (3) tongs, (4) ice scoop, (5) ice bucket, (6) jigger or measuring glass, (7) knife and cutting board, (8) muddler, and (9) pourer.

Glassware

People generally expect certain drinks to be served in certain kinds of glasses. The problem is that there are more standard bar glasses than most people (and many bars) care to purchase. In any event, Figure 1-5 shows most of the glasses that you're ever likely to use to serve drinks.

I have a few things to say about some of the glasses shown in Figure 1-5:

- ✔ **Brandy or cognac snifter:** Available in a wide range of sizes; the large, short-stemmed bowl should be cupped in the hand to warm the brandy or cognac.

- ✔ **Champagne glass:** The bowl is tapered to prevent bubbles from escaping.

- ✔ **Cocktail or martini glass:** Perfect for Martinis, Manhattans, Stingers, and many other classic drinks, this glass is available in 3 to 6 oz. sizes.

- ✔ **Cordial glass:** In addition to cordials, you can use this glass to serve straight-up drinks.

- ✔ **Highball and Collins glasses:** These glasses are the most versatile. Sizes range from 8 to 12 oz.

- ✔ **Red wine glass:** This glass is available in 5 to 10 oz. sizes. Note that the bowl is wider than the bowl of a white wine glass, allowing the wine to breathe.

- ✔ **Rocks glass:** Also known as an *old-fashioned glass,* sizes of this glass vary from 5 to 10 oz. Use the 5 or 6 oz. variety and add plenty of ice.

- ✔ **Shot glass:** You can also use the shot glass as a measuring tool. It's a must for every bar.

- ✔ **Stemless glasses:** These glasses have become popular in recent years, probably because they look elegant, even if they aren't as practical as the stemmed versions.

- ✔ **White wine glass:** This glass is available in 5 to 10 oz. sizes. I advise you to stick with the smaller wine glass.

If you're planning on creating a bar at home or serving cocktails at a party, keep your glass selection small. You can simplify by using two types of glasses: a white wine glass and a red wine glass. Both are shown in Figure 1-5. You can use these two glasses for every type of cocktail (including shots, even though a shot glass is essential for every bar), plus beer and wine. Also, if you use these two glass shapes, cleaning and storing your glasses is less complicated.

Figure 1-5: Glasses, glasses, glasses.

Chapter 2

Methods to the Madness

. . . .

. . . .

*M*aking good cocktails takes more effort than just pouring ingredients into a glass. This chapter shows you how to pull off some of the little touches that make both you and your drinks look better, with the ultimate result of happier guests.

Cutting Fruit (And One Veg)

Many drinks require fruit garnishes. Your guests expect the garnish, so you can't forgo it, and you have to do it well. Presentation counts — big time. You may mix the best drinks on the planet, but if they don't look good when you serve them, no one's going to want to drink them.

Okay, I've stepped away from the pulpit now. The next few diagrams and steps show you how to cut the most common garnishes.

Lemon twists

Figure 2-1 illustrates the procedure for cutting lemon twists.

1. Cut off both ends of the lemon.

2. **Insert a sharp knife or spoon between the rind and meat of the lemon and carefully separate them.**

3. **Cut the rind into strips.**

The outside of the lemon is where the flavor lies. When adding a lemon twist to a drink, slowly rim the edge of the glass with the outside of the lemon twist and then twist a drop into the cocktail.

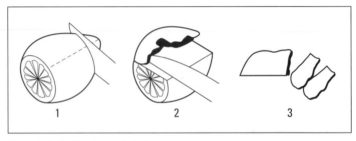

Figure 2-1: Cutting lemon twists.

Orange slices

The following steps for cutting orange slices are shown in Figure 2-2.

1. **With the ends of the orange removed, cut the orange in half.**

2. **Cut each half in half again (lengthwise).**

3. **Cut the orange quarters into wedges.**

Lime slices

The next few steps and Figure 2-3 show you how to cut lime slices.

1. **Cut off both ends of the lime.**

2. **Slice the lime in half.**

3. **Lay each half down and cut it into half-moon slices.**

Don't forget the Maraschino cherries

All kinds of drinks are garnished with Maraschino cherries, including the kid-friendly Shirley Temple and the more adult Manhattan. You can find Maraschino cherries in small jars at any food store, and the best thing about them is that you don't have to cut them before serving.

Lemon and lime wedges

Figure 2-4 illustrates the following steps for cutting wedges.

1. **Slice the lemon or lime in half the long way.**

2. **Lay the cut halves down and halve them again.**

3. **Cut wedges from the lemon or lime quarters.**

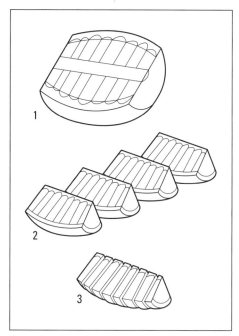

Figure 2-2: Cutting orange slices.

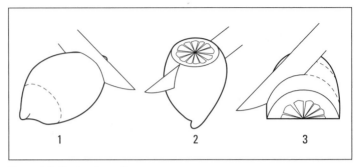

Figure 2-3: Cutting lime slices.

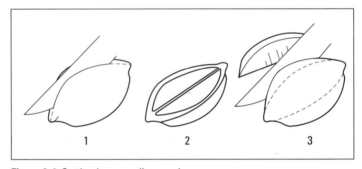

Figure 2-4: Cutting lemon or lime wedges.

Pineapple wedges

Figure 2-5 and the following steps show you how to cut pine-apple wedges.

1. **Cut off the top and bottom of the pineapple.**

2. **From top to bottom, cut the pineapple in half.**

3. **Lay the half pineapple down and cut it in half again.**

4. **Remove the core section of the pineapple quarters.**

5. **Cut wedges.**

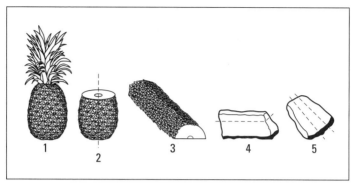

Figure 2-5: Cutting pineapple wedges.

Cucumbers

Long cucumber wedges make great garnishes for Bloody Marys and some Martinis. Here's how you slice them:

1. **Cut off the ends of the cucumber.**

2. **Cut the cucumber lengthwise into two pieces.**

3. **Cut the two pieces in half again.**

You now have four pieces of cucumber for garnish. You may also slice the cucumber in ¼-inch-thick wheels, but you probably knew that already.

Shaking a Drink

The main reasons for shaking drinks are to chill a cocktail, to mix ingredients, or to put a head on some cocktails.

As a general rule, you should shake all cloudy drinks (including cream drinks and sours), and you should stir all clear drinks. Never shake a cocktail that has carbonated water or soda. For some drinks, such as the Stinger or Martini, ask your guests whether they prefer them shaken or stirred.

To shake a cocktail in a Boston shaker, follow these steps:

1. **Put some ice cubes (if called for in the recipe) in the glass container.**

2. **Add the cocktail ingredients.**

3. **Place the metal container over the glass container.**

4. **Hold the metal and glass containers together with both hands and shake with an up-and-down motion.**

Make sure that you always point the shaker away from your guests. That way you avoid spilling anything on them if the shaker isn't properly sealed.

The two pieces of the shaker may stick together after you shake a drink. Never bang the shaker against the bar or any other surface or object; instead, gently tap it three or four times at the point where the glass and metal containers come in contact.

When pouring or straining the cocktail, always pour from the glass container.

Opening Wine and Champagne Bottles

Opening bottles doesn't take much skill — just a little practice. It's a no-brainer task, so if you don't get it right, you'll look like a fool.

Wine bottles

To open a wine bottle, you want to use a waiter's opener, which I show you in Chapter 1. Then go through these steps:

1. **Using the blade on the opener, cut the lead foil or capsule at the middle of the bulge near the bottle neck.**

2. **Remove the foil and wipe the bottle top with a cloth to remove any mold or foreign particles.**

3. **Line up the screw or worm directly over the bottle, and with gentle downward pressure, screw the worm clockwise into the cork.**

Don't break the end of the cork, and screw in just enough to extract the cork.

4. **Attach the lever of the opener to the lip on top of the bottle, and while holding the bottle firmly, slowly lift the cork straight up.**

5. **Wipe the neck of the bottle.**

6. **Present the cork to your guest and pour 1 ounce of wine into his or her glass.**

If the wine is to your guest's satisfaction, pour more. Keep your towel handy to wipe the neck of the bottle as you pour the wine for other guests.

Champagne and sparkling wine bottles

You don't use a corkscrew when opening sparkling wine bottles — you simply use your hands.

1. **Remove the wine hood and foil capsule.**

2. **Hold the bottle at an angle and point it away from you and anyone else (and anything valuable).**

3. **While holding the cork in one hand, twist the bottle with the other hand and gently remove the cork.**

Remember, twist the bottle, not the cork.

4. **Just before the cork is about to pop, place a bar towel over the cork and bottle and loosen it the rest of the way.**

The towel will catch the cork and prevent the cork from becoming a UFO.

Keep another towel handy in case the bottle bubbles over after you remove the cork. To avoid the bubbling, don't shake the bottle before opening.

Making Simple Syrup

Several cocktail recipes call for simple syrup. To make it, dissolve one part sugar in one part boiling water and reduce the mixture over low heat, stirring frequently, until it thickens. It shouldn't take more than a couple minutes.

Chapter 3

Setting Up Your Home Bar

. . . .

In This Chapter

▶ Thinking logistically when you set up your bar

▶ Purchasing the right products

▶ Figuring out how much to buy

. . . .

*W*hen doing any sort of entertaining, one of the biggest hassles is trying to figure out how to set up your bar and how much liquor you need to buy. If you throw parties all the time, or if you're trying to plan just one big party, this chapter can help.

Some Logistical Advice

Before I get into what and how much to buy, I'd like to provide some tips on how to set up a bar.

Directing traffic flow

Keep the bar as far as possible from your food and snacks. Doing so prevents large groups of people from staying in one area. If possible, base a wine and beer bar in one area and a cocktail bar in another.

Keeping your bar in or near the kitchen

Cleaning up spills is much easier in your kitchen. What's more, you do less running around when you're close to the sink and refrigerator. If you have to set up your bar in another location, put a small rug or cloth under and behind the bar to protect the floor or carpet. And no matter where your bar is, use a strong, steady table to avoid tipping or collapsing.

Serving smartly

Your party will run smoothly and your guests will be happy if you take the following suggestions to heart:

- Use nothing larger than a shot glass for shots, and don't serve doubles to your guests. You aren't doing anyone any favors by overserving. If a recipe calls for 1½ oz. of vodka, use just that amount. No mixed drink should exceed 2 oz. of liquor.

- Use lower-proof products if they're available. (See Chapter 5 for an explanation of *proof.*)

- Have punch available for those "light" drinkers.

- Have alcohol-free drinks available, including coffee and tea.

- Use only clean, fresh ice, and fresh fruit.

- If possible, chill glasses and don't put them out until five minutes before the party begins.

- When serving hot drinks, make sure that the cups or glasses have handles.

- Use a scoop, tongs, or a large spoon to serve ice. Never use your hands.

- If you don't have bottle pourers, rub wax paper over the tip of liquor bottles to prevent dripping.

- Close the bar 1 to 1½ hours before the end of the party.

- If possible, hire a professional bartender.

What You Need to Buy

When setting up your home bar, always use popular name brands. These brands aren't always the most expensive, but they tend to be the most recognizable.

The basic setup

A basic bar setup for your home and for spur-of-the-moment entertaining should consist of the following:

- One 750 ml bottle of the aperitif of your choice (Campari, Dubonnet, Lillet, and so on)
- One 750 ml bottle of sparkling wine or champagne
- Four 750 ml bottles of white domestic wine
- Two 750 ml bottles of red domestic wine
- One 750 ml bottle of dry vermouth
- One 750 ml bottle of sweet vermouth
- One 750 ml bottle of flavored vodka (stick to orange, lemon, raspberry, or vanilla flavor)
- One 750 ml bottle of vodka (domestic or imported)
- One 750 ml bottle of gin (domestic or imported)
- One 750 ml bottle of rum
- One 750 ml bottle of Scotch
- One 750 ml bottle of single-malt Scotch
- One 750 ml bottle of whiskey (domestic or imported)
- One 750 ml bottle of bourbon
- One 750 ml bottle of tequila
- One 750 ml bottle of brandy or cognac
- Twelve 12-oz. bottles of beer (domestic or imported)
- Three 750 ml bottles of the cordials of your choice (such as Irish cream, coffee liqueur or Kahlúa, Grand Marnier, triple sec, Cointreau, Sambuca, white or green crème de menthe, Galliano, B&B, Frangelico, amaretto, peach schnapps, and so on)

The approximate cost to set up this bar is between $250 and $300 using domestic and local brands. If you use premium brands, add 20 to 30 percent.

I recommend that you use mostly premium brands. You don't want your guests thinking that you'd serve them anything but the best.

A more complete bar

If you plan to serve more than the basics at your bar, add the following items to the basic bar outlined in the previous section, "The basic setup":

- ✔ One 750 ml bottle of Russian or imported vodka
- ✔ Two 750 ml bottles of flavored vodka (such as lemon, orange, vanilla, or berry)
- ✔ One 750 ml bottle of imported gin
- ✔ One 750 ml bottle of dark rum
- ✔ One 750 ml bottle of coconut-flavored rum
- ✔ One 750 ml or 1.5-liter bottle of 12-year-old Scotch
- ✔ One 750 ml or 1.5-liter bottle of single-malt Scotch
- ✔ One 750 ml bottle of Irish whiskey
- ✔ One 750 ml bottle of Canadian whisky
- ✔ One 750 ml bottle of Tennessee whiskey
- ✔ One 750 ml bottle of gold tequila
- ✔ One 750 ml or 1.5-liter bottle of V.S. or V.S.O.P. cognac
- ✔ One 750 ml bottle of port (imported)
- ✔ One 750 ml bottle of cream sherry
- ✔ One 750 ml bottle of Italian red wine
- ✔ One 750 ml bottle of French Bordeaux
- ✔ One 750 ml bottle of French Burgundy
- ✔ One 750 ml bottle of California white wine
- ✔ One 750 ml bottle of French champagne (nonvintage)
- ✔ Two 750 ml bottles of additional cordials
- ✔ Twelve 12-oz. bottles of imported beer
- ✔ Six 12-oz. bottles of light beer
- ✔ Six 12-oz. bottles of ale

The added cost of these items is about $300 to $400.

The ultimate bar

If money is no object and you want the most complete home bar, add the following items:

- ✔ Three 750 ml bottles of flavored vodka (such as lemon, orange, vanilla, or berry)
- ✔ One 750 ml bottle of imported or super-premium domestic vodka
- ✔ One 750 ml bottle of 15-year-old single-malt Scotch
- ✔ One 750 ml bottle of V.S.O.P. cognac
- ✔ One 750 ml bottle of armagnac
- ✔ One 750 ml or 1.5-liter bottle of imported brandy (from Germany, Spain, or Portugal)
- ✔ One 750 ml bottle of dark rum
- ✔ One 750 ml or 1.5-liter bottle of flavored rum
- ✔ One 750 ml or 1.5-liter bottle of gold tequila
- ✔ Two 750 ml bottles of additional cordials
- ✔ Two 750 ml bottles of vintage imported champagne
- ✔ Two 750 ml bottles of domestic champagne
- ✔ Two 750 ml bottles of French Bordeaux
- ✔ Two 750 ml bottles of French Burgundy
- ✔ Two 750 ml bottles of robust Italian red wine (Barolo)
- ✔ Two 750 ml bottles of California white wine
- ✔ Two 750 ml bottles of California red wine
- ✔ One 750 ml bottle of German white wine
- ✔ Six 12-oz. bottles of assorted microbrews
- ✔ Six cans (sizes vary depending on brand) of an energy drink (such as Red Bull or Rock Star)

The added cost of the ultimate bar is roughly $350 to $450.

Other supplies for your bar

You need one bottle of the following mixers for every five guests:

- Cola or diet cola
- Cranberry juice
- Ginger ale
- Grapefruit juice
- Lemon juice or lemon mix
- Lemon-Lime soda
- Lime juice
- Orange juice
- Pineapple juice
- Pomegranate juice
- Seltzer water or club soda
- Tomato juice
- Tonic water

You also need the following fruits and garnishes:

- Lemon twists
- Lime and lemon wedges
- Maraschino cherries
- Olives
- Orange slices

Finally, don't forget these items:

- Angostura bitters
- Salt and pepper
- Superfine sugar
- Tabasco sauce
- Worcestershire sauce

The Party Charts

I saved the best part of the chapter for last. Say you're throwing a party. How much liquor and supplies should you buy for the number of guests you invited? Tables 3-1 and 3-2 have all the answers.

How much liquor should you buy?

Table 3-1 shows the amount of liquor you should buy for the number of guests at your party. The left column lists the products, and the remaining columns list the number of bottles of that product you should purchase, depending on how many guests you're having. The last row of the table lists the total costs.

Table 3-1   How Much Liquor to Purchase for a Party

Product (750 ml Bottles)	10–30 Guests	30–40 Guests	40–60 Guests	60–100 Guests
White wine, domestic	5	5	6	8
White wine, imported	2	2	2	3
Red wine, domestic	1	2	3	3
Red wine, imported	1	1	2	2
Blush wine	1	2	2	2
Champagne, domestic	2	3	4	4
Champagne, imported	2	2	2	2
Vermouth, extra dry	1	1	2	2
Vermouth, red	1	1	1	1
Vodka	3	3	3	4

(continued)

Table 3-1 *(continued)*

Product (750 ml Bottles)	10–30 Guests	30–40 Guests	40–60 Guests	60–100 Guests
Rum	2	2	2	2
Gin	1	2	2	3
Scotch	1	2	2	3
Whiskey, American or Canadian	1	1	2	2
Bourbon	1	1	1	1
Irish whiskey	1	1	1	2
Tequila	2	2	2	3
Brandy/cognac	1	2	2	3
Aperitifs (your choice)	1	1	2	2
Cordials (your choice)	3	3	3	3
Beer (12-oz. bottles)	48	72	72	96
Total cost	**$500–$600**	**$600–$650**	**$650–$725**	**$725–$800**

With the exception of beer and wine, Table 3-1 is based on 1¾ oz. of liquor per drink. Cost totals are in U.S. dollars.

The number of products you purchase varies depending on the age of the crowd. If people between the ages of 21 and 35 dominate a crowd, increase the amount of vodka, rum, tequila, and beer by one half.

You should also consider the time of year. In the fall and winter, serve less beer. In the spring and summer, serve more beer, vodka, gin, and tequila.

Geographical location is also an important consideration when it comes to selecting your liquor stock for your guests. Consult a local bartender or liquor clerk to find out what the most popular products are in your area.

Add a little color to your rim

A great way to add color and fun to any cocktail is to use colored rim salts and sugars, such as the ones available from Stirrings. Stirrings offers 20 different flavored sugars to match just about any Martini you may be mixing, and the company also offers a Margarita rimmer made from mint, cilantro, lime, and sea salt. Check out `www.stirrings.com` for more info.

How many supplies should you buy?

Your bar needs more than just liquor. Table 3-2 lists the other supplies that you want to purchase. Again, the total costs (in U.S. dollars) are listed in the bottom row.

Table 3-2	Other Bar Supplies			
Product	**10–30 Guests**	**30–40 Guests**	**40–60 Guests**	**60–100 Guests**
Soda (2-liter bottles)				
Club soda/seltzer water	3	3	4	5
Ginger ale	2	2	2	3
Cola	3	3	3	4
Diet cola	3	3	3	4
Lemon-Lime soda	2	3	3	4
Tonic water	2	2	3	3
Juices (quarts)				
Tomato	2	2	3	3
Grapefruit	2	2	3	3
Orange	2	2	3	3
Cranberry	2	2	3	3

(continued)

Table 3-2 *(continued)*

Product	10–30 Guests	30–40 Guests	40–60 Guests	60–100 Guests
Miscellaneous Items				
Ice (trays)	10	15	20	30
Napkins (dozen)	4	4	6	8
Stirrers (1,000/box)	1	1	1	1
Angostura bitters (bottles)	1	1	1	2
Cream of coconut (cans)	1	2	2	2
Grenadine (bottles)	1	1	1	2
Horseradish (small jars)	1	1	1	2
Lime juice (bottles)	1	1	1	2
Lemons	3	4	5	6
Limes	2	3	3	4
Maraschino cherries (jars)	1	1	1	1
Olives (jars)	1	1	1	1
Oranges	1	2	2	3
Milk (quarts)	1	1	1	2
Mineral water (1-liter bottles)	2	3	4	5
Superfine sugar (boxes)	1	1	1	1
Tabasco sauce (bottles)	1	1	1	1
Worcestershire sauce (bottles)	1	1	1	1
Total cost	$45–$50	$50–$60	$60–$70	$70–$80

Chapter 4

Charts and Measures

● ●

In This Chapter

▶ Quantifying liquor from bottles to liters

▶ Knowing which wines to keep cool

▶ Counting calories and carbs

● ●

So how many ounces are in a jigger? How many glasses of beer can you pour from a keg? How many calories are in a shot of bourbon? The tables in this chapter answer these and many other burning questions.

Bottle-Related Measurements

Table 4-1 has some handy information about the capacities of standard distilled spirit bottles.

Table 4-1	Standard Bottles			
Bottle Size	**Fluid Ounces**	**Bottles/ Case**	**Liters/ Case**	**Gallons/ Case**
1.75 liters	59.2	6	10.50	2.77
1 liter	33.8	12	12.00	3.17
750 ml	25.4	12	9.00	2.38
500 ml	16.9	24	12.00	3.17
200 ml	6.8	48	9.60	2.54
50 ml	1.7	120	6.00	1.59

Wine bottles come in different sizes than distilled spirit bottles. Table 4-2 lists the capacities of standard wine bottles.

Table 4-2		Standard Wine Bottles		
Bottle Size	Fluid Ounces	Bottles/ Case	Liters/ Case	Gallons/ Case
4 liters	135.0	N/A	N/A	N/A
3 liters	101.0	4	12.00	3.17
1.5 liters	50.7	6	9.00	2.38
1 liter	33.8	12	12.00	3.17
750 ml	25.4	12	9.00	2.38
375 ml	12.7	24	9.00	2.38
187 ml	6.3	48	8.98	2.38
100 ml	3.4	60	6.00	1.59

Bar Measurements and Their Equivalents

You're likely to run across many of the measurements listed in Table 4-3.

Table 4-3	Standard Bar Measurements	
Measurement	Metric Equivalent	Standard Equivalent
1 dash	0.9 ml	$\frac{1}{32}$ oz.
1 teaspoon	3.7 ml	$\frac{1}{8}$ oz.
1 tablespoon	11.1 ml	$\frac{3}{8}$ oz.
1 pony	29.5 ml	1 oz.
1 jigger	44.5 ml	$1\frac{1}{2}$ oz.
1 miniature (nip)	59.2 ml	2 oz.
1 wine glass	119.0 ml	4 oz.
1 split	177.0 ml	6 oz.
1 half pint	257.0 ml	8 oz.
1 tenth	378.9 ml	12.8 oz.
1 "pint" (½ bottle of wine)	375.2 ml	12 oz.
1 pint	472.0 ml	16 oz.

Measurement	Metric Equivalent	Standard Equivalent
1 "quart" (1 bottle of wine)	739.0 ml	25 oz.
1 fifth	755.2 ml	25.6 oz.
1 quart	944.0 ml	32 oz.
1 imperial quart	1.14 liters	38.4 oz.
Magnum	1.53 liters	52 oz.
1 half gallon	1.89 liters	64 oz.
Jeroboam (4 bottles of wine)	3.08 liters	104 oz.
Tappit-hen	3.79 liters	128 oz.
1 gallon	3.79 liters	128 oz.
Rehoboam (6 bottles of wine)	4.43 liters	150 oz.
Methuselah (8 bottles of wine)	5.91 liters	200 oz.
Salmanazar (12 bottles of wine)	8.87 liters	300 oz.
Balthazar (16 bottles of wine)	11.83 liters	400 oz.
Nebuchadnezzar (20 bottles of wine)	14.78 liters	500 oz.

Beer Measurements

Ever wonder how much beer is in a keg? Table 4-4 tells you that and a whole lot more.

Table 4-4	Some Handy Beer Measurements	
Barrel Size	Gallons	Equivalent Measurement
1 barrel of beer	31.0 gallons	13.8 cases of 12-oz. cans or bottles
½ barrel of beer	15.5 gallons	1 keg
¼ barrel of beer	7.75 gallons	½ keg
⅛ barrel of beer	3.88 gallons	¼ keg

Drinks per Bottle

How many glasses can you get out of a standard spirit or wine bottle? Check out Table 4-5.

Table 4-5	The Number of Servings from Standard-Size Bottles		
Serving Size	*750 ml Bottle*	*1-Liter Bottle*	*1.75-Liter Bottle*
1 oz.	25	33	59
1¼ oz.	20	27	47
1½ oz.	17	22	39

Serving Temperatures for Wine

There's no sense serving good wine if you're not going to do so at the right temperature. Table 4-6 can help.

Table 4-6	Wine Serving Temperatures
Wine Type	*Temperature Range*
Full-bodied red wines	65°–68° F
Light-bodied red wines	60°–65° F
Dry white wines	50°–55° F
Sweet red and sweet white wines	42°–46° F
Sparkling wines and champagnes	42°–46° F

Calories and Carbohydrates

Most people watch what they eat, but many dieters sometimes forget to watch what they drink. Alcohol is a form of sugar, so it's high in calories. If you're counting calories or trying to keep tabs on your carbohydrate consumption, Table 4-7 can help. (For an explanation of proof, see Chapter 5.)

Table 4-7 The Number of Calories and Carbohydrates in Many Drinks

Drink	Calories	Carbohydrates (Grams)
Beer (12 oz.)		
Light beer	110	6.9
Typical beer	144	11.7
Bourbon (1 oz.)		
80 proof	65	trace
86 proof	70	trace
90 proof	74	trace
94 proof	77	trace
100 proof	83	trace
Brandy (1 oz.)		
80 proof	65	trace
86 proof	70	trace
90 proof	74	trace
94 proof	77	trace
100 proof	83	trace
Champagne (4 oz.)		
Brut	92	2.1
Extra Dry	97	2.1
Pink	98	3.7
Coffee Liqueur (1 oz.)		
53 proof	117	16.3
63 proof	107	11.2
Gin (1 oz.)		
80 proof	65	0.0
86 proof	70	0.0
90 proof	74	0.0
94 proof	77	0.0
100 proof	83	0.0

(continued)

Table 4-7 *(continued)*

Drink	Calories	Carbohydrates (Grams)
Rum (1 oz.)		
80 proof	65	0.0
86 proof	70	0.0
90 proof	74	0.0
94 proof	77	0.0
100 proof	83	0.0
Scotch (1 oz.)		
80 proof	65	trace
86 proof	70	trace
90 proof	74	trace
94 proof	77	trace
100 proof	83	trace
Tequila (1 oz.)		
80 proof	64	0.0
86 proof	69	0.0
90 proof	73	0.0
94 proof	76	0.0
100 proof	82	0.0
Vodka (1 oz.)		
80 proof	65	0.0
86 proof	70	0.0
90 proof	74	0.0
94 proof	77	0.0
100 proof	83	0.0
Whiskey (1 oz.)		
80 proof	65	0.0
86 proof	70	0.0
90 proof	74	0.0
94 proof	77	0.0
100 proof	83	0.0

Drink	Calories	Carbohydrates (Grams)
Wine (1 oz.)		
Aperitif	41	2.3
Port	41	2.3
Sherry	41	2.3
White or red table	29	1.2

A note about gluten

Many people have a problem consuming anything with gluten. If you're one of those people, you need to watch what you drink. Gluten is a protein in spelt, wheat, rye, kamut, triticale, and barley. Many beverages, especially rye, bourbon, and Scotch, are made from these products. Your best bet is to consult the label. Most products that do not contain gluten will say that they're gluten-free. For more information, check out *Living Gluten-Free For Dummies,* 2nd Edition, authored by Danna Korn and published by Wiley.

Part II
Short Shots from American Whiskey to Wine

The 5th Wave   By Rich Tennant

"I figured you for a vodka drinker. It too is completely tasteless."

In this part . . .

1 give you some background for just about every kind of liquor, including beer and wine. Each chapter tells you where a specific product comes from, how it's made, and how to store and serve it.

Chapter 5

American and Canadian Whisk(e)y

*T*his chapter deals with several kinds of whiskey: bourbon, Tennessee whiskey, rye whiskey, Canadian whisky, blended whiskey, and wheat and corn whiskies.

How Whiskey Is Made

Whiskey is distilled from grain. The type of grain or grains used determines the type of whiskey. After the grain is harvested, it's inspected, stored, and then ground into a meal and cooked to separate the starch. Malt is added, changing the starch to sugar. This mash is cooled and pumped into fermenters. Yeast is added to the mash and allowed to ferment, resulting in a mixture of grain residue, water, yeast cells, and alcohol. This mixture is then pumped into a still, where heat vaporizes the alcohol. The alcohol vapors are caught, cooled, condensed, and drawn off. This new, high-proof spirit is stored in large holding tanks. Water is added to lower the proof, and the whiskey is drawn into barrels, which are stored in a rackhouse for aging. After aging, the barrels of whiskey are drained into the tanks that feed the bottling line. In the case of blended whiskey (including Canadian), different whiskies are mixed together, and the grain spirits or other whiskies are added.

Some alcohol-related jargon

When you read about the production of alcoholic beverages, you see terms like *proof* and *distillation* thrown around. Here's what they mean.

Proof is the strength of an alcoholic beverage. In the United States, the scale is 200 degrees, with each degree equal to 0.5 percent alcohol by volume. So a 100-proof spirit is 50 percent alcohol. A 200-proof spirit is after-shave, or 100 percent alcohol.

Distillation is the process of converting a liquid by heating it into a gas or vapor, which is then condensed back into a liquid form. In the case of liquor production, the liquid is a blend of ingredients that have been fermented so that it contains some alcohol. When you heat this liquid, the alcohol it contains vaporizes first (because alcohol has a lower boiling point than, say, water). So the vapor that's trapped and later condensed back into a liquid has a much higher alcohol content than the original liquid.

Distillation is usually performed by a still. Stills come in two basic types:

- **The pot still:** A copper or copper-lined vessel with a large bottom and a long, tapered neck connected by a copper pipe to a cooling spiral tube, which is the condenser. As the liquid boils, it evaporates. The vapor rises up to the condenser, cools, and returns back to a liquid state with alcohol. Often, this process is repeated to achieve the right alcohol level.

- **The continuous still:** Also known as a *column still, patent still,* and *Coffey still,* the continuous still has tall copper columns that continually trickle liquid down over many steam-producing plates. The vapor is drawn into vents and condensed. A continuous still performs under the same principles as a pot still but can work with a constant flow of materials coming in and going out, which is great for mass production.

Bourbon

Bourbon is the best-known and probably the most popular whiskey produced in the United States. It has an amber color and a slightly sweet flavor. By law, straight bourbon must be made from at least 51 percent corn, and it must be aged in brand-new, charred oak barrels for at least two years. Although Tennessee whiskey doesn't have to be made this way, both Tennessee distilleries — George Dickel and Jack

Daniel's — also follow these guidelines. After aging, only pure water can be added to reduce the barrel proof strength to bottling (selling) proof. Scotch whiskies, Canadian whiskies, and Irish whiskies can have added caramel coloring, but bourbon can't.

A little history

Settlers on the East Coast of North America began making rye whiskey in the 1700s. They were mostly immigrants from Scotland, England, and Northern Ireland and weren't familiar with corn. In the 1790s, when the U.S. government imposed a tax on distilled spirits, the whiskey makers of Pennsylvania revolted, culminating in the Whiskey Rebellion of 1794. President Washington called out federal troops to put down the rebellion, and many distillers fled west to Kentucky, where the law wasn't imposed quite so strictly.

In Kentucky, early settlers had already begun making whiskey from corn, and the newcomers quickly learned how to use this American grain to make what would become known as *bourbon.* Its name came about because it was shipped from Bourbon County in Kentucky to places such as St. Louis and New Orleans, where it soon became known as *whiskey from Bourbon* and eventually *bourbon whiskey.*

Popular brands

When applicable, I list the varieties within each brand.

- ✔ **Baker's:** Aged for 7 years and bottled at 107 proof.
- ✔ **Basil Hayden's:** Aged for 7 years and 80 proof.
- ✔ **Blanton's Single Barrel Bourbon:** Produced in a variety of proofs and ages.
- ✔ **Booker's Bourbon:** Produced in a variety of proofs and ages.
- ✔ **Buffalo Trace Bourbon:** 90 proof and produced in a variety of ages.
- ✔ **Bulleit Bourbon:** Aged for 6 years and 90 proof.

✓ **Distillers' Masterpiece:** Available in 18- and 20-year-old versions. The 18-year-old is finished in cognac casks, and the 20-year-old is finished in Geyser Peak port wine casks.

✓ **Elijah Craig Bourbon:** 12 years old and 94 proof.

✓ **Evan Williams Black Label Kentucky Straight Bourbon Whiskey:** 7 years old and 86 proof.

✓ **Evan Williams Single Barrel Vintage Kentucky Straight Bourbon Whiskey:** Vintage-dated and 86.6 proof.

✓ **I.W. Harper Kentucky Straight Bourbon Whiskey:** 86 proof; very limited distribution.

✓ **Jim Beam:** 4 years old and 80 proof. Beam Choice: 5 years old and 80 proof.

✓ **Jim Beam Black:** Aged for 8 years and 86 proof.

✓ **Knob Creek:** Aged for 9 years and bottled at 100 proof.

✓ **Old Charter Kentucky Straight Bourbon Whiskey:** 8 years old and 80 proof; 10 years old and 86 proof. The Classic 90: 12 years old and 90 proof. Proprietor's Reserve: 13 years old and 90 proof.

✓ **Old Crow Bourbon:** Aged for 3 years and 80 proof.

✓ **Old Fitzgerald Kentucky Straight Bourbon Whiskey:** 86 and 90 proof. Very Special Old Fitzgerald (Bourbon Heritage Collection): 8 years old and 100 proof; very limited distribution.

✓ **Old Grand-Dad:** 86 proof. Bottled in Bond: 100 proof. 114 Barrel Proof.

✓ **Wild Turkey:** 80 proof. Wild Turkey Rare Breed: a blend of 6-, 8-, and 12-year-old stocks that's usually around 108 proof. Wild Turkey Old Number 8 Brand: 101 proof. Kentucky Spirit: 101 proof.

✓ **Woodford Reserve:** 7 years old and 90.4 proof.

Specialty bourbons

As you discover bourbon whiskey, you come across several different types within this category, including small batch and single barrel, which are more expensive and harder to find.

Small batch

A *small batch* bourbon is produced and distilled in small quantities of approximately 1,000 gallons or fewer. In other words, it's made in small batches, but you probably figured that out. The following are small batch bourbons:

- ✔ Baker's
- ✔ Basil Hayden's Small Batch
- ✔ Booker's Small Batch
- ✔ Elijah Craig
- ✔ Knob Creek
- ✔ Maker's Mark Kentucky Homemade Bourbon
- ✔ Old Rip Van Winkle and Pappy Van Winkle's Family Reserve
- ✔ Ridgemont Reserve 1792
- ✔ Woodford Reserve Distiller's Select

Single barrel

Single barrel bourbon also has a self-explanatory name. Each bottle contains bourbon whiskey from just one barrel, with no blending. Some single barrel bourbons include

- ✔ Benchmark/XO Single Barrel Kentucky Straight Bourbon
- ✔ Blanton's Single Barrel Kentucky Straight Bourbon
- ✔ Elijah Craig Single Barrel Kentucky Straight Bourbon
- ✔ Evan Williams Single Barrel Vintage Kentucky Straight Bourbon
- ✔ Henry McKenna Single Barrel Kentucky Straight Bourbon
- ✔ Jack Daniel's Single Barrel
- ✔ Wild Turkey Kentucky Spirit Single Barrel Kentucky Straight Bourbon

A limited number of distilleries produce a whiskey bottled at *barrel proof*, which enters the barrel at 125 proof and gains strength during aging, so it sometimes exceeds the 125-proof legal limit. Pretty potent stuff — drink at your own risk.

Tennessee Whiskey

Tennessee whiskey differs from bourbon in that it's mellowed (altered) through sugar-maple charcoal before it's aged. Although both whiskies are usually filtered before bottling, the sugar-maple charcoal adds a different flavor to Tennessee whiskey.

The following are the only two producers of Tennessee whiskey:

- **George Dickel Tennessee Whiskey:** Old No. 8 Brand: 80 proof. Old No. 12 Superior Brand: 90 proof. Barrel Reserve: 10 years old and 86 proof.

- **Jack Daniel's Tennessee Sour Mash Whiskey:** Black Label: 86 proof. Green Label: 80 proof, available only in the United States. Gentleman Jack: 80 proof.

Rye Whiskey

Distilled at no more than 160 proof, *rye whiskey* is a fermented mash or grain containing at least 51 percent rye. It's matured in new charred oak barrels for a minimum of two years. Rye has a strong, distinctive flavor. For quite some time, rye has taken a back seat to bourbon in the preferences of American whiskey drinkers, but rye has seen a resurgence lately. Whiskey connoisseurs are rediscovering the old brands, and new ones are popping up as well. Here's a sampling of what's available:

- **Jim Beam Rye:** 80 proof.

- **Michter's Straight Rye:** Aged in bourbon barrels for 4 years.

- **Old Overholt:** One of the early brands of American straight rye; 4 years old and 80 proof.

- **Redemption Rye:** 92 proof.

- **(ri)[1]:** New in 2008 by Jim Beam; bottled at 92 proof.

- **Rittenhouse:** 80 and 100 proof.

- **Russell's Reserve Rye:** 90 proof.

- **Templeton Rye:** 80 proof; produced in Iowa.

- **Thomas H. Handy Sazerac:** 127.5 proof whiskey.

- ✔ **Van Winkle Family Reserve Rye:** 95.6 proof and aged for 13 years.
- ✔ **WhistlePig Straight Rye:** 100 proof.
- ✔ **Wild Turkey Rye:** 80 proof.

Canadian Whisky

Canadian whisky (spelled without the *e*) is a blend of aged grain whisky and heavier flavored blended whiskies that's aged in oak casks for a minimum of three years. There are no limitations as to the grain, distilling proof, formula, or type of barrels used. Each distiller is allowed to make its own type of whisky. Most Canadian whisky is aged in white oak barrels. Canadian whiskies sold in the United States are blends bottled at a minimum of 80 proof and are generally three years old or older. Popular brands include

- ✔ **Black Velvet:** 80 proof and 3 years old.
- ✔ **Canadian Club:** 80 proof and 6 years old.
- ✔ **Canadian Mist:** 80 proof and 3 years old.
- ✔ **Crown Royal, Crown Royal Special Reserve, and Crown Royal XR:** All 80 proof.
- ✔ **Seagram's VO:** 86 proof; aged for 6 years (the *VO* means "Very Own" or "Very Old").
- ✔ **Tangle Ridge:** 100-percent rye whisky aged for 10 years in oak barrels, blended with sherry and other natural flavors, and then recased before bottling.

Blended Whiskey

American blended whiskey is a mixture of at least 20 percent bourbon, corn, or rye whiskies and neutral spirits or grain whiskey. Sometimes, additional coloring and enhancers are added. Blends are bottled at no less than 80 proof.

Whiskies blended with neutral spirits have a label on the back of the bottle that states the percentages of straight and neutral spirits. The most famous and biggest seller of blended whiskey is Seagram's 7 Crown. It, of course, is part of that famous drink, the Seven and Seven.

Other brands of blended whiskey include the following:

- Barton Reserve
- Carstairs
- Fleischmann's
- Imperial
- Mattingly & Moore

Wheat and Corn Whiskey

Wheat whiskey must contain 51 percent of a single type of grain and must be aged a minimum of two years in a new, charred, white oak barrel. As a commercial product, this type of whiskey is relatively new. (For all I know, some wheat farmers in the Midwest have been making this stuff for a couple of centuries, but you couldn't buy it at the local liquor store until recently.) The only brand available at press time is Bernheim Original Straight Wheat Whiskey (90 proof). More brands are likely to follow.

Corn whiskey is similar to bourbon, except that it must be made of a mash consisting of at least 81 percent corn. It's still called *moonshine* or *white lightning* in the southern United States. Available brands include

- Dixie Dew
- Georgia Moon
- J.W. Corn
- Mellow Corn

Storing and Serving Suggestions

American whiskey and Canadian whisky can be served straight, on ice, with water or seltzer, or mixed as a cocktail. Store an unopened bottle in a cool, dry place. After opening, a typical bottle should have a shelf life of at least two years.

Chapter 6

Aperitifs, Cordials, and Liqueurs

In This Chapter

▶ Serving up some tasty before-dinner drinks

▶ Exploring the vast world of cordials and liqueurs

*T*his chapter is a catchall for a handful of different liquor categories. Aperitifs were developed specifically as pre-meal beverages. Cordials and liqueurs have a variety of purposes. Some are great mixers, others are good after-dinner drinks, and a few make good aperitifs as well. Go figure.

Aperitifs: Great Ways to Whet Your Appetite

Aperitif comes from the Latin word *aperire,* meaning *to open.* An aperitif is usually any type of drink you'd have before a meal. Most aperitifs are usually low in alcohol and mild-tasting.

You can drink many of the cordials and liqueurs listed later in this chapter as aperitifs as well. I don't have much more to say about aperitifs other than to list the individual products that are available, such as the following:

▸ **Amer Picon (French):** A blend of African oranges, gentian root, quinine bark, and some alcohol. Usually served with club soda or seltzer water with lemon.

▸ **Campari (Italian):** A unique combination of fruits, spices, herbs, and roots.

✔ **Cynar (Italian):** A bittersweet aperitif that's made from artichokes. Best when served over ice with a twist of lemon or orange.

✔ **Dubonnet (American):** Produced in California and available in blond and red. Serve chilled.

✔ **Fernet-Branca (Italian):** A bitter, aromatic blend of approximately 40 herbs and spices (including myrrh, rhubarb, camomile, cardamom, and saffron) in a base of grape alcohol. Mint-flavored Fernet-Branca is also available. It's called Branca Menta.

✔ **Jägermeister (German):** Composed of 56 botanicals, including citrus peel, aniseed, licorice, poppy seeds, saffron, ginger, juniper berries, and ginseng.

✔ **Lillet (French):** Made in Bordeaux from a blend of 85 percent fine Bordeaux wines and 15 percent fruit liqueurs. Lillet Blanc is made from sauvignon blanc and semillon and has a golden color. Lillet Rouge is made from merlot and cabernet sauvignon and has a ruby-red color.

✔ **Pernod (French):** Comes from the essence of badiane (anise star) and from a spirit made from natural herbs, such as mint and balm.

✔ **Punt e Mes (Italian):** Vermouth with bitters and other botanicals added.

✔ **Ricard (French):** Made from anise, fennel (green anise), licorice, and other Provençal herbs.

✔ **Suze (French):** French bitters distilled from gentian root. Gentian is grown in the Auvergne and Jura regions and is a large, originally wild flower with golden petals.

Cordials and Liqueurs

Cordial comes from the Latin word *cor,* meaning *heart,* and *liqueur* is derived from the Latin meaning *melt* or *dissolve.* Both words are interchangeable, although liqueurs are more popular in Europe, and cordials are more popular in the United States. From this point on, I use the word *cordial* to describe both.

FABLES & LORE

What's Angostura?

Angostura aromatic bitters are a blend of rare tropical herbs and spices used to flavor and season a great variety of food dishes and certain alcoholic and nonalcoholic drinks.

Dr. Johann Siegert, surgeon-general in the army of the great liberator of South America, Simón Bolívar, first compounded the formula in 1824. Siegert's headquarters were in the port of Angostura in Venezuela, a city now known as Ciudad Bolívar. The doctor experimented for four years before finding the exact formula that he was after. He wanted to use the bitters to improve the appetite and well-being of his troops. Sailors pulling into the port discovered the bitters and bought bottles to carry away with them. Soon the fame of Angostura bitters spread around the world. Angostura bitters are used in many cocktails, including the Manhattan, the Old Fashioned, and the Rob Roy.

Cordials are made by infusing the flavor of fruits, herbs, spices, and other plants with a spirit, such as brandy or whiskey. As you discover from the list later in this chapter, cordials come in many different varieties. Most are sweet. In fact, cordials sold in the United States contain up to 35 percent sugar and must contain a minimum of 25 percent sugar by weight.

Within the cordial category are crèmes and fruit-flavored brandies. *Crèmes* have a high sugar content, which makes them, well, creamy. Usually, the name of such a cordial indicates what it tastes like. Crème de banana tastes like bananas, and apricot brandy tastes like apricots.

The world has more cordials than any one person can list. What I try to do here is describe the ones that you're likely to see in the recipes in this book. Someone somewhere probably makes a soy-sauce-and-aloe-flavored cordial, and maybe it tastes great, but nobody I know is ever going to ask for it, so I don't list it. Instead, I give you the following common cordials:

> ✓ **99 Bananas** is a rich-flavored, 99-proof banana cordial. Also available are 99 Apples, 99 Oranges, and 99 Blackberries.

✔ **Absente** is a product from France that's similar in flavor to absinthe but without the bad reputation or toxic side effects (see below).

✔ **Absinthe** is often called the Green Muse because of its pale greenish color and the dreamy state it induces in imbibers. Absinthe is 65 percent alcohol, or a whopping 130 proof. Because it contains wormwood (a plant that many believe is a narcotic and also toxic, causing death and/or madness), absinthe was for many years outlawed in most of the world. The fears over absinthe's alleged lethality were probably overstated, and absinthe is now widely available.

✔ **Agavero Tequila Liqueur** is a blend of blue Añejo and Reposado tequilas with natural damiana flower.

✔ **Akvavit** is a barley-and-potato distillate that's clear, colorless, and potent. It's a Scandinavian drink originally made in Aalborg, Denmark.

✔ **Alizé** is a blend of passion fruit juices and cognac. It's available in several varieties.

✔ **Amaretto** is an almond-flavored cordial.

✔ **Amarula Cream Liqueur** is made from the fruit of the marula tree from Africa and added to the highest quality cream.

✔ **Anisette** gets its name from the aniseed, which imparts its rich, licorice-like flavor to this cordial. Practically every Mediterranean country has a variation of the anise liqueur, such as Sambuca in Italy, Ouzo in Greece, and so on.

✔ **Applejack** is distilled from the mash of apples and is the best-known and most typical fruit brandy in the United States.

✔ **Baileys Irish Cream** is made from fresh dairy cream, Irish whiskey, and natural flavorings. The Irish whiskey acts as a preservative for the cream, which is why Baileys doesn't need to be refrigerated. It also comes in caramel and mint chocolate flavors.

✔ **Bärenjäger Honey Liqueur** is a honey liqueur made in Germany.

✔ **Benedictine** contains more than 27 herbs and spices, including cardamom, nutmeg, cloves, myrrh, and vanilla. B&B, which stands for Benedictine and Brandy, is a blend of Benedictine and cognac.

✔ **Black Haus** is a schnapps made from blackberries.

✔ **Blue Curaçao** is essentially the same as Orange Curaçao except that a deep blue color has been added, and it's slightly lower in proof. (See Chapter 5 for an explanation of proof.)

✔ **Bols** produces a complete line of flavored brandies and cordials.

✔ **Bunratty Meade** is a blend of honey, selected herbs, and wine.

✔ **Calvados** is an applejack made in Normandy and aged about four years.

✔ **Carolans Irish Cream** combines Irish spirits and whiskey with rich double cream and subtle flavors, principally honey.

✔ **Celtic Crossing** is created by combining Irish malt whiskies and cognac with a hint of honey.

✔ **Chambord** is made with framboise (small black raspberries) and other fruits and herbs combined with honey. It has a dark purple color.

✔ **Chartreuse** comes in green and yellow varieties and is made with more than 130 herbs and spices. It's normally sold at 4 years of age (aged in the bottle), but 12-year-old labels are also produced.

✔ **Chocoviac** is a smooth, aged cognac blended with dark chocolate from Switzerland and a rich vanilla from Madagascar.

✔ **CocoRibe** is a liqueur of wild island coconuts laced with Virgin Island rum.

✔ **Cointreau** is a clear cordial made from a blend of sweet and bitter oranges.

✔ **Crème de Cacao** is made from vanilla and cacao beans. It comes in white and brown varieties.

- **Crème de Cassis** is made from black currants imported from France and other selected fruits and berries.
- **Crème de Framboise** is a raspberry-flavored liqueur.
- **Crème de Menthe** is made from mint and spearmint. It comes in green and white (clear) varieties.
- **Crème de Noyaux** is made from a combination of sweet and bitter almonds.
- **Cuarenta Y Tres (Licor 43)** is made from a secret formula containing vanilla beans, citrus, and other fruits found in the Mediterranean, as well as carefully selected aromatic plants.
- **DeKuyper Schnapps** come in several flavors, including Blueberry, ButterShots, Hot Damn!, Key Largo, Old Tavern Rootbeer, Peachtree, Peppermint, Sour Apple, Tropical, Spearmint, and WilderBerry.
- **Der Lachs Goldwasser** is a mysterious blend of 25 herbs, spices, and real 22-karat gold flakes.
- **Domaine de Canton** is fresh baby ginger married with fine eau de vie (a clear, colorless fruit brandy), V.S.O.P., and X.O. Grande Champagne cognacs crafted with fresh Tahitian vanilla beans and Tunisian ginseng.
- **Drambuie** is made with the finest Highland malt whiskies, no less than 15 years old, heather honey, and special herbs that are prepared in secret.
- **Echte Kroatzbeere** is made with blackberries.
- **Fragoli** is made with hand-picked wild strawberries.
- **Frangelico** is made from wild hazelnuts blended with berries and flowers.
- **Galliano** is a golden-colored liqueur made with lavender, anise, yarrow musk, and juniper and blended with exotic flavors, such as vanilla and fragrant balm. In all, it contains more than 30 ingredients.
- **Godet Belgian White Chocolate Liqueur** is a blend of Belgian white chocolate and aged cognac.
- **Godiva Liqueur** is flavored with the same chocolate used in Godiva chocolate.
- **Goldschläger** is an 87-proof cinnamon schnapps liqueur imported from Switzerland. It features real flakes of 24-karat gold.

✔ **Grand Marnier** is made from wild oranges and cognac.

✔ **Hpnotiq** is a blend of cognac, triple-distilled vodka, and natural tropical fruit juices.

✔ **Illy Espresso Liqueur** is an espresso liqueur made in Italy.

✔ **Irish Mist** is a derivation of a heather wine.

✔ **Kahlúa** is made from coffee and the alcohol distilled from cane sugar. People also discern a chocolate flavor, but the recipe contains no chocolate. Its origin is a mystery. Some say Arabia; others say Turkey or Morocco. Today, as indicated by the sombrero on the label, it's made in Mexico using Mexican coffee beans.

✔ **KeKe Beach Key Lime Cream Liqueur** blends the flavor of Key lime pie with a hint of graham.

✔ **Kirsch** is distilled from cherries.

✔ **Kirschwasser** is a true fruit brandy or *eau de vie* distilled from fermented cherries and cherry pits. It's clear and dry.

✔ **Kummel** is made from caraway seeds, cumin, and aniseed. It's most esteemed as a digestive.

✔ **L'ile Supreme** combines tropical rum with an assortment of fruits, including orange, lychee, mango, lime, and goyavier.

✔ **Limoncello** is made from the finest grain spirits infused with the juice and peel of lemons from Italy's southern Amalfi coast.

✔ **Lochan Ora** is a Scotch whisky liqueur flavored with honey.

✔ **Luxardo** is the original maraschino liqueur.

✔ **Malibu** is a clear blend of coconut and Caribbean rum.

✔ **Marie Brizard Liqueurs** offers a complete line of extremely fine liqueurs from A to Z.

✔ **Midori** is a green, honeydew melon spirit.

✔ **Mozart Chocolate Liqueur** is made from praline-nougat and milk chocolate blended with kirsch.

✔ **Nassau Royale** is predominantly citrus-flavored with undertones of coffee.

✔ **Opal Nera** is black Sambuca with an added lemon twist.

✔ **Orange Curaçao** is made from the peel of the bittersweet Curaçao orange, which grows on the Dutch island of Curaçao in the West Indies.

✔ **Orangecello** is a combination of orange juice, orange peels, and grain spirits from Italy.

✔ **Ouzo** is an anise-based liqueur from Greece.

✔ **PAMA Pomegranate Liqueur** is made with all-natural California pomegranates.

✔ **Passoa Passion Fruit Liqueur** is a blend of Brazilian maracuja, or yellow passion fruit, with red berries and citrus and tropical fruits.

✔ **Patrón Citronge** is an orange-flavored liqueur from the famous tequila maker.

✔ **Pucker Flavored Cordials** are available in Raspberry, Peach, Watermelon, Sour Apple, Grape, Cheri-Beri, Strawberry Passion, and Island Blue.

✔ **Rock & Rye** is an old-time American favorite made with a special blend of aged rye whiskies and fresh fruit juices.

✔ **Rumple Minze** is a peppermint schnapps imported from Germany.

✔ **Sabra** is an Israeli chocolate-orange liqueur originally made in the 1960s from the sabra cactus that grows in Israel and around the southern and eastern Mediterranean. There is also a coffee version.

✔ **Sambuca** is made from two main ingredients, witch elderbush (*sambucus nigra,* hence the name of the drink) and licorice, which gives this liqueur its dominant taste. It's related to the licorice-flavored anise and pastis drinks of France, ouzo of Greece, mastika of the Balkans, and raki of Turkey.

✔ **Schönauer Apfel Schnapps** is produced from wheat and rye and then blended with the juices of apples from "Altes Land," one of the best-known fruit-growing areas of Germany.

✔ **Sloe Gin** has a confusing name. It's not a gin (although small amounts of gin are used in its making). *Sloe* comes from *sloeberry,* a small, deep-purple wild plum that grows principally in France.

✔ **Southern Comfort** is made from a secret recipe that contains bourbon, brandy, bitters, peaches, and herbs.

✔ **St-Germain Elderflower Liqueur** is made in France from freshly hand-picked elderflower blossoms.

✔ **Strega,** the Italian word for *witch,* is made from more than 70 botanicals.

✔ **Tequila Rose Cocoa Cream** adds the taste of fresh strawberries and chocolate to the cream of Tequila Rose.

✔ **Tequila Rose Java Cream** is the taste of coffee added to the cream of Tequila Rose.

✔ **Tequila Rose Strawberry Flavor Cream Liqueur and Tequila** is a blend of strawberry, cream, and a hint of tequila.

✔ **Tia Maria** is a Jamaican rum liqueur based on Blue Mountain coffee extracts and local spices.

✔ **Triple Sec** is made principally from imported orange peel, the wild Curaçao orange, and the sweet, aromatic Spanish Valencia. Triple sec means *triple dry* or *three distillations.*

✔ **Tuaca** is an aged brandy flavored with orange and other fruits and botanicals indigenous to the Tuscan region of Italy.

✔ **Ty-Ku Liqueur** is a sake and Asian vodka-based liqueur with more than 20 all-natural fruits and botanicals.

✔ **Vandermint** is a Dutch minted-chocolate liqueur.

✔ **Vermeer** is an outstanding Dutch chocolate cream liqueur.

✔ **Wild Spirit** is a special recipe of strong spirits, natural wild herbs, and a touch of fire-brewed cocoa.

✔ **Yukon Jack** is a Canadian whisky-based liqueur with citrus and herbs.

Storing and Serving Suggestions

As I mention earlier in this chapter, you should serve aperitifs before a meal. Most can be served either straight up or on the rocks.

Most cordials are served after dinner or mixed as cocktails and served over crushed ice as frappés.

Store an unopened aperitif, cordial, or liqueur bottle in a cool, dry area that's always out of direct light. After a bottle is opened, it should have a shelf life of three years.

Chapter 7

Beer

● ●

● ●

*B*asically, *beer* is an alcoholic beverage that's fermented and brewed from barley, hops, water, and yeast (along with corn and rice in some recipes). Beer has been brewed for thousands of years, and today, thousands of different varieties of beer are enjoyed throughout the world. The United States has more than 900 microbrews (made by small, independent brewers) alone. Germany brags of having more than 1,200 breweries.

Beer enjoys the distinction of coming to the Americas on the *Mayflower* and, in fact, seems to have played a part in the Pilgrims' decision to land at Plymouth Rock instead of farther south, as intended. A journal written by one of the passengers — which is now in the U.S. Library of Congress — states in an entry from 1620 that the *Mayflower* landed at Plymouth because "we could not now take time for further search or consideration, our victuals being much spent, especially our beer. . . ."

The first commercial brewery in America was founded in New Amsterdam (New York City) in 1613. Many patriots owned their own breweries, among them General Israel Putnam and William Penn. Thomas Jefferson was also interested in brewing and made beer at Monticello. George Washington even had his own brew house on the grounds of Mount Vernon, and his handwritten recipe for beer — dated 1757 and taken from his diary — is still preserved.

How Beer Is Made

The beer-brewing process begins with pure water, corn grits, and malted barley. Malted barley is the basic ingredient and is often referred to as the "soul of beer." It contributes to the color and characteristic flavor of beer. What does *malted* mean? It means that the barley has been steeped or soaked in water and allowed to *germinate,* or grow.

Brewing beer is a step-by-step process:

1. The corn grits and malt are cooked and blended to create mash.

2. A sugary liquid, called *wort,* is extracted from the mash. (The remaining solid portion of the mash, the brewer's grain, is sold as feed.)

3. The wort is transferred to the brew kettles, where it's boiled and hops are added. Hops are responsible for the rich aroma and the delicate bitterness in beer.

4. The wort then moves to the wort cooler.

5. Sterile air is added next, along with yeast, which converts sugar into alcohol and carbon dioxide. The wort moves to fermentation tanks for a carefully controlled time period.

Brewers can use two different categories of yeast: bottom and top.

- **Bottom yeast** settles to the bottom of the tank after converting all the sugar, and the resulting beer is a lager.

- **Top yeast** rises to the top of the tank when it's done with the sugar, and the beer it produces is an ale.

Types of Beer

You've probably seen some of the following terms on beer labels, or maybe you've heard them in beer commercials.

- ✔ **Ale** is top-fermented beer. It's a little bitter, usually tastes hoppy, and generally has a higher alcohol content than lagers.

- ✔ **Bitter** beer is a strong ale, usually English, with, as the name implies, a bittersweet taste.

- ✔ **Bock** beer is a dark, strong, slightly sweet lager brewed from caramelized malt.

- ✔ **Ice** beer is brewed at colder-than-normal temperatures and then chilled to below freezing, forming crystals. The crystals are filtered out, leaving a smoother-tasting beer with a slightly higher alcohol content.

- ✔ **Lager** is a bottom-fermented beer stored at very low (cold) temperatures for a long period of time (several months). The word *lager* is German for *to store.*

- ✔ **Lambic** beer is brewed in Belgium. Ingredients such as peaches, raspberries, cherries, and wheat are added during the brewing process.

- ✔ **Light** beer has fewer calories and less alcohol.

- ✔ **Low-calorie beer** has even fewer calories than light beer (and some would say even less flavor). These beers generally have 55–65 calories per serving.

- ✔ **Malt liquor** is fermented at a higher temperature than other beers, which results in a higher alcohol content.

- ✔ **Pilsner** is a light, hoppy, dry lager.

- ✔ **Sake** is beer brewed and processed from rice. (Some consider sake a wine.) Sake is served warm or at room temperature.

- ✔ **Stout** is an ale produced from heavily roasted barley. It's darker in color and has a slightly bitter flavor.

- ✔ **Trappist** beer is brewed in Belgium or the Netherlands by Trappist monks. It contains high levels of alcohol and is usually dark in color.

- ✔ **Wheat** beer is made, as you might expect, with wheat. It's usually garnished with a lemon and sometimes raspberry syrup.

Storing and Serving Suggestions

In the United States, beer is served cold (40 degrees Fahrenheit). Lower temperatures tend to dull the taste, so consider 40 degrees the lower limit. Store beer away from sunlight, or you'll have skunked beer, which is never pleasant. Most beers now have labels that say when they were brewed or when to remove them from the shelf.

For much more information on beer, check out *Homebrewing For Dummies* by Marty Nachel, published by the fine folks at Wiley Publishing, Inc.

Chapter 8

Brandy

● ●

● ●

*B*randy is made in most countries that produce wine. Brandy is derived from the Dutch term *brandewijn,* meaning *burnt wine.* The term was known as *branntwein* or *weinbrand* in Germany, *brandevin* in France, and *brandywine* in England. Today, the word has been shortened to *brandy.*

What Is Brandy?

Brandy is made by distilling wine or fruit and then aging it in oak barrels. The difference in brandy varies from country to country. Soil, climate, grapes, production methods, and blending give each brandy its own unique flavor and style.

When brandy is produced, it undergoes four basic processes: fermentation of the grape, distillation to brandy, aging in oak barrels, and blending by the master blender.

American Brandy

Brandy was introduced to California more than 200 years ago by Spanish missionaries. Taking advantage of the healthy soil, good climate, and water, American brandy production primarily occurs in the San Joaquin Valley. California produces the largest percentage of American brandy, and all California brandy has to be aged a minimum of two years. Here are some popular brands:

- **Carneros Alambic:** The first *alambic* (cognac-style) brandy in California.

- **Christian Brothers:** This brandy is processed and aged in Napa Valley.

- **E&J Gallo:** Gallo produces E&J Brandy (Gold), E&J V.S.O.P. Brandy, and E&J White Brandy.

- **Germain-Robin:** Another excellent alambic brandy from California.

- **Korbel:** A California brandy from the Korbel Distillery.

Brandies from Around the World

Check out the following list to find the names of just a few brands that are worth trying.

- **Asbach Uralt (Germany):** The top-selling brandy in Germany.

- **Aztec DeOro (Mexico):** A 12-year-old brandy made using the solera method. (See the sidebar, "The solera method," later in this chapter.)

- **Brandy de Jerez (Spain):** Produced in southern Spain.

- **Carlos I (Spain):** Ranked among the finest in the world.

- **Don Pedro (Mexico):** Pot-stilled and solera-aged.

- **Fellipe II (Spain):** The number-one-selling Spanish brandy in the United States.

- **Metaxa (Greece):** The most famous Greek brandy.

- **Presidente (Mexico):** The largest-selling brandy in Mexico and the world.

- **Stock 84 (Italy):** Produced by Stock Distillery of Trieste, Italy.

Peru and Chile both produce a clear, unaged brandy called *pisco,* which is made from muscat grapes.

Cognac and armagnac are two special types of French brandies. They're so special that I cover them in a separate chapter — Chapter 9 to be exact.

What the heck does alambic mean?

Alambic, the French word for *still,* is the word approved for label use by the U.S. Bureau of Alcohol, Tobacco, and Firearms (ATF). It denotes brandy distilled on a batch-process pot still rather than on a continued-column still. Cognac, armagnac, and high-quality fruit brandies are distilled on various types of pot stills. The major American alambic brandy producers, Germain-Robin and Carneros Alambic, use cognac stills. A cognac still entails two distillations, but small quantities have been made on single-distillation alsatian fruit stills by distillers of American fruit brandies, such as St. George Spirits.

Fruit Brandy

Fruit brandies are produced from all kinds of (guess what?) fruits. The fruit is washed and ground into a mash. Water and yeast are added and allowed to ferment. After the sugar metabolizes, the mash is pressed and the liquid is then distilled. Some fruit brandies are aged in oak barrels.

When shopping for fruit brandies, you may see the term *eau-de-vie,* which refers to any fruit brandy or any brandy not qualified as armagnac or cognac. Brandy snobs often throw around this term.

Some of the major fruit brandy types are

- ✔ **Applejack:** An apple brandy produced in the United States.
- ✔ **Calvados:** An apple brandy made from a variety of apples from northwestern France.
- ✔ **Framboise:** Made from raspberries.
- ✔ **Kirsch** and **Kirschwasser:** Made from cherries.
- ✔ **Poire:** Made from pears, usually from Switzerland and France. (Poire William is a pear brandy that contains a fully mature pear. While each pear is still on the branch, it's placed in the bottle. When the pear is mature, it's washed in the bottle, and the bottle is then filled with pear brandy.)
- ✔ **Slivovitz:** Made from plums, usually from Germany or Hungary.

The solera method

The *solera* method of making brandy is comprised of three aging stages:

1. The wine spirits are blended and placed for some months in barrels.

2. Half of the brandy in each barrel is then blended in another barrel containing older brandy.

3. Finally, half of that barrel is placed in yet another barrel containing even older brandy.

Fruit-Flavored Brandies

In the United States, fruit-flavored brandies are classified as *cordials* and are usually bottled at more than 70 proof. Sugar, natural coloring, fruit, and other flavorings are added. You can find brandies flavored with such diverse ingredients as apricots, bananas, coffee, and peaches.

Pomace Brandy

Pomace brandies are produced by the fermentation and distillation of grape seeds, stems, and anything that remains after grapes have been pressed and their juices extracted. Pomace brandies are neither aged nor colored. The most popular are grappa (Italian), marc (French), and orujo (Spanish).

Storing and Serving Suggestions

Brandy is traditionally served straight up in a snifter after dinner, but it's also mixed with water or soda and can be found in some famous cocktails, including the delicious Brandy Alexander. Store an unopened bottle out of sunlight. After opening, a bottle of brandy can last up to three years. Brandy doesn't improve with age in the bottle, so it will taste no better if you let it sit in the bottle in your basement for ten years.

Chapter 9

Cognac and Armagnac

· ·

In This Chapter

▶ Finding out where cognac and armagnac are made

▶ Deciphering the designations on labels

▶ Getting familiar with the well-known brands

▶ Finishing a meal with a warm drink

· ·

*F*rance produces two kinds of brandy: cognac and armagnac. Both are named after the region in which they're made, and both are delicious.

Cognac

Cognac can be produced only in the legally defined region of Cognac, France, located between the Atlantic and Massif Central — specifically, at the junction between the oceanic and continental climate zones. The region also straddles the dividing line between northern and southern climates. These four influences create a multitude of microclimates. In addition to the unique climate, the soil characteristics also foster a range of wine and, consequently, the cognac of each region. In 1909, the French government passed a law that only brandy produced in the "delimited area" surrounding the town of Cognac can be called *cognac.*

How cognac is made

The arduous, time-honored distilling and aging process is what makes cognac so special. The cognac you drink today was produced using methods dating back to the 17th century. The distillation of cognac is a two-stage process:

1. A first distillate, known as *brouillis,* is obtained, with an alcoholic strength of 28 to 32 percent.

2. The brouillis is returned to the boiler for a second heating, which produces a liquid known as *la bonne chauffe.* The beginning and the end of this second distillation (the head and tail) are discarded, leaving only the heart of the spirit, which becomes cognac.

The cognac is then sent to rest in oak casks made from wood from the Limousin and Troncais forests.

Maturing slowly over long years in cellars, the cognac acquires a smoothness and flavor beyond compare. The wood and the dark, saturated atmosphere of the cellars work together to develop the aroma of the cognac to its full potential. All cognac is aged a minimum of 30 months.

What are all those letters on the label?

When you shop for cognac, you see all kinds of designations on the labels of various brands — for example, Courvoisier V.S., Martell V.S.O.P., and Remy Martin X.O. The letters and phrases after the brand name are a general indication of the age (and, in turn, expensiveness) of the cognac.

Every major brand produces cognacs of different ages. When one of the following designations is used, it indicates the age of the youngest cognac used in the blend that makes up what's in the bottle.

- ✔ **V.S. (Very Superior)** or **Three Stars:** Cognac aged less than 4½ years.

- ✔ **V.S.O.P. (Very Superior Old Pale):** Cognac aged between 4½ and 6½ years. Sometimes called V.O. (Very Old) or Reserve.

- ✔ **X.O. (Extremely Old), Napoleon, Hors d'age, V.S.S.O.P., Cordon Bleu, Grand Reserve,** and **Royal:** Cognac aged at least 5½ years and up to 40 years.

Generally speaking, each cognac producer uses blends that are much older than the minimum required. In the most prestigious cognacs, some of the blends may have matured over several decades.

The angels' share

Aging cognac and armagnac is very expensive, not only because it ties up capital, but because millions of bottles per year disappear into the air through evaporation as the spirit sits in its oak casks. To make fine cognac and armagnac, you can't avoid this loss, and producers refer to it as the *angels' share.*

You're also going to see some of these names on the labels:

- ✓ **Grand Fine Champagne** or **Grande Champagne:** These identify cognacs made exclusively from grapes grown in the Grande Champagne region of Cognac.

- ✓ **Petite Fine Champagne** or **Petite Champagne:** These names mean that the cognac is a blend made from grapes grown in the Grande Champagne and Petite Champagne sections of Cognac. At least 50 percent of the blend must be from grapes grown in the Grande Champagne region.

The terms *fine cognac* and *grande fine,* which may also appear on cognac labels, have no legally defined meaning. The designations *extra old* (E.O.) and *very old pale* (V.O.P.) are not officially recognized by the Bureau du Cognac, which makes up all the names and rules.

You won't see vintage dates on cognac labels because in 1963, the French passed a law prohibiting the placement of vintage labels on cognac bottles. Go figure.

Popular brands

Even though all cognacs are produced in the same region, and even though every brand seems to have the same jumble of age designations on their labels, you may be surprised at the degree of distinctiveness among the brands. Some brands have a strong, room-filling aroma; some have a mild grape flavor; others have hints of caramel and vanilla. If you're a fan of cognac, my advice is that you not only try several different brands, but that you also try some of the variations within each brand.

If you're curious to find out what an older cognac (X.O. or better) tastes like, visit a decent bar and order a glass (and be prepared to pay $10–$20) before you decide to invest in an expensive bottle of cognac.

In the following list, the available styles for each brand are listed from the least expensive to the most expensive. All cognacs are 80 proof.

- **Alize** produces V.S. and V.S.O.P.

- **Camus** produces a range of cognacs including V.S., V.S.O.P., X.O., Extra, Borderies X.O., Ile de Ré Fine Island Cognac, Rarissimes, and Cuvée 3.128.

- **Courvoisier** produces V.S., V.S.O.P. Fine Champagne, V.S.O.P. Exclusif, Napoleon Fine Champagne, X.O. Imperial, Initiale Extra, Succession JS, and L'Esprit de Courvoisier.

- **Delamain** produces Pale and Dry X.O., Vesper, Très Vénérable, Extra, Millésimés, and Réserve de la Famille.

- **Hardy** produces Hardy Perfection Series: Air, Fire, Water, and Earth, Rosebud Family Reserve, Pearl Noces de Perle, Diamond Noces de Diamant, Captain Noces d'Or, Noces D'Or, X.O., Napoleon, V.S.O.P, V.S. Red Corner, and Hardy Vanille.

- **Hennessy** produces V.S., Privilège, X.O., Private Reserve 1873, and Richard Hennessy.

- **Hine Cognac** produces H by Hine, Rare V.S.O.P., Cigar, Antique X.O., Triomphe, Mariage, and Talent.

- **Martell** produces V.S., Médaillon V.S.O.P., Noblige, Cordon Bleu, X.O., Creation, and L'Art.

- **Remy Martin** produces Grand Cru, V.S.O.P., 1783 Accord Royal, X.O. Excellence, Extra, and Louis XIII de Remy Martin.

Armagnac

Armagnac, though less well-known than cognac, is France's oldest brandy and has been produced continuously since the 15th century (as early as 1422). It's distilled from premium white wine grown in the Armagnac region of southwest France.

How armagnac is made

Armagnac is a distillate produced from the continuous, or single, distillation process. Neutral white wine registering about 9 to 10 percent alcohol is heated in a traditional copper alambic pot still at a relatively low temperature. The vapors pass through the swan neck coils and produce a spirit of no more than 63 percent alcohol. This combination of low temperature and lower alcohol produces a spirit that retains more flavor and aroma elements in the brandy. The clear brandy is then put into casks traditional to the region — handcrafted 400-liter barrels made from Armagnac or Limousin oak. The aging process begins and can last from 1 to 50 years. The spirit takes on flavors of the wood and other special nuances as it matures, creating a brandy of complexity and distinction. It is then up to the cellar master to blend the separate barrels into a harmonious whole to create the full range of armagnacs.

How to read the label

The French government regulates armagnac labeling. The following designations are used:

- **V.S.** or **Three Stars:** The youngest brandy in the blend is at least 3 years old.

- **V.O. (Very Old), V.S.O.P. (Very Special Old Pale),** and **Reserve:** The youngest brandy in the blend is at least 4½ years old.

- **Extra, Napoleon, X.O.,** and **Vieille Reserve:** The youngest brandy is at least 5½ years old.

Unlike cognac, armagnac products may carry a vintage date. All nonvintage armagnacs contain much older brandies than indicated on the labels. Vintage armagnacs are the unblended product of a single year's production.

Popular brands

- **Armagnac Lapostolle X.O.** is matured for more than 30 years.

✔ **Janneau** produces V.S.O.P., Selection (aged 8 to 10 years), and Reserve de la Maison. A 1966 vintage is also sold.

✔ **Sempe** produces 6-year-old and 15-year-old varieties. Its Xtra Grand Reserve is a blend of brandies aged from 35 to 50 years.

Storing and Serving Suggestions

Cognac and armagnac are after-dinner drinks. Cognac is seldom mixed, but people have been known to drink it with soda or water. Both cognac and armagnac are excellent companions to coffee, tea, and cigars. They should be served at room temperature and in clear, crystal brandy snifters. Like all fine brandies, cognac and armagnac should be gently swirled in the glass and then sipped and savored. If stored in a cool, dry place, an opened bottle of either brandy should last for two years.

Chapter 10

Gin

*G*in is basically a distilled grain spirit flavored with extracts from different plants, mainly the juniper berry. The Dutch were the first to make gin and have been doing so since the late 1500s.

A Little History

Gin was invented by Franciscus de la Boe, also known as Dr. Sylvius. Why? Who knows but Mrs. Sylvius? Dr. Sylvius was a professor of medicine and a physician at Holland's University of Leyden. He used a juniper berry elixir known as *genievere* — French for *juniper*. He thought that juniper berries could assist in the treatment of kidney and bladder ailments.

British soldiers sampled his elixir when returning from the wars in the Netherlands and nicknamed it *Dutch courage*. When they brought the recipe back to England, they changed the name to *gen* and later to *gin,* which soon became the national drink of England.

Types of Gin

Although gin has been produced and consumed for centuries, the methods for making the quality gin that you drink today have been around only since the turn of the 20th century. Gin comes in many types; the most popular include the following:

- **London dry gin (English)** is distilled from a grain mixture that contains more barley than corn. It's distilled at a high proof and then redistilled with juniper berries.

- **Dutch gin or Holland gin** contains barley, malt, corn, and rye. It's distilled at a lower proof and then redistilled with juniper berries in another still at low proof. Dutch gins are usually slightly sweet.

- **Flavored gin** is a new product. It's basically gin to which natural flavorings have been added (lime, lemon, orange, and so on). The flavoring always appears on the bottle.

Popular Brands

The following are all London dry gins. Each brand has its own distinctive flavor that comes from a carefully guarded recipe.

- **Bafferts:** A London gin that's handcrafted with a closely guarded recipe.

- **Beefeater:** The only premium dry gin distillery in London.

- **Beefeater WET:** A lighter-tasting gin (70 proof) made with natural pear flavors.

- **Bluecoat:** An American gin distilled in Philadelphia.

- **Bols Genever:** A gin from Holland made with high-quality malt wine.

- **Bombay:** Made from a well-guarded recipe that dates back to 1761.

- **Bombay Sapphire:** Conceived by Michel Roux, president of Carillon Importers, Sapphire has more natural botanical ingredients than any other gin.

✔ **Boodles:** Named after the London club; one of the most popular gins in the United Kingdom.

✔ **Broker's:** Made from 100-percent English grain, quadruple-distilled, and flavored with ten botanicals.

✔ **Bulldog:** A London dry gin infused with poppy and dragon eye.

✔ **Citadelle:** Made in Cognac, France, with 19 exotic botanicals.

✔ **Cork Dry Gin:** An Irish gin distilled in Cork City.

✔ **Damrak:** A high-quality gin from Amsterdam.

✔ **Genevieve:** Made in the United States by Anchor Brewing Company in San Francisco. A throwback to the earliest forms of gin.

✔ **Gordon's:** First distilled more than 225 years ago in London by Alexander Gordon, who pioneered and perfected the making of an unsweetened gin with a smooth character and aromatic flavors known as London Dry.

✔ **G'Vine:** A gin from France made with a Ugni Blanc (Trebbiano grapes) base spirit, infused with green grape flowers.

✔ **Hendrick's:** A Scottish gin with juniper, coriander, rose petal, citrus, and an infusion of cucumber.

✔ **Magellan:** A French gin handcrafted in small batches using natural exotic botanicals from around the globe.

✔ **Martin Miller's:** A London dry gin, considered the world's first super-premium gin.

✔ **Plymouth:** Legend has it that a surgeon in the Royal Navy invented this gin to help the sailors make their Angostura bitters more palatable (pink gin).

✔ **Right:** An ultra-premium gin made with juniper, cardamom, and coriander leaf.

✔ **Seagram's Extra Dry:** A citrus-tasting golden gin.

✔ **Tanqueray:** Its unique green bottle is said to be inspired by an English fire hydrant.

✔ **Tanqueray No. Ten:** A super-premium gin from Tanqueray with a blend of fresh botanicals, including grapefruit and camomile. It's distilled four times.

Storing and Serving Suggestions

As you peruse the recipe section of this book (Chapter 17), you'll probably notice that gin appears in many cocktails, so choosing the right gin (that is, your favorite) can really affect your enjoyment of a given drink. Never, ever use cheap, nonpremium gin when making a drink. The results will be a disaster. Cheap gin tastes like disinfectant. Good gin has an herby, spicy, organic flavor, so stick to the premium brands such as those I list in this chapter.

When you're at a bar, don't order a Gin & Tonic because you'll end up with some cheap, awful bar (or *well*) gin. Order a Tanqueray & Tonic or a Sapphire & Tonic, and you'll get a decent drink. The same goes for gin Martinis: Always specify what brand of gin you want or you'll be sorry.

Store an unopened bottle of gin in a cool, dry place out of direct light. After opening a bottle, it should last about two years.

Famous gin-related lines

From one of the most romantic movies of all time, after Ingrid Bergman comes into Rick's bar in Casablanca, what does Humphrey Bogart say? "Of all the gin joints in all the towns in all the world, she walks into mine."

Eliza Doolittle makes this remark about someone's drinking at a fashionable horse race: "Gin was mother's milk to her."

Finally, a little poem:

I'm tired of gin
I'm tired of sin
And after last night
Oh boy, am I tired.

—Anonymous

Chapter 11

Irish Whiskey

*T*he Irish have been distilling whiskey for at least 600 years, if not longer. Though it's safe to say that Irish whiskey has a distinct character, it's also equally true to say that each brand of Irish whiskey is a unique product.

What Makes Irish Whiskey Taste So Yummy

Irish whiskey is triple-distilled from barley and other grains in pot stills and aged between five and ten years. One major difference between Scotch and Irish whiskey is that when drying the barley malt from which the whiskey is distilled, the Irish use coal instead of peat, which prevents the smoky flavor found in Scotch whisky.

What's more, Irish whiskey also gains a great deal of flavor from the casks in which it's aged. Depending on the brand, Irish whiskey is aged in casks that have held sherry, rum, or bourbon.

 For centuries, the Irish produced an illegal distilled spirit called *potcheen* (po-cheen), a colorless, unaged spirit that's high in alcohol content and similar to white lightning or moonshine in the southern United States. But as of March 17, 1997, it's legal and being produced and sold in Ireland and the rest of the world.

Popular Brands

You may be surprised at the variety of flavors among the brands of Irish whiskey:

- ✔ **Bushmills** produces Bushmills Premium, Black Bush Special, Bushmills Single Malt (10 years old), Bushmills Rare Single Irish Malt (16 years old), and a 21-year-old Single Malt Irish Whiskey.

- ✔ **Connemara** makes Pot Still Peated Single Malt Irish Whiskey, a unique product, being the only peated single malt on the market.

- ✔ **Danny Boy** is a 15-year-old Irish malt whiskey matured in the finest American white oak casks.

- ✔ **Jameson Irish Whiskey** is the world's largest-selling Irish whiskey. It's aged for 12 years and made from pure Irish water and a combination of malted and unmalted Irish barley. Jameson Gold is a blend of rare Irish whiskies, which range in age from 8 to 20 years.

- ✔ **Kilbeggan** is Gaelic for *little church*. What is now an idyllic village in the center of Ireland was for many years an active religious community built around a monastery. The first licensed whiskey distillery in the world was established in Kilbeggan in 1757.

- ✔ **Knappogue Castle Irish Single Malt Whiskey** is pot-stilled using only malted barley and bottled on a vintage basis. Knappogue also has a single malt whiskey.

- ✔ **Michael Collins** is double-distilled in pot stills. The final blend is aged from 4 to 12 years in oak casks.

- ✔ **Midleton** produces its Very Rare Irish Whiskey, a blend of triple-distilled whiskies ranging from 12 to 21 years old. It's matured exclusively in special, individually selected, bourbon-seasoned American oak casks. Midleton is a credit to the old sod.

- ✔ **Paddy** is named for Paddy Flaherty, a salesman for the Cork Distilleries Company in the 1920s.

- ✔ **Powers** was the first to introduce bottling in Ireland.

- ✔ **Redbreast Irish Whiskey** is a single, unblended whiskey, triple-distilled in oak casks for no less than 12 years.

- **Tullamore Dew** is famous for the slogan "Give every man his Dew."

- **The Tyrconnell Single Malt Irish Whiskey** is made from a mash of pure malted barley produced at a single distillery. (In contrast, other whiskies blend a variety of malt and grain products from several distilleries.)

- **The Wild Geese Irish Soldiers & Heroes** is produced using a special extended double distillation process to remove impurities and to achieve optimal alcohol content for maturation.

Storing and Serving Suggestions

The storage of Irish whiskey is very simple. An unopened bottle will last indefinitely because Irish whiskey doesn't mature after it's bottled. After a bottle is opened, it has a shelf life of about two years.

Chapter 12

Rum

· ·

In This Chapter

▶ Getting the background on rum

▶ Knowing the rum production process

▶ Looking at some well-known brands and flavors

▶ Serving it up

· ·

*R*um is a spirit distilled from sugar cane. It comes in light and dark varieties and is an ingredient in hundreds of cocktail recipes.

Rummaging through Rum History

Caribbean rum has been exported out of the islands for hundreds of years, linked to the tropical and subtropical climates where sugar cane thrives. It was Christopher Columbus himself who first brought sugar cane to the Caribbean from the Azores. But the origins of rum are far more ancient, dating back, most experts say, more than 2,000 years.

Sugar cane grew like a weed in parts of southern China and India, and Alexander the Great, after conquering India, brought with him to Egypt "the weed that gives honey without the help of bees." The Islamic people from the Middle Ages, known as the *Saracens,* passed on their knowledge of distilling sugar cane to the Moors, who made *arak* (a cane-based proto-rum) and planted sugar cane in Europe sometime after AD 636.

Columbus brought sugar cane to Puerto Rico on his second voyage in 1493. Later, Ponce de León, the first Spanish governor of the island, planted the first cane fields in Puerto Rico, which were soon to become vital to the local economy and to the world's palate for fine spirits. Some historians speculate that Ponce de León's legendary search for a mythical fountain of youth was, in fact, a much more practical search for a source of pure water to use in his distillation of rum.

The first sugar mill, a precursor to the Puerto Rican rum industry, was built in 1524, when the product of cane distillation was called *brebaje,* the word *rum* being a later addition brought by crusading English seamen.

The popularity of rum continued to spread during the early 19th century. Distilleries prospered and grew in Puerto Rico. In 1893, the first modern column still was introduced to Puerto Rico. With this innovation, the foundation was laid for the island to produce a more refined, smoother-tasting rum at a dramatically increased pace. Distilleries relocated from vast, outlying sugar plantations to more accessible sites and soon became centrally organized and managed. The first Puerto Rican rum for export to the continental United States was shipped in 1897 — some 18,000 gallons.

During the Prohibition period in the United States, most Puerto Rican rum distillers stayed in business — not by being rumrunners but by producing industrial alcohol. When Prohibition ended in 1933, Puerto Rico refocused on the potential of the American liquor market and slowly began to rebuild its shipments to U.S. ports. The island soon took steps to upgrade its rum production, and through special government funding and research, the island's rum was catapulted to the forefront of the world's rum production.

With the onset of World War II, manufacturers of U.S. distilled spirits were ordered to limit their production and manufacture of industrial alcohol for the war effort. However, because the territorial mandate didn't apply to Puerto Rico, demand for Puerto Rican rum increased. Sales were phenomenal throughout the war years, with Rum and Coke being the national drink during World War II. In 1952, about 100 different brands of Puerto Rican rum were on the market. Today, there are just 12.

Rum folklore

Legend has it that Paul Revere ordered a mug of rum before his famous ride from Boston to Lexington. And a Benjamin Franklin invention, the Rum Flip, made with rum and beer, was raised in 1773 in celebration after the Boston Tea Party.

Rum may have been the first of all shaken cocktails in the world: At Increase Arnold's Tavern in Providence, Rhode Island, thirsty patrons called for "rum, milk, sugar, cracked ice, shaken in a silver coffee pot until the frost is on the pot," topped with nutmeg and ginger.

Rums from Puerto Rico are the leaders in rum sales in the continental United States. A staggering 77 percent of all rum sold on the mainland comes from Puerto Rico.

How Rum Is Made

Rum is distilled from molasses, a sticky syrup that results when sugar cane is boiled down. When first distilled, the crude rum is between 130 and 180 proof. This rum is then aged for two to ten years to mellow it out. This aging process determines whether the rum is light or dark. Rum aged in charred oak casks becomes dark (caramel and other agents are added to affect its color). Rum aged in stainless steel tanks remains colorless.

Most light rum comes from Puerto Rico. Most dark rum comes from Jamaica, Haiti, and Martinique.

Popular Brands

Rum is produced throughout the Caribbean. Here are several popular brands:

- **10 Cane** (Trinidad)
- **Admiral Nelson Spiced Rum** (Puerto Rico)

- ✔ **Angostura** (Trinidad)
- ✔ **Appleton Estate** (Jamaica)
- ✔ **Bacardi** (Puerto Rico)
- ✔ **Brinley** (Saint Kitts)
- ✔ **Captain Morgan Original Spiced Rum** (Puerto Rico)
- ✔ **Castillo** (Puerto Rico)
- ✔ **Cavalier** (Antigua)
- ✔ **Cockspur** (Barbados)
- ✔ **Cruzan Rum** (U.S. Virgin Islands)
- ✔ **DonQ Rums** (Puerto Rico)
- ✔ **English Harbour** (Antigua)
- ✔ **Fernandes Vat 19 Rum** (Trinidad)
- ✔ **Gosling's Black Seal Rum** (Bermuda): Gosling also makes a Gold Rum and an Old Rum.
- ✔ **Gran Blason Añejo Especial** (Costa Rica)
- ✔ **Havana Club** (Cuba)
- ✔ **Matusalem** (Dominican Republic)
- ✔ **Mount Gay Rum** (Barbados)
- ✔ **Myers's Original Dark Rum** (Jamaica)
- ✔ **Ocumare** (Venezuela)
- ✔ **Oronoco** (Brazil)
- ✔ **Pampero** (Venezuela)
- ✔ **Pusser's** (Tortola, British Virgin Islands)
- ✔ **Pyrat** (Anguilla)
- ✔ **Rhum Barbancourt** (Haiti)
- ✔ **Ron Del Barrilito** (Puerto Rico)
- ✔ **Ron Rico** (Puerto Rico)
- ✔ **Royal Oak** (Trinidad)
- ✔ **Sailor Jerry** (U.S. Virgin Islands)
- ✔ **Sea Wynde** (Jamaica and Guyana)
- ✔ **Stroh** (Austria)

- 🖊 **Stubbs** (Australia)
- 🖊 **Tommy Bahama Rum** (Barbados)
- 🖊 **Whaler's** (Hawaii)
- 🖊 **Wray & Nephew** (Jamaica)
- 🖊 **Zaya Rum** (Trinidad)

Flavored Rums

Rums are now available in several different flavors; new flavors of rums come out every day. I suggest you check with your local liquor retailer or liquor wholesaler to see what's new. Here are some popular options:

- 🖊 **Bacardi** offers Bacardi Ciclon (90 percent Bacardi Gold rum and 10 percent blue agave tequila and a hint of lime), Bacardi Limón (a lemon-citrus-flavored rum), Bacardi Tropico (Bacardi Gold rum mixed with exotic fruit juices), Bacardi O (Bacardi rum infused with the essence of ripe oranges), Bacardi Razz (raspberry), Bacardi Vanila, Bacardi Coco (coconut), Bacardi Dragonberry, and Grand Melon (watermelon).

- 🖊 **Captain Morgan's Parrot Bay** offers coconut-, mango-, pineapple-, and passion fruit-flavored rums.

- 🖊 **Cocoribe** is a coconut-flavored rum.

- 🖊 **Cruzan Rums** have the following flavors: coconut, orange, pineapple, banana, vanilla, raspberry, mango, and citrus.

- 🖊 **Malibu** is a coconut-flavored rum.

- 🖊 **Tattoo** is a dark flavored rum from Captain Morgan.

- 🖊 **Whaler's** offers coconut, vanilla, and spiced rums.

Cachaça (aka Brazilian Rum)

Cachaça (pronounced kah-*shah*-sah) is a Brazilian sugar cane-based liquor. Even though I'm including cachaça in this chapter on rum, you shouldn't confuse it with rum, which is made from the molasses left over after sugar refinement.

Cachaça imported to the United States is taxed as rum and thus is often called Brazilian Rum.

Brazil consumes close to 360 million gallons of cachaça per year. It's the third most-consumed spirit in the world.

Cachaça must be aged for at least one year in barrels no larger than 700 liters. The barrels are made of cedar, jequitiba, and American and European oak. This barrel-aging gives the liquor a smoother taste.

Here are some popular cachaça brands:

- ✓ Boca Loca
- ✓ Cabana Cachaça
- ✓ Leblon
- ✓ Sagatiba Cachaça
- ✓ Samba

The most common cocktail made with cachaça is the Caipirinha. Check out the recipe in Chapter 17.

Storing and Serving Suggestions

You can serve rum straight, on ice, or mixed as a cocktail. The good old Rum and Coke is a popular choice. It's called a Cuba Libre when you add a lime. Store an unopened bottle in a cool, dry place. After opening, a typical bottle should have a shelf life of at least two years.

Chapter 13

Scotch Whisky

● ●

In This Chapter

▶ Noting the regional variations of Scotch

▶ Seeing how Scotch is made

▶ Listing some popular Scotch brands

▶ Savoring your Scotch

● ●

*S*cotch whisky (spelled without the *e* in *whiskey*) has a distinctive smoky flavor that's the result of both the choice of ingredients and the method of distillation.

Scotch whisky must be distilled in Scotland — but not necessarily bottled in Scotland. Some Scotch whiskies are distilled in Scotland but bottled in another country.

Types of Scotch Whisky

Two kinds of Scotch whisky are distilled: *malt whisky* (from barley) and *grain whisky* (from cereals). Malt whiskies are divided into four groups according to the geographical location of the distillery in which they're made. Figure 13-1 shows the four main areas of Scotch production.

▸ **Lowland malt whiskies:** Made south of an imaginary line drawn from Dundee in the east to Greenock in the west.

▸ **Highland malt whiskies:** Made north of the aforementioned line.

✔ **Speyside malt whiskies:** Made in the valley of the River Spey. Although these whiskies come from within the area of the Highland malt whiskies, the concentration of distilleries and the specific climatic conditions in Speyside produce whiskies of an identifiable character, which is why they're classified separately.

✔ **Islay malt whiskies:** Made on the island of Islay.

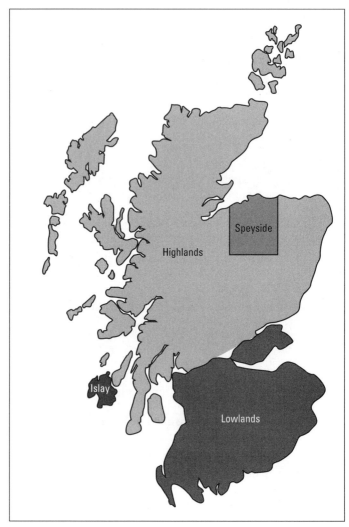

Figure 13-1: The four main Scotch-producing regions.

Each group has its own clearly defined characteristics, ranging from the gentle, lighter-flavored Lowland whiskies to those distilled on Islay, which are generally regarded as the heaviest malt whiskies.

Grain distilleries are mostly found in the central belt of Scotland, near the cities of Glasgow and Edinburgh. Single-grain whiskies display individual characteristics in the same way as malts, although the geographical influence isn't the same.

Married together, malt whiskies and grain whiskies create *blended* Scotch whisky, which accounts for 95 percent of world sales. As you may expect from the name, a *single-malt* Scotch whisky is made from one type of malt, and it's not blended with other malts or grain whiskies.

How Scotch Is Made

Scotch whisky made from malts dates back to 1494 to Friar John Cor and his fellow friars. Until the mid-1800s, nearly all Scotches were single-malt. Then, Andrew Usher came up with the idea of mixing malt whisky and grain whisky to create blended Scotch whisky. A blended whisky can have many (up to 50) different types of malt whiskies blended with grain whisky (from cereals).

1. The first stage of making Scotch whisky is the malting of barley. The barley is soaked and dried for germination. During this period, the starch in the barley converts to fermentable sugar.

2. To stop the germination, the malted barley is smoked, usually over peat fires in open malt kilns, giving Scotch whisky its smoky taste.

3. Then the barley is mixed with water and yeast. Fermentation takes place, and alcohol is the result. This liquid is then usually pumped into stills and double-distilled until the correct proof is attained.

4. After distillation, the whisky is placed in used American oak wine or bourbon barrels and then aged by law for a minimum of three years. Most Scotch whiskies age from five to ten years, sometimes much longer. It's said that the longer a whisky ages, the smoother it becomes.

Whisky doesn't improve with age after it's bottled.

After the whisky finishes aging in the barrel, each distiller then completes its own blending, filtering, and bottling. Scotland has more than 100 distilleries that produce more than 2,000 different Scotch whiskies.

Whisky can only be called *Scotch whisky* if it's distilled and matured for at least three years in Scotland.

Popular Blended Scotch Whiskies

These are the brands that you're most likely to find at your local bar or liquor store:

- **Ballantine's** is available in these varieties: Finest, 12 Year Old, Blended Malt 12 Year Old, 17 Year Old, 21 Year Old, and 30 Year Old.

- **Bell's** is available in Extra Special and Special Reserve Blended Malt.

- **Black & White** comes in a black bottle with a simple white label.

- **Black Bottle Blended Scotch Whisky** uses only malts from Islay.

- **Chivas Regal** is available in 12, 18, and 25 year old varieties.

- **Cutty Sark** is available in these varieties: Original, Black, Sark Malt, and 12, 15, 18, and 25 year old.

- **Dewar's** offers these varieties: White Label, 12 Year Old, 18 Year Old, and Signature.

- **The Famous Grouse** is available in 10, 12, and 15 year old varieties, along with Scottish Oak Finish, Bourbon Cask Finish, Snow Grouse, Black Snow Grouse, Famous Grouse, and Timorous Beasties Limited Edition.

- **Grant's** is available in several varieties: Family Reserve Blended, Ale Cask Reserve, Sherry Cask Reserve, Distillery Edition, and 12, 18, and 25 year old.

- **Johnnie Walker** offers these varieties: Red, Black, Green, Gold, Blue, and Swing.

✔ **Justerini & Brooks (J&B)** offers just one product, J&B Rare, which is blended from Speyside malt whiskies.

✔ **The Last Drop** uses nearly 70 different malt whiskies and 12 different grain whiskies to create its distinctive blend.

✔ **Pinch** is known as the **Dimple** everywhere in the world except in the United States.

✔ **Royal Salute** is available in these varieties: 21 Year Old, 100 Cask Selection, and 38 Year Old Stone of Destiny.

✔ **Scottish Leader Blended Scotch Whisky** contains malts from Aberfeldy, Caol Ila, Girvan, and North British grain.

✔ **Teacher's Highland Cream** is made with a blend of more than 30 different single malt whiskies.

✔ **Vat 69** is available in these varieties: Finest and Reserve de Luxe.

✔ **White Horse** is available in its standard blend and Extra Fine 12 Year Old.

Single-Malt Scotch

Single-malt Scotch whisky is unblended malt whisky from a single distillery. The water and malted barley, the raw materials of Scotch whisky, differ from distillery to distillery and region to region. In addition, the production methods, variations in topography and climate, and size and shape of the pot stills all contribute to the uniqueness of each distillery's single malt.

Scotland has more than 100 single-malt distilleries, so if you're a fan of single-malt Scotch whisky, it's unlikely that you'll run out of whiskies to sample and enjoy. The following is a listing of just a few brands worth trying:

✔ **Aberlour**

✔ **Balvenie**

✔ **Bowmore**

✔ **Bunnahabhain**

✔ **Cardhu**

✔ **Dalmore**

- Deanston
- Glenfiddich
- Glenlivet
- Glenmorangie
- Glenrothes
- Highland Park
- Isle of Jura
- Lagavulin
- Laphroaig
- Ledaig
- Macallan
- Oban
- Old Stillman's Dram
- Passport
- Pig's Nose
- Scapa
- Sheep Dip
- Singleton
- Speyburn
- Springbank
- Talisker
- Tobermory
- Whyte & Mackay

Storing and Serving Suggestions

Scotch can be served over ice, straight up, with water or club soda, or in a variety of mixed drinks. Single malts and aged Scotch whisky (over 12 years) can be served straight up or on the rocks with a splash of water. After opening, store a bottle of Scotch whisky in a cool, dry place out of direct light. It should have a shelf life of approximately two years.

Chapter 14

Tequila and Mezcal

· ·

In This Chapter

▶ Making tequila but only in Tequila

▶ Taking your pick of the popular brands

▶ Distilling mezcal from the agave plant, too

▶ Developing a taste for worms

· ·

*T*equila and mezcal are both products of Mexico, and both are made from the *agave plant.* Tequila is a much more popular beverage, and mezcal is famous for the worm in the bottle.

Tequila

Tequila can be traced back to almost AD 1000 and the Aztecs, when it was a milky drink known as *pulque.*

Since the 17th century and now by Mexican law, all tequila comes from a certain area known as Tequila, within the state of Jalisco. In this dry, volcanic soil of the Sierra Madre foothills, you can find the home of Tequila's largest producers.

Tequila is produced from the heart of one species of agave plant, the *Agave tequilana Weber,* or the blue variety. This heart is known as the *piña,* and it usually weighs between 80 and 150 pounds. The piña is steamed and shredded until the *aguamiel* (juice) runs off. This juice is then mixed with cane sugar and yeast and fermented for two to three days. The fermented juice is double-distilled in traditional copper pot stills to 90 proof or higher. Tequila must contain a minimum of 51 percent distillate from the blue agave plant.

Reading a tequila label

The Mexican Government established NORMA (Norma Oficial Mexicana de Calidad) on March 31, 1978, to set standards of quality for tequila production. On every bottle, the letters *NOM* must appear, followed by four numbers designating the distillery where the tequila was produced. Besides the brand name and NOM, the label must state the category of tequila, the proof, and whether the tequila is 100-percent agave.

Types of tequila

Tequila comes in four categories:

- ✔ **Tequila Blanco** (white, silver, or platinum tequila): This tequila comes fresh from the still and may be brought to commercial proof (salable proof or for sale commercially) with the addition of demineralized water.

- ✔ **Tequila Joven Abocado** (gold tequila): This is silver tequila with the addition of colorings and flavorings to mellow the flavor.

- ✔ **Tequila Reposado** ("reposed" or "rested" tequila): This tequila is aged for two months to a year in oak tanks or barrels. Flavorings and coloring agents may be added, as well as demineralized water, to bring the tequila to commercial proof.

- ✔ **Añejo** (aged tequila): This tequila is aged for at least one year in government-sealed oak barrels. Flavorings and coloring agents may be added, as well as demineralized water, to bring it to commercial proof. When tequilas of different ages are blended, the youngest age is designated.

Several tequila brands now offer flavored tequilas. Whether this trend catches on remains to be seen. Lemon, orange, and other citrus flavors are common, and you can also find such diverse flavors as chili pepper and chocolate if you're feeling adventurous.

Popular tequila brands

You're likely to find these brands at your local liquor store:

- **901 Tequila:** Justin Timberlake's line of ultra-premium tequila. Made from 100-percent blue weber agave and triple-distilled.

- **1800 Tequila:** 100-percent agave, double-distilled, and aged in French and American oak for six months.

- **Agavero:** Named after the blue agave plant, this tequila is a blend of selective 100-percent blue agave Añejo and Reposado.

- **Cabo Wabo:** Sammy Hagar's tequila. It was introduced to the United States around 1996, without Van Halen.

- **Cazadores Tequila:** 100-percent blue agave, this tequila rests for two months in new American white oak casks.

- **Chinaco:** An ultra-premium tequila.

- **Corazon de Agave:** An ultra-premium tequila made in Jalisco.

- **Corzo Tequila:** Comes in Añejo, Reposado, and Silver. Corzo uses more than twice the agave of other super-premium tequilas.

- **Don Julia:** 100-percent blue agave tequila. Available in Blanco, Reposado, Anejo, 1942, and Real.

- **El Tesoro de Don Felipe:** Estate-grown and bottled with no water added. Varieties include Añejo, Reposado, and Platinum.

- **Gran Centenario:** Handcrafted in Jalisco from 100-percent blue agave, this ultra-premium tequila is available in these varieties: Plata (silver), Reposado, Añejo, and Extra-Añejo.

- **Herradura:** The name is Spanish for *horseshoe*. It's available in Añejo, Reposado Gold, and Silver varieties.

- **Hotel California Tequila:** Ultra-premium artisanal tequila. Comes in Blanco, Reposado, and Añejo.

- **Jose Cuervo:** The world's oldest and largest tequila maker, and the oldest spirit company in North America. Available in these versions: Especial (Gold), Clasico, Tradicional, Black, and Reserva De La Familia.

- **Margaritaville Tequila:** Premium 80-proof tequila that comes in Gold and Silver.

- **Milagro Tequila:** Made in Jalisco using 100-percent estate-grown blue agave. Milagro makes a Silver, a Reposado, and an Añejo. The company also makes a Limon (from lemons) and a Mandarina (from oranges).

- **Paqui:** Handcrafted in small batches in the town of Tequila, Mexico.

- **Partida:** An authentic estate-grown tequila, available in Añejo, Blanco, and Reposado.

- **Patrón:** Available in Añejo, Silver, Reposado, Burdeos, and Gran Platinum versions, all containing 100-percent blue agave.

- **Pepe Lopez:** Available in de Oro (gold) and Superior Silver (white) labels.

- **Revolucion Tequila Extra Añejo:** 100-percent blue agave, distilled twice, and aged in 10-year-old oak barrels for a minimum of three years.

- **Sauza:** The first tequila exported to the United States. It's available in these versions: Tequila Blanco, Tequila Gold, Hacienda, Conmemorativo, Hornitos, and Tres Generaciones (available in Añejo, Reposado, and Plata).

- **Two Fingers:** Available in Gold, Limitado, and White. Named after a rogue entrepreneur, tequila producer, and occasional bandit from the Guadalajara area of Mexico who had only two fingers on his right hand (the index and thumb).

Messin' with Mezcal

The process of making *mezcal* hasn't changed much since the Spanish arrived in Mexico in the early 1800s and brought with them distillation technologies. The Aztecs near the mountaintop settlement of Monte Alban in Oaxaca had cultivated a certain species of agave plant for juice, which they fermented into what they called *pulque.* The Spaniards, wanting something much more potent, began to experiment with agave.

Mezcal, like tequila, is made from the agave plant, but the process is different. What's more, while tequila is made exclusively in the northwestern state of Jalisco, mezcal is exclusive to Oaxaca.

Mezcal has a high potency and a strong, smoky flavor. Distillers insist that the drink has medicinal and tonic qualities. In Mexico, tribal women drink mezcal to withstand the pain of childbirth, and laborers drink it for added strength.

The famous worm

Worms live in the agave plant and are hand-harvested during the rainy summer season. They're stored in mezcal, drained and sorted, and placed in bottles near the end of the process. The worm is what makes mezcal unique; it's added as a reminder that it comes from the same plant from which the alcohol is made.

Apocryphal legends note that the worm gives strength to anyone brave enough to gulp it down. Some even believe it acts as an aphrodisiac. Like the drink itself, the worm is something of an acquired taste.

A few brands

The number of mezcal brands is much smaller than the number of tequila brands. Here are a few:

- ✓ **Gusano Rojo Mezcal**
- ✓ **Ilegal Mezcal**
- ✓ **Miguel de la Vega Mezcal**
- ✓ **Monte Alban**

Storing and Serving Suggestions

The traditional way to drink straight tequila requires a little coordination and a steady hand. Place salt on the web of the hand between your thumb and forefinger. Hold a wedge of lime or lemon with the same two fingers and have a 1-ounce shot glass filled with tequila in the other hand. In one quick, continuous motion, lick the salt, drink the tequila, and bite the lime or lemon wedge.

Tequila also appears in many popular cocktails, including the Margarita.

You drink mezcal straight, without the salt or citrus. Some folks drink it with a dram of water, but not in Mexico.

An opened bottle of tequila or mezcal has a shelf life of many years if kept in a cool, dry place.

Chapter 15

Vodka

● ●

In This Chapter

▶ Distilling vodka from potatoes, grains, and beets

▶ Sampling vodka brands from all over the world

▶ Having fun with fruity flavors

● ●

*V*odka, a clear, almost flavorless spirit, is usually thought of as the national spirit of Russia and other Slavic nations. Both Russia and Poland claim the invention of vodka and explain that the name is a diminutive of the word *voda,* meaning *little water.* Slavic countries have been producing vodka for more than 600 years.

How Vodka Is Made

Vodka was originally distilled only from potatoes, but today, it's also made from grain — mostly wheat, rye, and corn. But distillers don't seem at all hindered by tradition — in Turkey, they use beets! Vodkas are distilled at a very high proof (190 or higher), and most are filtered through activated charcoal. Certain charcoals are so important to the making of vodka that distillers patent them. High-end vodkas are triple- and even quadruple-distilled, and some are filtered through fine quartz sand.

Popular Brands

Vodka is now produced in almost every country in the world, and each location tends to put its spin on the classic. You may want to sample some of the following brands to see whether you can find differences:

- **42Below:** An award-winning, 84-proof vodka from New Zealand.

- **360 Vodka:** An eco-friendly, green-packaged vodka that's quadruple-distilled.

- **Absolut:** From Sweden.

- **Artic:** Wheat vodka from Italy.

- **Belvedere:** From Poland.

- **Blavod:** 80-proof black vodka distilled in the United Kingdom.

- **Boru:** Made in Ireland from grain and pure Irish water.

- **Chopin:** From Poland; made with potatoes.

- **Cîroc:** Made from snap-frost grapes in southwestern France and distilled five times.

- **Crystal Head:** Made with water from a deep aquifer in Newfoundland and sold in a cool skull-shaped bottle.

- **Danzka:** Made with wheat from Denmark.

- **Double Cross:** An award-winning, seven-time distilled vodka produced in the Slovak Republic.

- **Ed Hardy:** Made with wheat from France.

- **EFFEN:** A Dutch vodka. In a bar, if you order a cocktail made with EFFEN, you're supposed to say, "Give me an EFFEN Screwdriver," or, "I'd like an EFFEN Cape Cod." Get it?

- **Finlandia:** Classic Finlandia is imported from Finland. It's made from spring water and barley.

- **Fris:** Produced in Scandinavia.

- **Gilbey's:** An American vodka.

- **Glacier:** Distilled in Rigby, Idaho, using Idaho potatoes and water from the Rocky Mountains.

- **Gordon's:** Has been distilled in the United States since 1957.

- **Grey Goose:** From France, made from fine grain and mineral water that's naturally filtered with champagne limestone.

- **Hamptons:** From the Hamptons in New York.

✔ **Hangar One:** An 80-proof vodka made with American wheat and Viognier grapes (a white wine grape).

✔ **Iceberg Vodka:** Made from the waters of icebergs from the coast of Greenland.

✔ **Jewel of Russia:** Made with only natural ingredients from an ancient recipe.

✔ **Ketel One:** From Holland, Ketel One is handmade in small batches according to the techniques and secret family recipe developed by the Nolet family more than 300 years ago.

✔ **Kremlyovskaya:** "Kremly" is made in the Vladimir region of Russia.

✔ **Level Vodka:** An ultra-premium vodka from the makers of Absolut.

✔ **Luksusowa:** An original potato vodka (unlike most vodkas, which are grain-based), made in Poland.

✔ **McCormick Vodka:** Quadruple-distilled vodka made from American grain.

✔ **Nikoli:** A very inexpensive vodka made in the United States.

✔ **Pearl:** Made from Canadian Rocky Mountain spring water and distilled from Canadian winter wheat.

✔ **Pink:** Made with wheat from the Netherlands.

✔ **Rain Organics:** 80-proof organic vodka distilled seven times, made with organic white corn.

✔ **Reyka:** From Iceland.

✔ **Russian Standard:** The number-one premium brand in Russia. Employing a unique blend of century-old tradition and a passionate attention to detail, it's made using only the finest Russian ingredients.

✔ **Seagram's Vodka:** A very popular vodka from Canada.

✔ **SKYY:** An American vodka made with 100-percent pure mountain water.

✔ **Smirnoff:** From the United States, the largest-selling vodka in the world.

✔ **Snow Leopard:** Made from spelt grain from Poland.

✔ **Snow Queen:** Made with organic wheat from Kazakhstan.

How that Russian drink got going in the United States

American John Martin of Heublein Inc. is credited with encouraging Americans to drink vodka. In the summer of 1946, he and his friend Jack Morgan, the owner of the Cock 'n' Bull Restaurant in Los Angeles, were discussing his Smirnoff Vodka when Jack remembered that he had an overstock of ginger beer. Jack and John mixed the two, added a dash of lime juice, and thus created the Moscow Mule. It spread rapidly, promoted by Heublein ("It leaves you breathless!"), who had it served in a copper mug. Smirnoff Vodka was in high demand and is still the number-one-selling vodka in the United States.

✔ **Sobieski:** The number-one premium vodka in Poland. Made with Dankowski rye.

✔ **Square One:** A certified organic, 80-proof vodka made with organically grown America rye.

✔ **Stolichnaya:** A Russian vodka also known as "Stoli."

✔ **Svedka:** Imported from Sweden.

✔ **Tanqueray Sterling:** An English vodka from the makers of Tanqueray gin.

✔ **Three Olives Vodka:** Imported from England.

✔ **Tito's Handmade Vodka:** Produced in Texas's first and oldest legal distillery, Tito's Handmade Vodka is distilled six times.

✔ **Ultimat:** A rich, smooth-tasting, ultra-premium vodka made from wheat, rye, and potatoes.

✔ **UV Vodka:** A four-time distilled corn vodka made in the United States.

✔ **Vermont Vodka:** Available in a Gold variety distilled from the sugar of maple sap and a White variety distilled from pure milk sugar.

✔ **Vincent Van Gogh Vodka:** From Holland, handcrafted using small batches of the finest grains.

- **VOX:** Distilled five times in the Netherlands from 100-percent wheat.
- **Wyborowa:** From Poland.
- **Xellent:** A Swiss vodka.

Flavored Vodkas

Flavored vodkas, which have become quite popular, are made with the addition of natural flavoring ingredients. Scores of flavored vodkas are available, from apple to Zubrowka. (Once sold with a single blade of grass in each bottle, Zubrowka is no longer available with grass in the United States, as some believed the grass contained a toxic compound, but you can still get it *sans flora*.) New flavors of vodka come out seemingly every day. The following is a list of some of the most popular flavored vodkas:

- **4 Orange Premium Vodka** is the world's first and only super-premium vodka distilled from pure Florida oranges.
- **Absolut** offers these flavors: Apeach, Berri Açaí, Citron, Kurant, Mandrin, Mango, Pears, Peppar, Raspberri, Ruby Red, and Vanilia.
- **Bakon Vodka** is a bacon-flavored vodka made from potatoes and the essence of bacon.
- **EFFEN Black Cherry** combines natural black cherry and vanilla flavors.
- **Finlandia** offers Cranberry, Lime, and Tangerine.
- **Firefly** offers Lemon Tea, Mint Tea, Peach Tea, Raspberry Tea, and Sweet Tea Vodka.
- **Gordon's** offers Citrus and Wildberry.
- **Grey Goose** offers Le Citron, L'Orange, and La Poire.
- **Ketel One** offers Citroen and Oranje.
- **Seagram's** offers Peach Tea and Sweet Tea.
- **SKYY** offers Cherry, Citrus, Ginger, Grape, Passion Fruit, Pineapple, and Raspberry flavors.

- ✔ **Smirnoff** offers Black Cherry, Black Ice, Blueberry, Cranberry, Green Apple, Raspberry, Strawberry, Vanilla, and Watermelon.

- ✔ **Sobieski** offers Karamel, Cytron, Vanilia, Raspberry, and Orange.

- ✔ **Square One** offers Cucumber and Botanical vodkas.

- ✔ **Stoli** offers Blakberi, Blue (a sweet vodka with a hint of vanilla), Blueberi, Citros, Cranberi, Gala Applik, Ohranj, Peachik, Razberi, Strasberi, and Vanil.

- ✔ **Three Olives** is offered in Berry, Cherry, Chocolate, Citrus, Grape, Green Apple, Orange, Raspberry, and more.

- ✔ **UV Vodka** offers Apple, Blue, Citruv, Cherry, Lemonade, Grape, Orange, and Vanilla.

- ✔ **Vincent Van Gogh** offers Acai-Blueberry, Banana, Black Cherry, Double Espresso, Dutch Chocolate, Espresso, Grape, Mango, Mojito Mint, Pineapple, Pomegranate, and more.

- ✔ **VOX Raspberry** has the flavor of fresh raspberries.

Storing and Serving Vodka

Store at least one bottle in the freezer or refrigerator. It won't freeze because of the high alcohol content. Serve vodka neat (aka straight up) in a small cordial glass, especially with caviar, smoked fish, salmon, sardines, steak tartare, and spicy foods.

Vodka is one of the most mixable and versatile of spirits and is used in hundreds of cocktail recipes. When an opened bottle is refrigerated or stored in a cool, dry place, it should last up to three years.

Chapter 16

Wine

· ·

In This Chapter

▶ Discovering wine varieties (there's more than just red and white)

▶ Exploring port and sherry

▶ Checking out sparkling wines and vermouth

· ·

*W*ine, as most of you know, is made from fermented grapes. It comes in red, white, or rosé (pink or blush) varieties. Winemaking dates back to roughly 3000 BC, and it's here to stay.

Wines from Around the World

Climate is a big factor in making good wine. To grow wine-worthy grapes, summers can't be too hot and autumns need to be cool. Light rainfall is necessary in the winter and spring, and the rain needs to taper off in the summer and fall. Harsh, cold winters with hail, frost, and heavy winds are bad for growing grapes.

The type of grape determines the type of wine, and only certain types of grapes grow in certain climates. To make matters even more complicated, the soil of a particular region plays a big role in how its grapes turn out. So while the climate in certain regions of California and France may be perfect for, say, chardonnay grapes, the soil in those regions affects the grapes to the point that the resulting wines from each region are different.

Many wines receive their names from the grape from which they're produced. See the following list of some popular wines named after grapes:

- Barbera (red): Italy
- Cabernet Sauvignon (red): France, United States
- Camay (red): France, United States
- Chardonnay (white): France, United States, Argentina, Australia, South America
- Chenin Blanc (white): France, United States
- Gewürztraminer (white): Germany
- Grenache (rosé): France, United States
- Merlot (red): France, United States, South America
- Pinot Noir (red): France, United States
- Reisling (white): Germany, United States, France
- Sauvignon Blanc (white): France, United States
- Semillon (white): France, United States, Australia
- Zinfandel (red and white): United States

Some popular French wines are as follows. They're named after the region of France from which they originate.

- Alsace (white)
- Beaujolais (red) from Burgundy
- Bordeaux (red and white)
- Burgundy (red and white)
- Rhône (red)
- Sauterne (white) from Bordeaux

The following is a list of some German wines that are worth noting (all are white):

- Gewürztraminer
- Johannisberg Riesling
- Spalleseen

Italy produces all kinds of regional wines:

- ✔ **Barbaresco** (red) from Piedmont
- ✔ **Barbera** (red) from Piedmont
- ✔ **Bardolino** (red) from Veneto
- ✔ **Barolo** (red) from Piedmont
- ✔ **Chianti** (red) from Tuscany
- ✔ **Orvieto** (white) from Umbria
- ✔ **Pinot Grigio** (white) from Trentino
- ✔ **Riserva** (red) from Tuscany
- ✔ **Soave** (white) from Veneto
- ✔ **Valpolicella** (red) from Veneto

Australia's wines are growing in popularity. Here are the names of just a few:

- ✔ **Grange** (red)
- ✔ **Grenache** (red)
- ✔ **Semillon** (white)
- ✔ **Shiraz** (or **Syrah**) (red)

Some South American wines include

- ✔ **Chandonnay** (white)
- ✔ **Malbec** (red) from Argentina
- ✔ **Merlot** (red) from Chile
- ✔ **Torrontes** (white) from Argentina

In the United States, California produces 90 percent of all wine. Most California wine comes from Napa Valley or Sonoma Valley, and those areas produce both red and white wines in varieties too numerous to list.

Port

Port is a sweet, fortified wine to which brandy is added. It's named for *Oporto* — a city in northern Portugal. It's made from grapes grown in some 72,000 acres of vineyards in a designated area along the Douro River, known as the *Alto Douro*.

Although many wines are sold as port throughout the world, authentic port wine is the unique product of Portugal. By law, it must be made only from approved grape varieties native to the Alto Douro district and grown nowhere else in the country.

Fortification with brandy gives port extra strength and, more important, preserves the fresh flavor of grapes that makes port so delicious.

Port comes in three varieties:

- **Ruby:** Dark in color and fairly sweet.
- **Tawny:** Lighter in color and drier because it's aged in casks longer.
- **Vintage port:** Released only in certain exceptional years; the fullest and sweetest of all ports.

The following are some popular brands:

- **Cockburn's**
- **Croft**
- **Royal Oporto**
- **Sandeman**

Port is a great after-dinner drink. It also goes well with cheese and cigars. An opened bottle of port has a shelf life of four to six months.

Sherry

The English discovered the wines of Jerez, Spain, calling them *jerries,* and the word later evolved into *sherry.* Sherry is a fortified wine to which grape brandy is added. No longer limited to production in Spain, sherry is now produced all over the world.

Sherry comes in five basic styles:

- ✔ **Fino:** Light and very dry; usually served chilled as an aperitif.
- ✔ **Manzanilla:** Pale, dry, and light-bodied; also served chilled as an aperitif.
- ✔ **Amontillado:** Medium-dry and full-bodied; perfect between meals or with soup and cheese.
- ✔ **Oloroso:** Gold in color with a strong bouquet; more hardy than Amontillado.
- ✔ **Cream:** A smooth, sweet wine. Cream sherry is what results when Oloroso is blended with a sweetening wine, such as Moscatel. Cream is the largest-selling sherry. It can be served at any time, chilled or over ice.

The following are popular sherry brands:

- ✔ **Dry Sack**
- ✔ **Gonzalez Byass**
- ✔ **Harveys Bristol Cream**
- ✔ **Savory & James**

Sparkling Wines

A monk whose name is now familiar — Dom Perignon — developed the first sparkling wine in the 1600s in the Champagne region of France. Without going into all the details, he developed a method of bottling wine so that carbon dioxide, a product of fermentation, remains in the bottle with the wine, and the result is the presence of bubbles.

Sparkling wine made in the Champagne region is called, of course, *champagne.* It's made with a mix of different grapes (including pinot noir, pinot meunier, and chardonnay) through a process called *méthod champenoise,* which is quite costly and time-consuming. Sparkling wines from other places in the world are made in different ways with different grapes. For example, prosecco is an Italian sparkling wine made from glera grapes. But you can find sparkling wines from places such as California that are made using the *méthod champenoise.*

Champagne and other sparkling wines should be stored in a cool, dark place away from heat, light, vibrations, and severe temperature variations. Unlike the best wines from Bordeaux or California, sparkling wines are ready for consumption when they're shipped to the market. However, some wine lovers also enjoy cellaring their champagnes for a few extra years.

Before serving, chill the wine well, but don't freeze it. Placing the bottle in a bucket filled with ice and water for 30 to 40 minutes is the best way to chill champagne. You can also chill a bottle by refrigerating it for several hours, but don't keep bottles in the fridge for extended periods of time. The excessive cold and the vibration of the motor will cause the flavor to go a little flat.

Champagne is best served in tall flute or tulip glasses at a temperature of 42 to 47 degrees Fahrenheit. Tiny bubbles will rise in a continuous stream. When serving, pour a small quantity of champagne into each glass and allow it to settle. Then fill each glass two-thirds full.

For much more information on how to buy and serve champagne, check out *Champagne For Dummies* by Ed McCarthy (Wiley).

Vermouth

Vermouth originated in the 18th century, when wine growers in the foothills of the French and Italian Alps developed a method of enhancing the taste of sour or uncompromising wines with the infusion of a variety of sweeteners, spices, herbs, roots, seeds, flowers, and peels. Just a few of the herbs and spices used to flavor and aromatize the wine include cloves, bitter orange peel, nutmeg, gentian, camomile, and wormwood, which in German is *wermut,* from which vermouth got its name. After it's flavored, the wine is clarified, pasteurized, and fortified to an alcoholic content of about 18 percent — close to that of sherry.

The standard classification of vermouth is white/dry and red/sweet, but exceptions do exist, including a half-sweet variety known as rosé. And though most dry vermouths are considered French and sweet vermouths are considered Italian, both types are produced in France and Italy, as well as throughout the world, including in the United States.

Vermouth is an ingredient in many cocktails, and just as carefully as you select other liquor to pour at the bar, so you should take care and time in selecting a good vermouth. Choose the brand of vermouth that tastes best to you — crisp and light, not too heavy or burnt. Check out the following list of popular brands:

- ✔ **Boissiere**
- ✔ **Cinzano**
- ✔ **Martini & Rossi**
- ✔ **Noilly Prat**
- ✔ **Stock**

You need to refrigerate a bottle of vermouth after opening. The shelf life of an open bottle, when refrigerated, is approximately one year.

One Final Word on Wines

I haven't said nearly as much about wine as I would like. The fact is, people have written whole books on single types of wine, so it's sort of foolish for me to even pretend to give a comprehensive overview in a single chapter. The focus of this book, after all, is cocktail recipes.

A great introduction to buying, serving, and drinking wine is *Wine For Dummies,* 4th Edition, by Ed McCarthy and Mary Ewing-Mulligan (Wiley). It's full of useful and interesting information, and it makes a great companion to this book.

Part III
The Recipes

"This time, let's keep the eye of newt out of the punch."

In this part . . .

Chapter 17 presents around a thousand great cocktail recipes, listed in alphabetical order. Chapter 18 offers over 20 interesting martinis. Then I serve up some punch, holiday cocktails, and tasty nonalcoholic drinks, all of which will come in handy for your next party.

Chapter 17

Recipes from A to Z

In This Chapter

▶ Many, many cocktail recipes

▶ A few stories to keep things interesting

*Y*ou probably bought this book just for this chapter, which lists the recipes for about a thousand drinks. Some are classic drinks that you've probably heard of; others are new and trendy. Most are quite good; some are strange concoctions that few people like.

This cute little icon to the right of the drink name indicates a classic drink. The appropriate glass for each drink is shown to the left of its list of ingredients. I put little stories and anecdotes in sidebars — the text that's set apart in gray boxes.

If you're looking for nonalcoholic drinks, see Chapter 20. You won't find punches in this chapter either. They're in Chapter 19.

One final note: Just in case you don't know, the term *straight up* means *without ice.*

A Tinker Tall

1¼ oz. Irish Mist	Combine ingredients with lots of ice
3 oz. Ginger Ale	in a tall glass.
3 oz. Club Soda	

A-Bomb #1

½ oz. Ultimat Vodka
½ oz. Coffee Liqueur
½ oz. Irish Cream
½ oz. Orange Liqueur

Shake with ice, strain, and serve in a highball glass.

A-Bomb #2

½ oz. Baileys Irish Cream
½ oz. Kahlúa
½ oz. Stolichnaya
¼ oz. Tia Maria

Shake with ice and strain.

You can also serve this one in a rocks glass.

Absente Frappé

2 oz. Grande Absente
½ oz. Anisette
4 oz. Soda Water or Seltzer

Combine ingredients in a tall glass with a mountain of crushed ice.

This is the hot new recipe out of the French Quarter.

Absohot

1½ shot Absolut Peppar Vodka
1 dash Hot Sauce

Combine ingredients in a shot glass and serve with a beer chaser.

This one really is hot.

Absolut Citron Rickey

1¼ oz. Absolut Citron Vodka
Club Soda

In a glass filled with ice, add Vodka. Fill with Club Soda and garnish with a Lemon.

A classic cocktail with a summer twist.

Absolut Quaalude

1 oz. Baileys Irish Cream
1 oz. Frangelico
1 oz. Absolut Vodka

Shake ingredients with ice and strain into a glass filled with ice.

Absolution

| 1 oz. Absolut Vodka
5 oz. Champagne | In a fluted champagne glass, add ingredients. Cut a Lemon Peel in the form of a ring to represent a halo. The Lemon Peel can be either wrapped around the top of the glass or floated on top of the Champagne. |

Created by Jimmy Caulfield at the River Café, New York, New York.

Acapulco Gold

| 1¼ oz. Jose Cuervo Especial Tequila
⅝ oz. Grand Marnier
1 oz. Sweet & Sour Mix | Blend with ice. |

After 5

| 1 oz. Irish Cream
1 oz. Rumple Minze | Pour the ingredients in a shot glass. |

After 8

| ½ oz. Irish Cream
½ oz. Coffee Liqueur
½ oz. Green Crème de Menthe | Shake with ice. Strain into a shot glass. |

The After Ten

| 1 oz. Galliano
1 oz. Remy Martin Cognac
3 oz. Coffee | Rim glass with Brown Sugar. Add freshly brewed coffee and top with whipped cream. |

Alabama Slammer

| 1 oz. Amaretto
1 oz. Sloe Gin
1 oz. Southern Comfort
splash Lemon Juice | Shake ingredients and serve in a shot glass. |

One of the first popular shots. Cover with napkins or a coaster. You can also serve this one over ice in a highball glass.

A

The Alamo Splash

1½ oz. Jose Cuervo Gold Tequila
1 oz. Orange Juice
½ oz. Pineapple Juice
splash 7-Up

Mix well with cracked ice, strain, and serve right from a glass in a thin, well-aimed stream directly into the recipient's mouth.

Alaska

1¾ oz. Cork Dry Gin
¼ oz. Yellow Chartreuse

Shake with ice and strain into a shot glass.

Albuquerque Real

1½ oz. Jose Cuervo Especial
      Tequila
½ oz. Triple Sec
½ oz. Sweet & Sour Mix
¼ oz. Cranberry Juice
splash Grand Marnier

Stir all but Grand Marnier in the glass. Float the Grand Marnier on top.

You can also serve this one in a cocktail glass.

Algonquin

1½ oz. Blended Whiskey
1 oz. Dry Vermouth
1 oz. Pineapple Juice
3 Ice Cubes

Combine all ingredients in a shaker and shake. Strain into chilled cocktail glass.

Could be named for the famous round table.

Alice in Wonderland

½ oz. Herradura Tequila
½ oz. Tia Maria
½ oz. Grand Marnier

Shake with ice and strain into shot glass.

This one will get the Cheshire Cat smiling.

Almond Lemonade

1¼ oz. Vodka
¼ oz. Amaretto
Lemonade

Shake with ice and strain into a shot glass.

Summer in Italy.

Ambrosia

1 oz. Applejack
1 oz. Brandy
¼ oz. Cointreau
¼ oz. Lemon Juice
2 oz. Champagne

Shake the first four ingredients over ice and strain into a champagne flute. Fill with Champagne.

This drink was created at Arnaud's restaurant in New Orleans immediately following the end of Prohibition. The word "ambrosia" comes from the Greek mabrotos, meaning "immortal."

Ambush

1 oz. Bushmills Irish Whiskey
1 oz. Amaretto
5 oz. Coffee

Serve hot in mug. Top with whipped cream if desired.

Americano

1 oz. Martini & Rossi Rosso
   Vermouth
1 oz. Campari
Club Soda

Build with ice in a highball glass. Top with Club Soda and a twist.

A classic from Italy.

Angel's Delight

½ oz. Grenadine
½ oz. Triple Sec
½ oz. Sloe Gin
½ oz. Heavy Cream

Layer this drink in the order listed. Start with Grenadine on the bottom and finish with Cream on top.

Angostura Costa Del Sol

1½ oz. Cream Sherry
2 oz. Orange Juice
2 oz. Cream
2 dashes Angostura

Shake with ice and serve in a rocks or highball glass.

Anti-Freeze

1½ oz. Vodka
½ oz. Midori

Shake with ice, strain, and serve.

You can also serve this one in a rocks glass.

Apple Kir

1 oz. Jose Cuervo Gold Tequila
½ oz. Crème de Cassis
1 oz. Apple Juice
1 tsp. Fresh Lemon Juice

Mix in a rocks glass over ice. Garnish with a Lemon Wedge.

Apple Pie

½ oz. Apple Schnapps
½ oz. Vodka
½ oz. Pineapple Juice
dash Powdered Cinnamon

Shake with ice and strain into a shot glass.

Applejack Cobbler

2½ oz. Laird's Applejack
½ oz. Simple Syrup
2 or 3 thinly cut Apple Slices

Pour ingredients over crushed ice and stir very briefly. Garnish with the Apple Slices.

Appletini

1½ oz. DeKuyper Pucker Sour Apple
1½ oz. VOX Vodka

Shake with ice and strain into a chilled martini glass. Garnish with an Apple Slice.

Apricot Sour

2 tbsp. Lemon Juice
½ tsp. Superfine Sugar
2 oz. Apricot Brandy
3–4 Ice Cubes

Combine all ingredients in a shaker and shake vigorously. Strain into a chilled cocktail glass. Garnish with Lemon.

The hot drink of the '60s.

Aunt Rose

1¼ oz. Irish Mist
2 oz. Cranberry Juice
2 oz. Orange Juice

Shake. Serve in a tall glass with ice.

Yes, there is an Aunt Rose from Ireland.

Aviation

2 oz. Plymouth Gin
1 oz. Fresh-Squeezed Lemon
    Juice
¼ oz. Maraschino Liqueur
dash Simple Syrup

Fill mixing glass with ice. Add
ingredients and shake well. Strain
into a martini glass. Add Lemon Zest
for garnish.

B & B

1 oz. Benedictine
1 oz. Brandy

Stir and serve in a snifter.

An easy one to remember.

B-52

½ oz. Grand Marnier
½ oz. Kahlúa
½ oz. Baileys Irish Cream

Shake with ice. Strain or serve over
ice.

You can also serve this one as a shot.

B-52 with Bombay Doors

½ oz. Kahlúa
½ oz. Baileys Irish Cream
½ oz. Grand Marnier
½ oz. Bombay Gin

Shake with ice and strain into a shot
glass.

Keep the door open.

Bacardi & Cola

1½ oz. Bacardi Light or Dark Rum
Cola

Pour Rum into tall glass filled with ice. Fill with your favorite Cola and garnish with a squeeze of a Lemon.

Bacardi & Tonic

1¼ oz. Bacardi Light Rum
Tonic

Pour Rum into a tall glass filled with ice. Fill with Tonic.

A change in mixer.

Bacardi Blossom

1¼ oz. Bacardi Light Rum
1 oz. Orange Juice
½ oz. Lemon Juice
½ tsp. Sugar

Blend with crushed ice and pour.

Sweet as a spring flower.

Bacardi Champagne Cocktail

1 oz. Bacardi Silver Rum
1 tsp. Sugar
dash Bitters
Champagne

In a Champage flute, mix Rum, Sugar, and Bitters. Fill with Champagne.

Bacardi Cocktail

1¼ oz. Bacardi Light Rum
1 oz. Rose's Lime Juice
½ tsp. Sugar
½ oz. Rose's Grenadine

Mix in a shaker with ice and strain into a chilled cocktail glass.

The New York Supreme Court ruled in 1936 that a Bacardi Cocktail is not a Bacardi Cocktail unless it's made with Bacardi Rum. You can also serve this one over ice in a rocks glass.

Bacardi Collins

1½ to 2 oz. Bacardi Light Rum
2 tsp. Frozen Lemonade or
   Limeade Concentrate
½ tsp. Sugar
Club Soda

Combine first two ingredients in a tall glass with ice. Fill with Club Soda.

A Collins with rum instead of gin, whiskey, vodka, and so on.

Bacardi Daiquiri

1¼ oz. Bacardi Light Rum
½ oz. Lemon Juice
½ tsp. Sugar

Mix in shaker with ice and strain into a chilled cocktail glass.

The original Daiquiri was made with Bacardi Rum in 1896. You can add bananas, orange juice, peaches, and any other fruit that you enjoy. You can also serve this one in a highball glass over ice.

Bacardi Dragon Berry Dragon Serum

2 oz. Bacardi Dragon Berry
   Flavored Rum
1½ oz. Orange Juice
1½ oz. Cranberry Juice

Pour ingredients over ice in a tall glass and garnish with an Orange Wedge.

Bacardi Dry Martini

2 oz. Bacardi Light Rum
½ oz. Martini & Rossi Dry
   Vermouth

Shake with ice and strain.

A new Caribbean classic. You can also serve this one over ice in a highball glass.

Bacardi Fizz

1¼ oz. Bacardi Light Rum
¼ oz. Lemon Juice
¼ oz. Rose's Grenadine
Club Soda

Pour Rum and Lemon Juice in a highball glass filled with ice. Add the Grenadine and fill with Club Soda.

Bacardi Grand Melón & Cranberry

2 oz. Bacardi Grand Melón
4 oz. Cranberry Juice

Pour ingredients over ice. Garnish with fresh Watermelon.

Bacardi Hemingway

1½ oz. Bacardi Light Rum
Juice of ½ Lime
¼ oz. Grapefruit Juice
¼ oz. Maraschino Liqueur

Mix with ice and serve.

Ernest would have written about this one.

Bacardi Limón Martini

2 oz. Bacardi Limón
dash Martini & Rossi Extra Dry
  Vermouth
splash Cranberry Juice

Stir in a cocktail glass. Garnish with Lemon.

It's a new twist on an old classic. First invented at the Heart and Soul in San Francisco, California.

Bacardi Sunset

1¼ oz. Bacardi Light Rum
3 oz. Orange Juice
squeeze of Lime

Combine in a tall glass with crushed ice. Add a squeeze of Lime. Garnish with an Orange Wheel.

What a way to end the day.

Bagpiper

1½ oz. 100 Pipers Scotch
3 oz. Coffee

Stir in an Irish coffee glass and top with whipped cream.

Bailey Shillelagh

1 part Baileys Irish Cream
1 part Romana Sambuca

Pour ingredients in a shot glass.

Baileys & Coffee

1½ oz. Baileys Irish Cream
5 oz. Coffee

Pour the Irish Cream into a cup of steaming Coffee.

Easy enough.

Baileys Alexander

1½ oz. Baileys Irish Cream
½ oz. Cognac

Shake well with ice and serve over ice.

You can also strain this one into a cocktail glass.

Baileys Banana Blaster

1 oz. Baileys Irish Cream
1 oz. Malibu Rum
½ oz. Banana Liqueur or
   ½ Banana

Blend with ice until smooth.

You can also serve this one in a margarita glass.

Baileys Chocolate Covered Cherry

½ oz. Grenadine
½ oz. Kahlúa
½ oz. Baileys Irish Cream

Layer Grenadine, Kahlúa, and then Irish Cream in a shot glass.

You can also serve this one over ice in a rocks glass (without layering the ingredients, of course).

Baileys Coconut Frappé

2 oz. Baileys Irish Cream
1 oz. Malibu Rum
2 oz. Milk

Shake or blend until frothy; pour over ice and garnish with Toasted Coconut.

You can also serve this one in a cocktail glass.

Baileys Dublin Double

1 part Baileys Irish Cream
1 part Di Saronno Amaretto

Pour ingredients in a shot glass.

B

Baileys Eggnog

1 oz. Baileys Irish Cream
½ oz. Irish Whiskey
1 Medium Egg
2 cups Milk
dash Nutmeg

Mix with cracked ice in a shaker, strain, and serve in a glass. Sprinkle Nutmeg on top.

Baileys Fizz

2 oz. Baileys Irish Cream
3 oz. Club Soda

Combine ingredients and pour over crushed ice.

Baileys Float

2 oz. Baileys Irish Cream
2 scoops Softened Ice Cream

Blend ingredients until frothy. Top with one more scoop of Ice Cream.

Baileys French Dream

1½ oz. Baileys Irish Cream
½ oz. Raspberry Liqueur
2 oz. Half & Half
4 oz. Ice Cubes

Blend for 30 seconds and serve.

Baileys Hot Milk Punch

1 oz. Baileys Irish Cream
¼ oz. Cognac
1½ tsp. Sugar
3 oz. Hot Milk
dash Freshly Ground Nutmeg

Combine Baileys, Cognac, and Sugar. Add Hot Milk and stir. Sprinkle with Nutmeg.

Baileys Iced Cappuccino

5 oz. Double-Strength Coffee
½ cup Ice
2 oz. Baileys Irish Cream
1 oz. Half & Half
2 tsp. Sugar

Brew a pot of double-strength Coffee and set aside to cool. In a blender, combine the other ingredients. Blend for 10 seconds and pour into a 10 oz. glass filled with ice. Top with a dollop of Whipped Cream and sprinkle of Cinnamon, if desired.

Baileys Irish Coffee

3 oz. Freshly Brewed Coffee
2 oz. Baileys Irish Cream
½ oz. Irish Whiskey
1 tbsp. Whipped Sweetened
   Cream

After brewing Coffee, combine with Irish Cream and Whiskey. Top with Cream.

Baileys Irish Mudslide

1 oz. Baileys Irish Cream
1 oz. Coffee Liqueur
1 oz. Vodka

Mix ingredients and pour into a rocks glass.

You can also blend the ingredients with ice and serve the drink as a frozen beverage in a margarita glass.

Baileys Malibu Slide

1 oz. Baileys Irish Cream
1 oz. Kahlúa
1 oz. Malibu Rum

Blend with ice and serve in a rocks glass.

You can also serve this one in a margarita glass.

Baileys Mint Kiss

1 oz. Baileys Irish Cream
3 oz. Coffee
½ oz. Rumple Minze
½ oz. Peppermint Schnapps

Combine ingredients. Top with fresh Whipped Cream.

You can also serve this drink in a margarita glass.

Baileys O'

½ oz. Baileys Irish Cream
½ oz. Stolichnaya Vodka
½ oz. Stoli Ohranj Vodka

Combine in a shot glass.

Baileys Roma

1 oz. Baileys Irish Cream
1 oz. Romana Sambuca

Pour over ice and serve.

It's the Irish and Italian together again.

Bald Head Martini

2 oz. Beefeater Gin
¼ oz. French Vermouth
¼ oz. Italian Vermouth
2 dashes Pernod

Stir gently with ice. Strain or serve on the rocks. Sprinkle the oil from a twist of Lemon Peel on top.

Bamboo Cocktail

1½ oz. Sherry
¾ oz. Dry Vermouth
dash Angostura Bitters

Stir with ice and strain.

This drink was invented around 1910 by bartender Charlie Mahoney of the Hoffman House in New York, New York.

Banana Boat

¾ oz. Malibu Rum
¾ oz. Hiram Walker Banana
   Liqueur
¼ oz. Pineapple Juice

Combine in a shot glass.

Day-o – Day-o!

Banana Daiquiri

1¼ oz. Light Rum
¼ oz. Lemon Juice or Rose's
   Lime Juice
½ tsp. Sugar
1 Banana

Blend with ice and serve.

Peel the banana, of course.

Banana Man

1 oz. Bacardi Light Rum
¼ oz. Hiram Walker Banana
   Liqueur
½ oz. Lemon Juice or Rose's
   Lime Juice

Blend with ice and serve.

Banana Rum Cream

1½ oz. Puerto Rican Dark Rum
½ oz. Crème de Banana
1 oz. Light Cream

Shake well. Serve straight up or with ice.

The Barbados Cocktail

2 oz. Mount Gay Rum
½ oz. Cointreau
½ oz. Sweet & Sour

Shake with ice and serve.

Barnumenthe & Baileys

1½ oz. Baileys Irish Cream
½ oz. White Crème de Menthe

Combine in a rocks glass over cracked ice.

Serve this one when the circus is in town.

Barracuda

1¼ oz. Ronrico Dark Rum
1 oz. Pineapple Juice
½ oz. Rose's Lime Juice
¼ tsp. Sugar
Champagne

Shake everything but the Champagne. Serve in a champagne glass and fill to the top with Champagne.

Bat Bite

1¼ oz. Bacardi Silver Rum
4 oz. Cranberry Juice

Pour ingredients in a glass filled with ice. Squeeze and drop in one Lime or Lemon Wedge. Stir and serve.

Bay Breeze

1½ oz. Absolut Vodka
3 oz. Pineapple Juice
1 oz. Cranberry Juice

Stir. Serve over ice.

Quite refreshing.

Beach Bum

1 oz. Sobieski Vodka
1½ oz. Midori
1 oz. Cranberry Juice

Mix in a shaker with ice. Strain.

Beach Party

1¼ oz. Bacardi Light or Dark Rum
1 oz. Pineapple Juice
1 oz. Orange Juice
1 oz. Rose's Grenadine

Blend with ice.

Keep the sand out of this one.

Beachcomber

1½ oz. Puerto Rican White Rum
¾ oz. Rose's Lime Juice
¼ oz. Triple Sec
dash Maraschino Liqueur

Shake. Serve straight up or
with ice.

Beam Me Up Scotty

1 oz. Kahlúa
1 oz. Baileys Irish Cream
1 oz. Hiram Walker Crème de
    Banana

Shake with ice and strain into a shot
glass.

It's bar wars.

Beefeater Lemoneater

2 oz. Beefeater Gin
Lemonade

Add Gin to a glass filled with ice. Fill
with Lemonade.

Beefeater Red Coat

1½ oz. Beefeater Gin
5 oz. Cranberry Juice

Serve in a tall glass over ice.

Bee's Kiss

1 oz. Puerto Rican White Rum
¼ oz. Myers's Dark Rum
¾ oz. Cream
2 bar spoons Honey

Shake. Serve over ice.

Bellini

1 Peach Half
Simple Syrup
Champagne

Muddle the Peach in a champagne
glass with a little Simple Syrup. Fill
the glass with Champagne.

*Invented at Harry's Bar in Venice, Italy, by Giuseppi Cipriani on the
occasion of an exhibition of the work of Venetian painter Bellini.*

Bellini Easy

1 oz. Peach Schnapps
3 oz. Champagne

Pour Schnapps in a champagne glass
and add Champagne.

Bermuda Rose

1 oz. Bombay Gin
¼ oz. Apricot Flavored Brandy
½ oz. Rose's Lime Juice
dash Rose's Grenadine

Shake with ice and strain.

Bermuda Rum Swizzle

1 oz. Gosling's Black Seal Rum
1 oz. Gosling's Gold
   Bermuda Rum
2 oz. Orange Juice
2 oz. Pineapple Juice
dash Grenadine
dash Angostura Bitters

Churn vigorously with ice. Strain into
a highball glass with ice. Garnish
with an Orange Slice.

Between the Sheets

1 oz. Remy Martin Cognac
1 oz. Cointreau
1 oz. Bacardi Light Rum
dash Lemon Juice

Shake with ice. Strain into a
sugar-rimmed glass.

Bewitched

1 oz. B&B
1 oz. Vodka
1 oz. Cream

Stir over ice or shake with ice and pour.

Big Apple Mojito

12 Mint Leaves
½ tsp. Sugar
½ Lime
2 oz. Bacardi Big Apple Rum
3 oz. Club Soda

Place Mint Leaves, Sugar, and Lime in a glass. Crush well with a pestle. Add Bacardi Big Apple Rum. Top off with Club Soda. Stir well, and garnish with sprigs of Mint and a Lime Wheel or Green Apple Slices.

Bitch on Wheels

¼ oz. Martini & Rossi Extra Dry Vermouth
1 oz. Bombay Gin
¼ oz. Pernod
¼ oz. White Crème de Menthe

Shake ingredients with ice and strain into a chilled cocktail glass.

Invented at Stars in San Francisco, California.

Black and Tan

1½ oz. Irish Whiskey
1 oz. Jamaican Dark Rum
½ oz. Lime Juice
½ oz. Orange Juice
½ tsp. Superfine Sugar
6–8 Ice Cubes
4 oz. Chilled Ginger Ale

Combine Irish Whiskey, Rum, Lime and Orange Juice, Sugar, and 3 to 4 Ice Cubes in shaker and shake vigorously. Put the remaining ice in a glass. Strain the mixture into the glass and fill with Ginger Ale.

Black Buck

1¼ oz. Bacardi Black Rum
Ginger Ale

Pour Rum in a tall glass with ice. Fill with Ginger Ale and garnish with Lemon.

Black Currant Martini

1 oz. Godiva Liqueur
1 oz. Seagram's Gin
¼ oz. Crème de Cassis
⅙ oz. Lemon Juice
⅙ oz. Lime Juice

Combine ingredients with ice, shake well, and strain into a cocktail glass. Garnish with a Cherry.

Black Devil

1½ oz. Puerto Rican Light Rum
½ oz. Dry Vermouth
1 Pitted Black Olive

Stir well with ice and strain.

A hot drink.

Black Ice

1 oz. Opal Nera Sambuca
1 oz. Vodka
¼ oz. Crème de Menthe

Shake with ice and strain.

You can also serve this one over ice in a highball glass.

Black Magic

½ oz. Vodka
¾ oz. Coffee Liqueur
dash Lemon Juice

Mix the first two ingredients with cracked ice in a shaker. Add a dash of Lemon Juice.

Black Manhattan

1½ oz. Bushmills Black Bush Irish Whiskey
¼ oz. Sweet Vermouth

Fill mixing glass with ice. Add Irish Whiskey and Sweet Vermouth. Stir and strain into a chilled cocktail glass filled with ice. Garnish with a Cherry.

Black Maria

1 oz. Myers's Dark Rum
¾ oz. Tia Maria
1 bar spoon Sugar
½ cup Cold Coffee
Lemon Peel

Stir with ice and strain into a cocktail glass.

You can also serve this drink over ice in a highball glass.

Black Martini

1½ oz. Absolut Kurant
splash Chambord

Stir ingredients and serve straight up
or over ice.

Invented at the Continental Cafe in Philadelphia, Pennsylvania.

Black Orchid

1 oz. Sobieski Vodka
½ oz. Blue Curaçao
1½ oz. Cranberry Juice

Build over ice in a 7 oz. rocks glass.

A flower very rare and a drink very sweet.

Black Russian

1½ oz. Vodka
¾ oz. Kahlúa

Add Vodka and then Kahlúa to
a glass filled with cubed ice. Stir
briskly. Garnish with a Swizzle Stick.
Add cream for a White Russian.

You should use Russian Vodka.

Black Tie Martini

1½ oz. SKYY Vodka
spritz Campari
spritz Chivas
2 Cocktail Onions
1 Black Olive

Stir and serve straight up or over ice.

Invented at the Continental Cafe in Philadelphia, Pennsylvania.

Black Velvet (also known as a Bismarck or Champagne Velvet)

2 oz. Guinness Stout
2 oz. Champagne

Layer the Champagne over the
Guinness in a champagne flute.

Blackthorn #1

1½ oz. Irish Whiskey
1½ oz. Dry Vermouth
3–4 dashes Pernod
3–4 dashes Angostura Bitters

Shake or blend with ice. Pour into a chilled rocks glass. Sloe Gin can be used in place of Irish Whiskey.

Blackthorn #2

1½ oz. Bushmills Irish Whiskey
½ oz. Noilly Prat Dry Vermouth
dash Anisette

Stir with ice. Serve in a cocktail glass.

Blarney Cocktail

1½ oz. Irish Whiskey
1 oz. Italian Vermouth
splash Green Crème de Menthe

Shake well with ice. Strain into a cocktail glass. Serve with a Green Cherry.

Blarney Stone Cocktail

2 oz. Irish Whiskey
½ tsp. Pernod
½ tsp. Triple Sec
¼ tsp. Grenadine
1 dash Angostura Bitters

Shake with ice and strain. Serve with a twist of Orange Peel and an Olive.

Blighter Bob

1 oz. Puerto Rican Light Rum
½ oz. Puerto Rican Dark Rum
½ oz. Crème de Cassis
1 oz. Orange Juice
2 dashes Orange Bitters
2 oz. Ginger Ale

Stir and serve straight up or with ice. Garnish with a Lemon Twist.

Blizzard

1¼ oz. Vodka
Fresca

Add Vodka to a tall glass filled with ice. Fill with Fresca.

Nice and cold.

Blonde Ambition

2 oz. SKYY Infusions Pineapple
1 oz. fresh Lime Juice
¾ Triple Sec
¾ oz. Crème de Cacao

Combine all ingredients in a cocktail shaker with ice. Shake vigorously and strain into a martini glass. Garnish with a Lime Wedge.

Blood Ohranj Martini

3 parts Stoli Ohranj Vodka
1 part Campari
splash Club Soda

Stir ingredients with ice.

Bloody Bull

1¼ oz. Vodka
2½ oz. Tomato Juice
1½ oz. Beef Bouillon
1–2 tsp. Lemon Juice
dash Worcestershire Sauce
dash Tabasco Sauce
dash Pepper

Combine with ice in a shaker. Strain into a coffee glass.

Bloody Caesar

1¼ oz. Vodka
2½ oz. Clamato Juice
dash Tabasco Sauce
dash Worcestershire Sauce
dash Pepper and Salt

Pour Vodka into a glass with ice and fill with Clamato Juice. Add a dash of Tabasco, Worcestershire, Pepper, and Salt. Garnish with a Celery Stalk or a Lime Wheel.

A popular drink in Canada.

Bloody Mary

1¼ oz. Vodka
2½ oz. Tomato Juice
dash Worcestershire Sauce
dash Tabasco Sauce
dash Salt and Pepper
dash Lemon Juice

Pour Vodka over ice in a glass. Fill with Tomato Juice. Add a dash or two of Worcestershire Sauce, Lemon Juice, and Tabasco Sauce. Stir and garnish with a Celery Stalk. For those who enjoy their Bloody Marys extremely spicy, add more Tabasco or even Horseradish.

The most famous of the "Hair of the Dog" morning-after cocktails.

Bloody Molly

1½ oz. Jameson Irish Whiskey
3 oz. Tomato Juice (seasoned
   to taste) or prepared Bloody
   Mary Mix
dash Lemon Juice

Combine in a tall glass over ice and
stir. Garnish with a Celery Heart.

Irish Whiskey and Tomato Juice? Hmmmm.

The Bloomin' Apple

1¼ oz. Jameson Irish Whiskey
2 oz. Apple Juice
dash Cointreau

Combine in a mixing glass with ice
and stir. Pour into a highball glass and
garnish with a slice of Orange Peel.

Blue Blazer

2 oz. Irish Whiskey
¼ oz. Clear Honey
½ oz. Lemon Juice
3 oz. Water

Pour all ingredients into a pan and
heat very gently until the Honey has
dissolved. Place a teaspoon into a
short tumbler and pour drink carefully
into the glass (the spoon keeps the
glass from cracking). Serve with
Cinnamon Sticks.

Blue Blocker

1 oz. Stoli Ohranj Vodka
½ oz. Blue Curaçao

Combine over ice and stir.

You can also serve this drink in a shot glass (without ice).

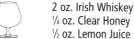

C'mon baby, light my fire

Jerry Thomas (nicknamed *Professor*)
created the Blue Blazer in 1849
at the El Dorado Saloon in San
Francisco, California. Perfecting
his technique, Thomas made this
drink famous: He ignited the whiskey and tossed the flaming liquid
between two silver tankards,
thus mixing the ingredients while
illuminating the bar with liquid fire.

Blue Fin

2 oz. Citrus Vodka
1 oz. Hpnotiq
3 oz. White Cranberry Juice

Shake with ice and pour into a rocks glass. Garnish with Gummy Fish.

If you don't have Gummy Fish on hand, goldfish crackers aren't an acceptable substitute.

Blue Kamikazi

1 oz. Absolut Vodka
¼ oz. Rose's Lime Juice
¼ oz. Hiram Walker Blue Curaçao

Shake with ice and strain into a shot glass.

Blue Lagoon

1½ oz. Sobieski Vodka
½ oz. Blue Curaçao
3 oz. Lemonade

Combine ingredients over ice in a highball glass. Garnish with a Cherry.

Created around 1960 at Harry's Bar in Paris, France, by Harry's son, Andy MacElhone.

Blue Tap

1½ oz. Agavero Tequila
½ oz. Blue Curaçao
4 oz. Pineapple Juice

Combine ingredients over ice in a tall glass.

Blue Whale

1 oz. Puerto Rican Rum
¼ oz. Blue Curaçao
¼ oz. Pineapple Juice

Shake with ice and strain into a shot glass.

A big drink in a small glass.

Blueberry Mojito

¼ cup Fresh Blueberries
4 Mint Leaves
½ oz. Lime Juice
2 tbsp. Sugar
2 oz. Soda Water
1 oz. Light Puerto Rican Rum

Place Fresh Blueberries and Mint Leaves in bottom of glass. Add Lime Juice and Sugar. Muddle. Add Soda Water and Light Rum. Garnish with Mint Leaves.

B

Bobby Burns

1 oz. Scotch
¼ oz. Rosso Vermouth
3 dashes Benedictine

Build in a cocktail glass over ice. Stir and serve.

A great Scotsman.

Bocci Ball

½ oz. Di Saronno Amaretto
½ oz. Stolichnaya Vodka
½ oz. Orange Juice

Shake with ice. Serve straight up in a shot glass.

You can also serve this one over ice in a rocks glass.

Boilermaker

1¼ oz. Irish Whiskey
10 oz. Beer

Serve Whiskey in a shot glass with a glass of Beer on the side as a chaser.

Bolero

1½ oz. Rhum Barbancourt
½ oz. Calvados
2 tsp. Sweet Vermouth
dash Bitters

Stir. Serve straight up or with ice.

You can also serve this drink as a shot.

Bonbini

1 oz. Bacardi Light or Dark Rum
¼ oz. Orange Curaçao
dash Bitters

Stir and serve with ice.

Bongo Drum

1 oz. Bacardi Light Rum
Pineapple Juice
¼ oz. Blackberry Flavored Brandy

Pour Rum into a tall glass filled with ice. Fill with Pineapple Juice. Float the Brandy on top.

Boogie-Woogie

3 oz. Grey Goose Vodka
L'Orange
5 oz. Grapefruit Juice
1 oz. Lemon Juice
dash Bitters

Mix with ice and garnish with a Twist of Lime.

Boston Breeze

1 oz. Coco Lopez Cream of
Coconut
1¼ oz. Cruzan Rum
3 oz. Cranberry Juice
1 cup Ice

Blend and serve in a margarita glass.

Bourbon Sling

1 tsp. Superfine Sugar
2 tsp. Water
1 oz. Lemon Juice
2 oz. Bourbon

In a shaker half-filled with ice cubes, combine the Sugar, Water, Lemon Juice, and Bourbon. Shake well. Strain into a glass. Top with a Lemon Twist.

Bourbon Street

1½ oz. Bourbon
½ oz. Di Saronno Amaretto

Shake with ice and strain into a shot glass.

Brain Hemorrhage

1 oz. Baileys Irish Cream
1 oz. Peach or Strawberry
Schnapps

Float Irish Cream on top of Schnapps. Drop Grenadine to form the hemorrage.

This will keep you thinking.

Brain Hemorrhage

1½ oz. Irish Cream
1 oz. Peach Schnapps
dash Grenadine

Combine in a shot glass.

Brainstorm

1¾ oz. Irish Whiskey
¼ oz. Dry Vermouth
dash Benedictine

Stir all ingredients and strain into a
cocktail glass. Decorate with a twist
of Orange Peel.

Brandy Alexander

1½ oz. Brandy or Cognac
½ oz. Dark Crème de Cacao
1 oz. Sweet Cream or Ice Cream

Shake with ice. Strain.

A sweet and tasty classic.

Brass Knuckle

1 oz. Bourbon
½ oz. Triple Sec
2 oz. Sweetened Lemon Mix

Shake with ice and serve in a highball
glass with ice.

Brave Bull

1½ oz. Tequila
½ oz. Coffee Liqueur

Stir and serve over ice.

You can also serve this one as a shot.

Brazilian Rose

3 oz. Guava Juice
splash Triple Sec
2 oz. Leblon Cachaça

Pour the Guava Juice and Triple Sec
into a shaker. Fill the shaker with
ice and add Leblon Cachaça. Shake
vigorously. Serve in a martini glass.
Garnish with a Rose Petal.

Breakfast Martini

2 oz. Plymouth Gin
1 oz. Cointreau
1 oz. Fresh-Squeezed Lemon
Juice
1 tsp. Orange Marmalade

Fill mixing glass with ice. Add
ingredients and shake well. Strain
into a martini glass.

Created by Salvatore Calabrese of London, England.

Bronx

1½ oz. Gin
½ oz. Dry Vermouth
½ oz. Sweet Vermouth
½ oz. Fresh Orange Juice

Shake with ice and strain.

Brown Derby

1¼ oz. Puerto Rican Dark Rum
½ oz. Lime Juice
⅙ oz. Maple Syrup

Shake with ice. Serve straight up or
over ice.

Bubble Gum #1

½ oz. Melon Liqueur
½ oz. Vodka
½ oz. Crème de Banana
½ oz. Orange Juice
dash Rose's Grenadine

Serve in a shot glass.

Bubble Gum #2

1 oz. Finlandia Cranberry
Vodka
¼ oz. Peach Schnapps
¼ oz. Crème de Banana
1 oz. Orange Juice

Shake. Serve with ice.

Buck-a-Roo

1¼ oz. Bacardi Light or Dark
Rum
Root Beer

Pour Rum into a Collins glass filled
with ice. Fill with Root Beer.

Bucking Irish

1¼ oz. Irish Whiskey
5 oz. Ginger Ale

Combine in an ice-filled Collins glass. Garnish with a Lemon Twist.

Buff Martini

5 parts Finlandia Vodka
1 part Baileys Irish Cream
1 part Kahlúa

Stir gently with ice and strain. Add a sprinkle of freshly ground Coffee or Cinnamon.

Bullshot

1½ oz. Vodka
1 tsp. Lemon Juice
dash Worcestershire
dash Tabasco
4 oz. Chilled Beef Bouillon
dash Salt and Pepper

Shake and serve in a glass. Garnish with a Lemon Wedge.

One of the "Hair of the Dog" hangover cures, along with the Bloody Mary.

Bungi Jumper

1¼ oz. Irish Mist
4 oz. Orange Juice
½ oz. Cream
splash Amaretto

Mix all but the Amaretto in a highball glass. Float the Amaretto on top. Serve straight up or over ice.

Stretch this one for awhile.

Bunratty Peg

1½ oz. Irish Whiskey
¾ oz. Irish Mist
¼ oz. Amaretto or Drambuie

Stir with ice and strain into a chilled cocktail glass.

You can also serve this drink with ice in a rocks glass.

Bushmills Fuzzy Valencia

1½ oz. Bushmills Irish Whiskey
¾ oz. Amaretto
5 oz. Orange Juice

Serve in a tall glass over ice.

Bushmills Hot Irish Tea

1½ oz. Bushmills Irish Whiskey
4 oz. Hot Tea

In a mug, stir the ingredients well.
Add a Cinnamon Stick.

Definitely not for the morning.

Bushmills O'thentic Irish Kiss

1½ oz. Bushmills Irish Whiskey
1 oz. Peach Schnapps
2 oz. Orange Juice
5 oz. Ginger Ale

Combine over ice in a highball glass
and garnish with a Lime Wedge.

Bushmills Summer Sour

1¼ oz. Bushmills Irish Whiskey
2 oz. Orange Juice
2 oz. Sweet & Sour Mix

Shake. Serve over ice in a Collins
glass.

Bushmills Surprise

1 oz. Bushmills Irish Whiskey
½ oz. Triple Sec
2 oz. Lemon Juice

Shake well with ice and strain into a
cocktail glass.

Bushmills Tea

1½ oz. Bushmills Irish Whiskey
6 oz. Iced Tea

Combine in a tall glass over ice.
Garnish with a Lemon Twist.

Bushmills Triple Treat

1½ oz. Bushmills Irish Whiskey
¾ oz. Amaretto
5 oz. Orange Juice

Combine in a tall glass over ice.

Bushranger

1 oz. Dubonnet
1 oz. Puerto Rican White Rum
2 dashes Angostura Bitters

Stir and serve over ice.

Bushwacker

2 oz. Coco Lopez Cream of
   Coconut
2 oz. Half & Half
1 oz. Kahlúa
½ oz. Dark Crème de Cacao
½ oz. Rum
1 cup Ice

Blend and serve in a margarita glass.

Butterscotch Bomber

½ oz. Vodka
½ oz. Baileys Irish Cream
½ oz. Butterscotch Schnapps

Shake with ice and serve in a shot
glass.

You can also serve this one over ice in a highball glass.

Buttery Finger

¼ oz. Irish Cream
¼ oz. 360 Vodka
¼ oz. Butterscotch Schnapps
¼ oz. Coffee-Flavored Liqueur

Combine in a shot glass.

You can also serve this drink over ice in a highball glass.

Buttery Nipple

⅓ oz. Irish Cream
⅓ oz. Vodka
⅓ oz. Butterscotch Schnapps

Combine in a shot glass.

Cabopolitan

1 oz. Cabo Wabo Blanco
   Tequila
3 oz. Cranberry Juice
splash Lime Juice

Combine Tequila, Cranberry Juice,
and a splash of fresh Lime Juice.
Shake and serve in a chilled martini
glass.

A Mexican take on the classic Cosmopolitan.

Cafe Cooler

5 oz. Coffee
½ oz. Romana Sambuca
½ oz. Half & Half
dash Brown Sugar

Pour Coffee over ice. Add Sambuca and Half & Half. Add Brown Sugar to taste.

Caffé Europa

1 oz. Galliano
1 oz. Cointreau
3 oz. Coffee

Add freshly brewed coffee and top with whipped cream.

Caipirinha

½ Lime
2 tsp. Superfine Sugar
2 oz. Leblon Cachaça

Cut the Lime into 4 wedges. Muddle the Lime and Sugar in a shaker. Fill the shaker with ice and add Leblon Cachaça. Shake vigorously. Serve in a rocks glass. Garnish with a Lime Slice.

Caipírissima

5 freshly cut Lime Wedges
1½ oz. Oronoco Rum
splash freshly squeezed Lime
    Juice
1 tbsp. Refined Sugar

Muddle 4 Lime Wedges in a shaker. Add Rum, Lime Juice, and 1 tablespoon of Refined Sugar, and shake vigorously with ice. Strain contents into a chilled martini glass and garnish with Lime Wedge.

If you like Mojitos, give this one a try.

Caipiroska

½ oz. Simple Sugar
½ Lime cut into wedges
2 oz. Vodka
small spoonful of Brown Sugar

Pour the Sugar onto the Lime Wedges in an old-fashioned glass. Muddle well before adding Vodka and filling with crushed ice. Stir all ingredients together well. Top with more crushed ice.

Cajun Martini

2 oz. Absolut Peppar Vodka
¼ oz. Dry Vermouth

Serve chilled and straight up. Garnish with a Habanero-Stuffed Olive.

Created at the Continental Cafe in Philadelphia, Pennsylvania.

Cameron's Kick

¾ oz. Irish Whiskey
¾ oz. Scotch Whisky
Juice of ¼ Lemon
2 dashes Angostura Bitters

Shake well with cracked ice and strain into a cocktail glass.

Camino Reál

1½ oz. Gran Centenario Plata
  or Reposado Tequila
½ oz. Banana Liqueur
1 oz. Orange Juice
dash Lime Juice
dash Coconut Milk

Shake or blend. Garnish with a Lime Slice.

Campari & Soda

2 oz. Campari
Club Soda

Top Campari with Club Soda in a Collins glass. Add a Lemon Twist.

Can-Can

1 oz. Tequila
½ oz. French Vermouth
2 oz. Grapefruit Juice
1 tsp. Sugar
Orange Twist

Shake together over ice and serve with a twist.

Candy Apple

1 oz. Apple Schnapps
1 oz. Cinnamon Schnapps
1 oz. Apple Juice

Shake with ice and strain into a shot glass.

Candy Ass

1 oz. Chambord
1 oz. Mozart

Shake with ice and strain into a shot glass.

Cannonball

1½ oz. Captain Morgan Spiced Rum
3 oz. Pineapple Juice
¼ oz. White Crème de Menthe

Pour the Rum and Pineapple Juice over ice. Float the Crème de Menthe on top.

Big noise in a rocks glass.

Canton Sunrise

1½ oz. Canton Delicate Ginger Liqueur
1½ oz. Orange Juice
splash Grenadine

Combine over ice.

Cape Codder #1

1¼ oz. Vodka
3 oz. Cranberry Juice
dash Lime Juice

Combine in a chilled cocktail glass over ice. Garnish with a Lime Wedge.

Cape Codder #2

1½ oz. Vodka
4 oz. Cranberry Juice
Club Soda

Combine Vodka and Cranberry Juice over ice in a tall glass. Fill with Club Soda. Garnish with an Orange Slice.

Captain & Cola

1½ oz. Captain Morgan Spiced Rum
3 oz. Cola

Stir in a tall glass with ice.

Captain & OJ

1¼ oz. Captain Morgan Spiced Rum
5 oz. Orange Juice

Combine in a tall glass with ice.

Captain Morgan Sour

1¼ oz. Captain Morgan Spiced
   Rum
1 oz. Lemon Juice
1 tsp. Sugar

Shake and serve over ice or
straight up.

Captain's Berry Daiquiri

1¼ oz. Captain Morgan Spiced
   Rum
½ cup Strawberries or
   Raspberries
1 tsp. Lime Juice
½ tsp. Sugar
½ cup Crushed Ice

Blend. Garnish with Berries.

Captain's Colada

1¼ oz. Captain Morgan Spiced
   Rum
1 oz. Cream of Coconut
3 oz. Pineapple Juice
   (unsweetened)
½ cup Crushed Ice

Blend. Garnish with a Pineapple
Spear.

Captain's Cream Soda

¼ oz. Captain Morgan Spiced
   Rum
5 oz. Lemon-Lime Soda

Combine in a Collins glass with
ice. Garnish with a Lemon or Lime
Twist.

Captain's Cruiser

1¼ oz. Captain Morgan's
   Parrot Bay Rum
3 oz. Tropicana Orange Juice
2 oz. Pineapple Juice

Mix in a shaker. Pour over ice in a
tall glass.

Captain's Daiquiri

1¼ oz. Captain Morgan Spiced
   Rum
2 tsp. Lime Juice
½ tsp. Sugar

Shake or blend with ice. Garnish
with a Lime Wedge.

Captain's Morgarita

1 oz. Captain Morgan Spiced
  Rum
½ oz. Triple Sec
16 oz. Frozen Limeade
1 cup Ice Cubes

Blend until smooth.

Captain's Seabreeze

1¼ oz. Captain Morgan Spiced
  Rum
5 oz. Cranberry Juice

Serve over ice in a tall glass.

Captain's Spiced Ginger Ale

1¼ oz. Captain Morgan Spiced
  Rum
5 oz. Seagram's Ginger Ale

Serve over ice in a tall glass.

Captain's Tropical Spiced Tea

1¼ oz. Captain Morgan Spiced
  Rum
5 oz. Iced Tea
½ tsp. Lemon Juice

Serve over ice in a tall glass. Garnish
with a Lemon Wedge.

Caramel Apple

½ oz. 99 Apples Schnapps
1 oz. Butterscotch Schnapps

Shake with ice and strain to serve as
a shooter.

Caribbean Cruise Shooter

½ oz. Baileys Irish Cream
½ oz. Kahlúa Coffee Liqueur
½ oz. Malibu Rum

Shake with ice and strain into a shot
glass.

Caribbean Grasshopper

1½ oz. Coco Lopez Cream of
  Coconut
1 oz. White Crème de Cacao
½ oz. Green Crème de Menthe

Combine ingredients. Serve straight
up or over ice.

Caribbean Joy

1¼ oz. Castillo Silver Rum
1 oz. Pineapple Juice
¾ oz. Lemon Juice

Shake and serve over ice.

Carolaretto

1½ oz. Carolans Irish Cream
1½ oz. Amaretto

Shake or stir over ice.

Carrot Cake

¾ oz. Goldschläger
¾ oz. Baileys Irish Cream
¾ oz. Coffee Liqueur

Shake with ice. Pour over rocks or
serve straight up.

Cassis Cocktail

1 oz. Maker's Mark Bourbon
½ oz. Dry Vermouth
1 tsp. Crème de Cassis

Shake with cracked ice. Strain into a
chilled cocktail glass.

The Catalina Margarita

1¼ oz. Jose Cuervo Gold Tequila
1 oz. Peach Schnapps
1 oz. Blue Curaçao
4 oz. Sweet & Sour Mix

Blend with crushed ice.

Cavalier

1½ oz. Sauza Tequila
½ oz. Galliano
1½ oz. Orange Juice
½ oz. Cream

Blend with crushed ice and strain
into a cocktail glass.

CC & Soda

1¾ oz. Canadian Club Whisky
3 oz. Club Soda

Serve in a Collins glass with ice.

A Canadian favorite.

Celtic Bull

1½ oz. Irish Whiskey
2 oz. Beef Consommé or
   Bouillon
2 oz. Tomato Juice
1–2 dashes Worcestershire
   Sauce
dash Tabasco Sauce
dash Freshly Ground Pepper

Mix all ingredients with cracked ice
in a shaker or blender. Pour into a
chilled highball glass.

A variation of the Bloody Bull, which is derived from the Bloody Mary.

Cement Mixer

¾ shot Irish Cream
¼ shot Rose's Lime Juice

Pour ingredients directly into the
glass. Let the drink stand for 5
seconds and it will coagulate.

This drink will stick to your ribs.

Chambord Iceberg

½ oz. Chambord
½ oz. Iceberg Vodka

Combine in a champagne glass
packed to the top with ice.

Chambord Kamikazi

1 oz. Vodka
½ oz. Chambord
¼ oz. Triple Sec
¼ oz. Lime Juice

Shake with ice and strain into a shot
glass.

Tastes sort of like a Purple Hooter.

Champagne Cocktail

3 oz. Champagne, chilled
1 cube Sugar
dash Angostura Bitters

Stir ingredients slowly. Garnish with
a Lemon Twist.

How can you do this to champagne?

Champerelle

½ oz. Cointreau
½ oz. Anisette
½ oz. Green Chartreuse
½ oz. Cognac

Layer this drink in the order listed.
Start with Cointreau on the bottom
and finish with Cognac on top.

Champs Élysées

½ oz. Grenadine
½ oz. Brown Crème de Cacao
½ oz. Orange Curaçao
½ oz. Green Crème de Menthe
½ oz. Cognac

Layer this drink in the order listed.
Start with Grenadine on the bottom
and finish with Cognac on top.

Chamu

½ oz. Chambord
1 oz. Malibu Rum
½ oz. Vodka
3 oz. Pineapple Juice

Combine ingredients in a tall glass
with ice. Fill with Pineapple Juice.

Cherried Cream Rum

1½ oz. Rhum Barbancourt
½ oz. Cherry Brandy
½ oz. Light Cream

Shake with ice and strain.

Cherry Blossom

1 oz. Cherry Marnier
1 tsp. Superfine Sugar
1½ oz. Brandy
3–4 dashes Grenadine
3–4 dashes Triple Sec or
   Curaçao
½ oz. Lemon Juice
3–4 Ice Cubes

Moisten the rim of a cocktail glass
with a drop of Cherry Marnier and
Sugar Frost. Combine all ingredients
in a shaker and shake vigorously.
Strain drink into the prepared
cocktail glass.

Cherry Bomb

½ oz. Cherry Brandy
1 oz. Rum
½ oz. Sour Mix

Shake with ice and strain into a shot
glass.

Chi-Chi

1 oz. Coco Lopez Cream of
   Coconut
2 oz. Pineapple Juice
1½ oz. Vodka
1 cup Ice

Blend until smooth.

Move over rum, vodka is in this one.

Chicago Style

¾ oz. Bacardi Light Rum
¼ oz. Hiram Walker Triple Sec
¼ oz. Hiram Walker Anisette
¼ oz. Lemon or Lime Juice

Blend with ice.

The windy one.

The Chimayo Cocktail

1¼ oz. Herradura Silver Tequila
¼ oz. Crème de Cassis
1 oz. Fresh Apple Cider or
   Apple Juice
¼ oz. Lemon Juice

Fill a glass with ice. Pour the
ingredients over ice and stir. Garnish
with an Apple Wedge.

China Beach

¾ oz. Canton Delicate Ginger
   Liqueur
1 oz. Cranberry Juice
splash Vodka

Shake with ice and serve over ice.

Chinese Torture

1 part Domaine de Canton
   Delicate Ginger Liqueur
1 part Bacardi 151 Rum

Shake with ice and strain into a shot
glass.

Chip Shot

¾ oz. Devonshire Irish Cream
¾ oz. Tuaca
1½ oz. Coffee

Combine in a glass and stir.

Perfect after golf or cookies.

Chocolate Covered Cherry

2 oz. Chocoviac
½ oz. Cherry Soda

Garnish with a Maraschino Cherry.
Serve as a shot or on the rocks.

Chocolate Martini Cocktail

Cocoa Powder to rim glass
2 oz. Bacardi O
1 oz. Light Crème de Cacao
splash Disaronno Originale
    Amaretto
Chocolate Kiss

Rim a martini glass with Cocoa
Powder. In a shaker with ice,
combine the Bacardi O, Crème
de Cacao, and Amaretto. Strain
into the martini glass. Drop in the
Chocolate Kiss.

Chocolate Martini #1

1 oz. Absolut Vodka
½ oz. Godiva Chocolate
    Liqueur

Shake over ice; strain into a chilled
cocktail glass with a Lemon Twist
garnish.

For your sweet tooth.

Chocolate Martini #2

1½ oz. Absolut Kurant Vodka
dash White Crème de Cacao

Pour Kurant and Crème de Cacao
over ice. Shake or stir well. Strain
and serve in a chocolate-rimmed
cocktail glass straight up or over
ice. Garnish with an Orange Peel.

*To rim the glass, first rub a piece of orange around the top of the glass
and then gently place the glass upside down in a plate of unsweetened
chocolate powder.*

Ciclón Heat Storm

1½ oz. Ciclón
3 shakes Tabasco

Add the Tabasco to the Ciclón in a
shot glass.

For fire-breathers only.

Cilver Citron

1¼ oz. Absolut Citron
2 oz. Chilled Champagne

Combine in a champagne glass.

Ciroc Caribbean

2 oz. Ciroc Coconut
4 oz. Pineapple Juice

Combine in a tall glass with ice.

Ciroc Red Berry Repartee

2 oz. Ciroc Red Berry
4 oz. Lemon-Lime Soda
dash Grenadine

Combine in a tall glass with ice.

Citron Cooler

1¼ oz. Absolut Citron Vodka
½ oz. Fresh Lime Juice
Tonic

Pour Citron and Lime Juice over ice
in a tall glass. Fill with Tonic. Garnish
with a Lime Wedge.

Citron Kamikazi

¾ oz. Absolut Citron Vodka
¾ oz. Triple Sec
Lime Juice

Pour Citron, Triple Sec, and Lime
Juice over ice in a glass. Shake well
and strain into a glass. Serve straight
up or over ice. Garnish with a Lime
Wedge.

Citron Martini

1¼ oz. Absolut Citron Vodka
dash Extra Dry Vermouth

Pour Citron and Vermouth over ice.
Shake or stir well. Strain and serve
in a cocktail glass straight up or over
ice. Garnish with a Twist or an Olive.

A real twist to the classic Martini.

Citroska

2 oz. Stoli Citros Vodka
¼ oz. Simple Syrup
3 oz. Lemon-Lime Soda

Add Simple Syrup to a highball glass.
Fill with ice, add Vodka, and fill with
Soda. Garnish with a Mint Sprig.

Clam Voyage

1 oz. Bacardi Light or Dark
    Rum
¼ oz. Apple Flavored Brandy
1 oz. Orange Juice
dash Orange Bitters

Blend with ice and serve in a
margarita glass.

Claridge

½ oz. Cork Dry Gin
½ oz. Dry Vermouth
½ oz. Cointreau
½ oz. Apricot Brandy

Mix with ice. Serve over ice or
straight up.

Coco Loco (Crazy Coconut)

1½ oz. Herradura Tequila
3 oz. Pineapple Juice
2 oz. Coco Lopez Cream of
    Coconut

Blend. Garnish with a Pineapple
Spear.

Coco Margarita

1¼ oz. 1800 Tequila
1 oz. Sweet & Sour Mix
1½ oz. Pineapple Juice
½ oz. Fresh Lime Juice
½ oz. Coco Lopez Cream of
    Coconut

Shake or blend ingredients. Garnish
with fresh Pineapple.

Cocolou

1½ oz. Carolans Irish Cream
1½ oz. Crème de Cacao

Stir well over ice.

And this has not a drop of coconut.

Cocomistico

½ oz. Jose Cuervo Mistico
½ oz. Baileys Irish Cream
½ oz. Godiva Liqueur
1 oz. Half & Half

Shake ingredients and strain into a
rocks glass.

Cocomotion

4 oz. Coco Lopez Cream of
    Coconut
2 oz. Lime Juice
1½ oz. Puerto Rican Dark Rum
1½ cups Ice

Blend and serve in a margarita glass.

Coconut Almond Margarita

1¼ oz. 1800 Tequila
2½ oz. Sweet & Sour Mix
½ oz. Cream of Coconut
¼ oz. Amaretto Liqueur
½ oz. Fresh Lime Juice

Shake and serve over ice. Garnish
with a wedge of Lime.

You can also blend the ingredients with ice.

Coconut Bellini

2 oz. Coco Lopez Cream of
    Coconut
3 oz. Champagne
2 oz. Peach Puree
½ oz. Peach Schnapps
1 cup Ice

Blend until smooth.

This famous Bellini is made with Coco Lopez.

Coffee Cream Cooler

1¼ oz. Bacardi Light or
    Dark Rum
Cold Coffee
Cream

Pour Rum into a tall glass half filled
with ice. Fill with cold Coffee and
Cream to desired proportions.

Cointreau Santa Fe Margarita

1½ oz. Jose Cuervo Gold
    Tequila
¾ oz. Cointreau
2 oz. Sweet & Sour Mix
2 oz. Cranberry Juice

Blend ingredients and serve in a
margarita glass.

Cointreau Strawberry Margarita

1¼ oz. Jose Cuervo Gold Tequila
¾ oz. Cointreau
2 oz. Sweet & Sour Mix
3 oz. Frozen Strawberries

Blend ingredients and serve in a
margarita glass.

Cold in Ireland

3 slices of Fresh Ginger
1 oz. Honey Syrup
2 oz. Glenlivet Single Malt
    Scotch Whisky
¾ oz. Fresh Lemon Juice

In a shaker, muddle Ginger with
Honey Syrup. Add remaining
ingredients and shake. Strain over
fresh ice into a tumbler. Garnish
with Crystallized Ginger on a pick.

Cold Irish

1½ oz. Irish Whiskey
½ oz. Irish Mist
Coffee Soda
Whipped Cream
2–3 drops Crème de Cacao

Pour the Irish Whiskey and the Irish
Mist over ice. Fill with Coffee Soda
and stir. Touch up the Whipped
Cream with the Crème de Cacao
and use it to top the drink.

Colorado Bulldog

1½ oz. Coffee Liqueur
4 oz. Cream
splash Cola

Pour first two ingredients over ice.
Add a splash of Cola. Stir briefly.

*There is another name for this drink. You've heard it but won't see it in
print.*

Colosseum Cooler

1 oz. Romana Sambuca
3 oz. Cranberry Juice
Club Soda

Combine Sambuca and Cranberry
Juice in a tall glass. Fill with Soda
and garnish with a Lime Wedge.

Columbus Cocktail

1½ oz. Puerto Rican Golden
    Rum
¾ oz. Apricot Brandy
Juice of ½ Lime

Mix or blend with crushed ice.

Commando Fix

2 oz. Irish Whiskey
¼ oz. Cointreau
½ oz. Lime Juice
1–2 dashes Raspberry Liqueur

Fill a glass with ice. Add Irish Whiskey, Cointreau, and Lime Juice. Stir slowly. Dot the surface of the drink with Raspberry Liqueur.

Commodore

1 part Bourbon
1 part Crème de Cacao
1 part Sweetened Lemon Juice
1 dash Grenadine

Shake with ice and serve over ice.

Conchita

1¼ oz. Tequila
½ oz. Lemon Juice
6 oz. Grapefruit Juice

Combine first two ingredients in a chilled highball glass. Fill with Grapefruit Juice and stir.

Continental

1 oz. Bacardi Light Rum
¼ oz. Green Crème de Menthe
¾ oz. Rose's Lime Juice
¼ tsp. Sugar (optional)

Blend with ice.

The Coolidge Cooler

1½ oz. Vermont White Vodka
½ oz. American Whiskey
2 oz. Orange Juice
2 oz Club Soda

Combine ingredients and top with Club Soda.

Cool Citron

1 oz. Absolut Citron Vodka
½ oz. White Crème de Menthe

Shake and serve over ice.

Cool Mist

2 oz. Irish Mist
Tonic Water

Combine in a tall glass with crushed
ice. Add a Shamrock for a garnish.

Copper Illusion Martini

1 oz. Gin
½ oz. Grand Marnier
½ oz. Campari

Stir ingredients and garnish with an
Orange Slice.

Invented at the Gallery Lounge at the Sheraton in Seattle, Washington.

Copperhead

1¼ oz. Vodka
Ginger Ale

Combine in a tall glass filled with ice.
Add a squeeze of Lime and garnish
with a Lime Wedge.

Cork Comfort

1½ oz. Irish Whiskey
¾ oz. Sweet Vermouth
3–4 dashes Angostura Bitters
3–4 dashes Southern Comfort

Shake with ice or blend. Pour into a
chilled rocks glass.

Corkscrew

¾ oz. Bacardi Light Rum
¼ oz. Asbach Uralt
¼ oz. Port Wine
½ oz. Lemon or Rose's Lime
Juice

Stir. Serve over ice.

Cosmo Kazi

2 oz. Vodka
½ oz. Cointreau
dash Lime Juice
splash Cranberry Juice

Combine ingredients and pour over
ice.

A red, nonshot variation of the Kamikazi.

Cosmopolitan Martini

2 oz. Vodka
½ oz. Cointreau
Juice of ¼ Lime
½ oz. Cranberry Juice

Shake with ice and strain.

There are many variations of the Martini. This one works.

Cossack Charge

1½ oz. Vodka
½ oz. Cognac
½ oz. Cherry Brandy

Mix all ingredients with cracked ice in a shaker or blender and pour into a chilled cocktail glass.

Cow Puncher

1 oz. Bacardi Light or
  Dark Rum
1 oz. White Crème de Cacao
Milk

Pour Rum and Crème de Cacao into a tall glass half filled with ice. Fill with Milk.

Cowboy

2 oz. Jim Beam Bourbon
4 oz. Milk

In an ice-filled shaker, shake the Bourbon with Milk. Strain into a Collins glass.

A great way to add calcium to your diet.

Cowcatcher

1 oz. O'Mara's Irish Country
  Cream
1 oz. Sambuca Sarti

Mix together. Pour over ice and serve.

Cran Razz

2 oz. Two Fingers Tequila
2 oz. Cranberry Juice
1 oz. Raspberry Liqueur

In a shaker, mix all ingredients. Serve over ice.

Cran-Rum Twister

2 oz. Puerto Rican Light Rum
3 oz. Cranberry Juice
Lemon-Lime Soda

Combine the first two ingredients in a tall glass with ice. Fill with Lemon-Lime Soda and garnish with a Lemon Slice.

Cranberry Cocktail

2 oz. Finlandia Cranberry Vodka

Serve alone over ice or with splash of Club Soda.

Cranberry Martini

1 oz. Godiva Liqueur
1 oz. Absolut Vodka
1 oz. Cranberry Juice

Combine with ice and shake well. Garnish with a Lime Twist.

Cranberry Sauce Martini

1 oz. Stoli Ohranj Vodka
¼ oz. Cranberry Juice

Shake with ice and strain or serve over ice. Garnish with Cranberries that have been soaked in Simple Syrup.

Cranpeppar

1¼ oz. Absolut Peppar Vodka
Cranberry Juice

Pour Vodka over ice in a tall glass. Fill with Cranberry Juice.

Crantini

2 oz. Bacardi Limón Rum
touch Martini & Rossi Extra Dry Vermouth
splash Cranberry Juice

Shake and serve straight up. Garnish with Cranberries and a Lemon Twist.

Invented at Mr. Babbington's in New York, New York.

Cream Whiskey

1 oz. Carolans Irish Cream
1½ oz. Rye Whiskey

Stir well over ice.

Creamed Sherry

2 oz. Carolans Irish Cream
½ oz. Duff Gordon Cream
  Sherry

Stir well over ice.

Creamy Orange Treat #1

1½ oz. Stoli Ohranj Vodka
½ oz. Irish Cream

Combine over ice.

Creamy Orange Treat #2

1 oz. Liquore Galliano
1 oz. Half & Half or Heavy
  Cream
Orange Juice

Combine over ice.

Creamy Orange-Vanilla Smoothie

½ oz. Absolut Vanilia
1 oz. Absolut Mandrin
1½ medium scoops Vanilla Ice
  Cream

Blend ingredients. Pour over ice.
Garnish with Orange Peel.

Creature from the Black Lagoon

1 oz. Jägermeister
1 oz. Romana Black

Shake with ice and strain into a shot
glass.

Back to the water.

Creole

1¾ oz. Puerto Rican White
  Rum
2 splashes Lemon Juice
3½ oz. Beef Bouillon
dash Pepper
dash Salt
dash Tabasco Sauce
dash Worcestershire Sauce

Combine over ice.

Crest of the Wave

1¼ oz. Bombay Gin
1½ oz. Grapefruit Juice
1½ oz. Cranberry Juice

Combine in a tall glass over ice.

Cricket

¾ oz. Bacardi Light Rum
¼ oz. White Crème de Cacao
¼ oz. Green Crème de Menthe
1 oz. Cream

Blend ingredients with ice.

Cripple Creek

½ oz. Herradura Tequila
½ oz. Benchmark Bourbon
1 oz. Orange Juice
½ oz. Galliano

Shake the first three ingredients and
strain into a glass. Float the Galliano
on top.

Crocodile Bite

1¼ oz. Jameson Irish Whiskey
2 oz. Orange Juice
1 oz. Grand Marnier
1 bottle 7-Up

Combine in a tall glass with ice.
Garnish with a slice of Orange or
Lemon and serve with straws.

Are there crocodiles in Ireland?

Cuba Libre

1¾ oz. Bacardi Rum
Cola
Juice of ¼ Lime

Add Rum to a glass filled with ice.
Fill with Cola. Add Lime Juice and
stir.

Rum & Coke with a lime.

Cuervo Alexander

1 oz. Jose Cuervo Gold Tequila
1 oz. Coffee-Flavored Liqueur
1 oz. Wild Cherry Brandy
2 scoops Vanilla Ice Cream

Blend until smooth.

A little kick to the Brandy Alexander.

Cuervo Side-Out

1½ oz. Jose Cuervo Gold
    Tequila
1 oz. Triple Sec
2 oz. Cranberry Juice
1½ oz. Lime Juice

Blend.

Cuervo Sunrise

1½ oz. Jose Cuervo Gold
    Tequila
3 oz. Cranberry Juice
½ oz. Lime Juice
½ oz. Grenadine

Shake and serve over ice. Garnish
with a Lime.

Cuervo Traditional Aztec Ruin

½ oz. Jose Cuervo Traditional
    Tequila
½ oz. Rose's Lime Juice

Shake with ice and strain into a
shot glass.

Cuervo Traditional Aztec Sky

¾ oz. Jose Cuervo Traditional
    Tequila
¾ oz. Blue Curaçao

Shake with ice and strain into a
shot glass.

FABLES & LORE

Cuba Libre lore

This drink is a political statement as well as a cocktail. It translates to *Free Cuba*, a status that the country enjoyed in 1898 at the end of the Spanish-American War. Cuban-American relations were friendly around the turn of the century, when a U.S. Army lieutenant in Havana mixed some light native rum with a new-fangled American soft drink called Coca-Cola and braced the libation with a lime.

D

Cuervo Tropical

1½ oz. Jose Cuervo Gold Tequila
3 oz. Orange Juice
1 tsp. Lemon Juice
½ oz. Grenadine

Mix in highball glass filled with cracked ice. Garnish with half an Orange Slice and a Cherry.

Cutthroat

1¼ oz. Finlandia Cranberry Vodka
Orange Juice

Add Vodka to a tall glass with ice. Fill with Orange Juice.

Sort of a cranberry screwdriver.

Czar

1 oz. Stoli Persik Vodka
1 oz. Stoli Cranberi Vodka
1 oz. Pineapple Juice
1 oz. Cranberry Juice

Shake all ingredients with ice. Strain into a rocks glass.

Daiquiri

1¼ oz. Light Rum
½ oz. Sweetened Lemon Juice

Shake or blend with ice.

Dalmore Apple Cider

2 oz. Dalmore 12 Year Old
    Scotch
3 oz. Hot Apple Cider

Combine and serve in a tall, stemmed mug. Garnish with Whipped Cream and a Cinnamon Stick.

Dancing Leprechaun

1½ oz. Irish Whiskey
1½ oz. Lemon Juice
Club Soda
Ginger Ale

Combine the Whiskey and the Lemon Juice. Shake with ice. Strain and add ice. Fill the glass with equal parts Club Soda and Ginger Ale. Stir gently. Touch it up with a twist of Lemon.

D

Dark & Stormy

1½ oz. Gosling's Black Seal
    Rum
4 oz. Ginger Beer

Pour the Rum over ice and top with Ginger Beer. Garnish with Lime or Lemon Wedge (optional).

Bermuda's national drink.

Dean Martini

2 oz. Ketel One Vodka, chilled
Olive
1 Lucky (cigarette)
1 book of matches

Pour the Vodka into a cocktail glass and garnish with an Olive. Place the Cigarette and Matches on the side.

Invented at the Continental Cafe in Philadelphia, Pennsylvania.

Dempsey Rum Runner

1 shot Hendrick's Gin
1 tsp./pkt. Sugar
dash Bitters
3 oz. Pineapple Juice

Shake well and serve.

Derry Delight

2 oz. O'Mara's Irish Country
    Cream
2 oz. Half & Half

Shake together well and pour over ice.

Derry Delight with a Kick

1½ oz. O'Mara's Irish Country
   Cream
½ oz. Copa De Oro Coffee
   Liqueur
½ oz. Burnett's Vodka
2 oz. Half & Half

Shake together well; pour over ice.

Dewar's Summer Splash

1½ oz. Dewar's
3 oz. Ginger Ale
dash Lime Juice

Combine over ice. Garnish with a
Lime Slice.

Dewey Martini

1½ oz. Absolut Vodka
dash Martini & Rossi Extra Dry
   Vermouth
dash Orange Bitters

Shake and strain into a cocktail
glass or serve over ice.

Dillatini Martini

1½ oz. Absolut Vodka
dash Martini & Rossi Extra Dry
   Vermouth
Dilly Bean

Shake and strain into a cocktail
glass or serve over ice.

Try and find a Dilly Bean.

Dingle Dram

1½ oz. Irish Whiskey
½ oz. Irish Mist
Coffee Soda
dash Crème de Cacao
Whipped Cream

Pour Irish Whiskey and Irish Mist
into a chilled highball glass along
with several ice cubes. Fill with
Coffee Soda. Stir gently. Add a float
of Crème de Cacao. Top with dollop
of Whipped Cream.

Dirty Harry

1 oz. Grand Marnier
1 oz. Tia Maria

Shake with ice and strain.

Do you feel lucky? This will make your day.

Disarita Margarita

1 oz. Jose Cuervo 1800
  Tequila
½ oz. Di Saronno Amaretto
3 oz. Margarita Mix
½ cup Crushed Ice

Blend. Garnish with Lime.

Her Italian sister.

Disaronno Italian Punch

1½ oz. Disaronno
1 oz. Bacardi Limón
3 oz. Cranberry Juice

Combine ingredients in a glass over ice. Garnish with skewered Cranberries.

Dixie Dew

1½ oz. Bourbon
½ oz. White Crème de Menthe
½ tsp. Cointreau or Triple Sec

In a mixing glass half-filled with ice cubes, combine all the ingredients. Stir well. Strain into a cocktail glass.

Dixie Stinger

3 oz. Bourbon
½ oz. White Crème de Menthe
½ tsp. Southern Comfort

In a shaker half-filled with ice cubes, combine all the ingredients. Shake well. Strain into a cocktail glass.

Dizzy Lizzy

1½ oz. Bourbon
1½ oz. Sherry
dash Lemon Juice
Club Soda

Combine first three ingredients in a tall glass with ice. Fill with Club Soda.

Double Gold

½ oz. Jose Cuervo Gold Tequila
½ oz. Goldschläger

Shake with ice and strain into a shot glass.

Dragon Berry Arnold Palmer

2 oz. Bacardi Dragon Berry
    Flavored Rum
1½ oz. Lemonade
1½ oz. Iced Tea

Pour ingredients over ice in a tall glass and garnish with a Lemon Wedge.

Dream Shake

1 oz. Baileys Irish Cream
1 oz. Tia Maria

Shake with ice and strain into a shot glass.

Dublin Handshake

½ oz. Baileys Irish Cream
½ oz. Irish Whiskey
¾ oz. Sloe Gin

Shake with crushed ice. Strain into a cocktail glass.

Dubonnet Cocktail

1½ oz. Dubonnet
½ oz. Gin
dash Angostura Bitters

Combine over ice and garnish with a Lemon Twist.

Duck Pin

1 oz. Chambord
1 oz. Southern Comfort
½ oz. Pineapple Juice

Shake with ice and strain into a shot glass.

Eclipse

1½ oz. Bushmills Black Bush
    Irish Whiskey
Seltzer Water

Fill a highball glass with ice. Add Irish Whiskey. Fill with Seltzer Water and stir. Garnish with an Orange Slice.

Egg Nog

1¼ oz. Bacardi Light or Dark
    Rum
1 Egg
1 tsp. Sugar
1 oz. Milk

Mix in a shaker and strain into a glass. Sprinkle with Nutmeg.

1800 Bite the Berry

1¼ oz. 1800 Tequila
½ oz. Triple Sec
¼ oz. Raspberry Liqueur
2½ oz. Sweet & Sour Mix
2 oz. Cranberry Juice

Combine in a rocks glass. Garnish with an Orange Slice.

1800 Lemon Drop

1¼ oz. 1800 Tequila
½ oz. Triple Sec
1 oz. Sweet & Sour Mix
1 oz. Lemon-Lime Soda
splash Fresh Lemon Juice

Combine in a rocks glass and stir. Add a Lemon Juice float. Garnish with Lemon.

E

Electric Lemonade

1¼ oz. Vodka
½ oz. Blue Curaçao
2 oz. Sweet & Sour Mix
splash 7-Up

Blend. Pour over ice in a tall glass and garnish with a Lemon Slice.

Electric Peach

1 oz. Vodka
¼ oz. Peach Schnapps
½ oz. Cranberry Juice Cocktail
¼ oz. Orange Juice

Blend. Pour over ice in a tall glass and garnish with a Lemon Slice.

Elegant Martini (Gin)

1¾ oz. Bombay Sapphire Gin
½ oz. Martini & Rossi Dry
    Vermouth
¼ oz. Grand Marnier
dash Grand Marnier (on top)

Stir the first three ingredients with ice. Strain or serve on ice. Float Grand Marnier on top.

Elegant Martini (Vodka)

1½ oz. Absolut Vodka
dash Martini & Rossi Extra Dry
Vermouth
¼ oz. Grand Marnier
dash Grand Marnier

Stir the first three ingredients with
ice. Serve on ice or straight up.
Float Grand Marnier on top.

Elephant's Ear Martini

1 oz. Dry Gin
¾ oz. Martini & Rossi Dry
Vermouth
¾ oz. Dubonnet

Stir with ice. Serve on ice or
straight up.

Did I hear this drink right?

Emerald City Martini

1¾ oz. Fris Vodka
¼ oz. Midori

Stir with ice. Serve on ice or straight
up and garnish with a Lime Wheel.

Emerald Isle

¾ shot Irish Whiskey
¾ shot Green Crème de
Menthe
2 scoops Vanilla Ice Cream
Soda Water

Blend the first three ingredients
and then add Soda Water. Stir after
adding Soda Water.

It's green.

Emerald Martini

2 oz. Bacardi Limón
splash Martini & Rossi Extra
Dry Vermouth
splash Midori

Stir with ice. Serve on ice or
straight up.

Invented at the Heart and Soul in San Francisco, California.

Erie Tour

1 oz. Irish Mist
1 oz. Carolans Irish Cream
1 oz. Irish Whiskey

Combine over ice.

Extra Nutty Irishman

1 oz. Irish Mist
1 oz. Frangelico
1 oz. Carolans Irish Cream
Whipped Cream

Shake. Top with Whipped Cream.
Serve in a goblet-type glass.

Extreme Waborita

2 oz. Cabo Wabo Reposado
    Tequila
splash Blue Curaçao
splash Grand Marnier
1 oz. Cointreau
1 oz. Lime Juice

Combine ingredients in a shaker
half-filled with ice. Shake well.
Strain into a salt-rimmed martini
glass.

Eye Drop

1 oz. Rumple Minze
1 oz. Stolichnaya Vodka
1 oz. Ouzo

Shake with ice and strain into a
shot glass.

Eyes R Smilin'

1 oz. Baileys Irish Cream
1 oz. Vodka
½ oz. Gin
½ oz. Triple Sec

Build over ice. Stir and serve.

Fascinator Martini

1½ oz. Absolut Vodka
dash Martini & Rossi Extra Dry
    Vermouth
dash Pernod and Mint Sprig

Stir and serve straight up or over
ice. Garnish with a Mint Sprig.

You can also serve this one over ice in a highball glass.

The Fashionista

¾ oz. Pomegranate Juice
3 oz. Moët Impérial
A Pink Rose Petal for garnish

Pour the Pomegranate Juice into a glass. Fill with Moët Impérial. Stir gently with a long spoon. Place a Pink Rose Petal over the drink.

Fatmancillo

1 oz. Giori Lemoncillo
¾ oz. Frangelico Liqueur
½ oz. Kahlúa

Shake with ice. Garnish with Shaved Chocolate.

Fifth Avenue

1 oz. Dark Crème de Cacao
1 oz. Apricot Brandy
1 oz. Cream

Layer this drink in the order listed. Start with Crème de Cacao on the bottom and finish with Cream on top.

Fifty-Fifty

1½ oz. Beefeater Gin
1½ oz. Vermouth

Stir ingredients over ice in a shaker and strain into a chilled martini glass. Garnish with an Olive.

A very wet Martini.

'57 T-Bird with Honolulu License Plates

1 part Orange Liqueur
1 part Dark Rum
1 part Sloe Gin
1 part Orange Juice

Shake with ice and strain into a shot glass.

Get a designated driver.

'57 T-Bird with Texas License Plates

1 oz. Cointreau
½ oz. Dark Rum
½ oz. Sloe Gin
½ oz. Grapefruit Juice

Shake with ice and strain into a shot glass.

Fire

1¼ oz. Stoli Ohranj Vodka
¼ oz. Cinnamon Schnapps

Combine over ice.

A hot one.

Fire Fly

1¼ oz. Vodka
2 oz. Grapefruit Juice
dash Grenadine

Combine Vodka and Grapefruit
Juice in a tall glass over ice. Add
Grenadine.

Fireball

2 oz. Cinnamon Schnapps
dash Tabasco

Combine in a shot glass.

Firebird

1¼ oz. Absolut Peppar Vodka
4 oz. Cranberry Juice

Combine over ice.

The First Lady

2 oz. Templeton Rye Whiskey
1 oz. Cointreau
splash Orange Juice
Orange Wheel

Combine Rye Whiskey, Cointreau,
and Orange Juice in a shaker.
Shake well and strain. Serve up in
a martini glass and garnish with an
Orange Wheel.

Fizz

1¼ oz. Bacardi Light Rum
¼ oz. Lemon Juice
¼ oz. Rose's Grenadine
4 oz. Club Soda

Pour Rum and Lemon Juice into a
highball glass filled with ice. Add
Grenadine and fill with Club Soda.

Flamingo

1½ oz. Rhum Barbancourt
dash Grenadine
1 oz. Pineapple Juice
Juice of ¼ Lime

Shake and serve over ice.

Flirting with the Sandpiper

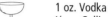

1½ oz. Puerto Rican Light Rum
½ oz. Cherry Brandy
3 oz. Orange Juice
2 dashes Orange Bitter

Stir well. Serve over ice.

Flying Kangaroo

1 oz. Vodka
¼ oz. Galliano
1 oz. Rhum Barbancourt
1½ oz. Pineapple Juice
¾ oz. Orange Juice
¾ oz. Coconut Cream
½ oz. Cream

Shake or blend with ice.

Foggy Day Martini

1½ oz. Dry Gin
¼ oz. Pernod
twist of Lemon Peel

Shake and pour over ice or serve
straight up. Garnish with a
Lemon Peel Twist.

F

Fool's Gold

1 oz. Vodka
1 oz. Galliano

Shake with ice and strain into a
shot glass.

43 Amigos

1½ oz. Jose Cuervo Gold
  Tequila
½ oz. Licor 43
½ oz. Triple Sec
½ oz. Lime Juice

Shake. Strain into a chilled martini
glass. Garnish with a Lime Wedge.

43 Caipirinha

3 Lime Wedges
3 Orange Slices
1½ oz. Cachaça
1 oz. Licor 43

Muddle Lime and Orange in a
mixing glass. Add Cachaça and
Licor 43. Shake well and pour into
a rocks glass.

Four Leaf Clover

1¼ oz. Bushmills Irish Whiskey
2 oz. Orange Juice
2 oz. Sweet & Sour
splash Green Crème de Menthe

Shake first three ingredients and
top with Crème de Menthe. Serve
over ice or straight up.

Don't overlook this one.

Fourth Degree Martini

¾ oz. Dry Gin
¾ oz. Dry Vermouth
¾ oz. Sweet Vermouth
¼ oz. Pernod

Stir gently with ice; serve straight
up or over ice. Garnish with a
Lemon Peel Twist.

Fourth of July

⅓ shot Grenadine
⅓ shot Vodka
⅓ shot Blue Curaçao

Layer this drink in the order listed.
Start with Grenadine on the bottom
and finish with Blue Curaçao on top.

Frangelico Classic Hazelnut Martini

1½ oz. Stoli Vodka
1 oz. Frangelico

Shake with ice and strain in a
martini glass garnished with a
Chocolate Rim.

Freddy Fudpucker

1¾ oz. Jose Cuervo Tequila
3 oz. Orange Juice
¼ oz. Liquore Galliano

Stir Tequila and Orange Juice in
a rocks glass. Top with Galliano.

Yes, there was this guy named Freddy.

French Colada

1½ oz. Puerto Rican White Rum
¾ oz. Cognac
1 scoop Crushed Ice
¾ oz. Sweet Cream
¾ oz. Coco Lopez Cream of
    Coconut
1½ oz. Pineapple Juice
splash Crème de Cassis

Blend with ice.

French Connection

½ oz. Cognac
½ oz. Grand Marnier

Serve straight up in a brandy snifter
or shake with ice and strain.

You can also serve this drink as a shot.

French Cosmopolitan

2 oz. Grey Goose Vodka
L'Orange
½ oz. Triple Sec
½ oz Peach Schnapps

Shake with ice. Garnish with an
Orange Peel.

French Kiss

1½ oz. Martini & Rossi Rosso
Vermouth
1½ oz. Martini & Rossi Dry
Vermouth

Combine over ice. Add a twist of
Lemon Peel for garnish.

French Kiss Martini

2 oz. Stolichnaya Ohranj
Vodka
¼ oz. Lillet

Stir gently with ice. Serve straight
up or over ice.

French 75

1½ oz. Cognac
½ tsp. Lemon Juice
½ tsp. Powdered Sugar
Champagne

Combine everything but Champagne.
Shake and pour in a champagne
glass. Fill with Champagne. Garnish
with a Lemon Twist.

French Tickler

1 part Goldschläger
1 part Grand Marnier

Shake with ice and strain into a
shot glass.

Frisco Cocktail

1¼ oz. Templeton Rye Whiskey
¾ oz. Benedictine

Stir with cracked ice and strain.
Serve with a twist of Lemon Peel.

FABLES & LORE

The origins of the French 75

If you request this drink, you may receive a mix of gin and champagne. In the French trenches of World War I, gin was scarce, but cognac and champagne were not. American soldiers soon discovered that a combination of the two produced an effect similar to getting zapped by an artillery piece known as French 75.

F

Fru-Fru

¾ oz. Banana Liqueur
1 oz. Peach Schnapps
dash Rose's Lime Juice
1 oz. Pineapple Juice

Shake with ice and strain into a glass.

Fruity Irishman

2 oz. Baileys Irish Cream
½ oz. Midori Melon Liqueur

Stir well over ice.

You can serve this one without ice in a shot glass.

Fudgesicle

1 oz. Vodka
¼ oz. Crème de Cacao
¼ oz. Chocolate Syrup

Shake and serve over ice.

Fuzzy Navel ⑦

1¼ oz. Peach Schnapps
3 oz. Orange Juice

Pour Schnapps over ice in a rocks glass. Fill with Orange Juice and stir well.

This famous drink was invented by National Distillers, which is now Jim Beam.

The origin of the Fuzzy Navel

Twenty years ago, at a private bar on Park Avenue in New York City, two lovers of the drink, Jack Doyle, who worked for the DeKuyper company, and Ray Foley, a bartender from New Jersey, were trying to create a cocktail for a brand new product, DeKuyper Peachtree Schnapps. Jack was mixing it with orange juice and Ray was cutting an orange for garnish when Jack made the remark that he could still smell the fuzz of the DeKuyper Peachtree Schnapps through the orange juice. Ray looked at the orange, saw the word "navel" printed on the skin, and they had their name: the Fuzzy Navel.

Fuzzy Rita

1½ oz. Jose Cuervo Gold Tequila
½ oz. Peach Liqueur
½ oz. Cointreau
1½ oz. Lime Juice

Combine over ice in a tall glass.

Margarita's cousin.

G & C

1 oz. Galliano
1 oz. Cognac

Shake with ice and strain into a shot glass.

Galliano Hot Shot

1 oz. Galliano
1 oz. Hot Coffee
dash Whipped Cream

Combine in a shot glass.

Hot and sweet.

Gangster's Martini

3 oz. Templeton Rye Whiskey, chilled
1 tsp. Water

Combine in a martini glass. Scan the room and serve.

Gator

¼ oz. Vodka
¼ oz. Gin
¼ oz. Rum
¼ oz. Scotch
¼ oz. Blackberry Brandy
¼ oz. Blue Curaçao
¼ oz. Triple Sec
¼ oz. Sweet & Sour Mix
1½ oz. Orange Juice
1½ oz. 7-Up

Shake the ingredients with ice and strain into shot glasses.

This cocktail should be green when all is said and done. It's not practical to make just one, by the way. This recipe will make about 3 shots.

Gentle Bull

1½ oz. Two Fingers Tequila
1 oz. Heavy Cream
¾ oz. Coffee Liqueur
1 scoop Crushed Ice
Whipped Cream

Shake. Top with Whipped Cream and a Cherry.

George Bush

Crushed Ice
1½ oz. Bushmills Irish Whiskey
1 strip Lemon Peel
3–4 oz. Ginger Ale

Fill a glass with crushed ice to the ¾ level. Add Irish Whiskey. Twist Lemon Peel over the drink to release its oil; then drop it in. Top with Ginger Ale.

Who's George Bush?

German Chocolate Cake

1 oz. Malibu Rum
½ oz. Crème de Cacao
½ oz. Frangelico
½ oz. Half & Half

Shake with ice. Pour over rocks or serve straight up.

G

Gibson

2 oz. Dry Gin
dash Martini & Rossi Extra Dry
   Vermouth
Cocktail Onion

Stir with ice. Add the Cocktail
Onion. Serve straight up or on ice.

Gimlet

1¼ oz. Vodka
½ oz. Fresh Lime Juice

Mix Vodka and Lime Juice in a
glass with ice. Strain and serve in a
cocktail glass. Garnish with a Lime
Twist.

You can also serve this one on ice in a highball glass.

Gin & Tonic

1¼ oz. Gin
Tonic

In a glass fllled with ice, add Gin
and fill with Tonic. Add a Lime
Wedge.

Gin Cocktail

1 oz. Gin
2 oz. Dubonnet

Stir over ice. Add a Lemon Twist.

Also known as the Dubonnet Cocktail.

Gin Fizz

2 oz. Gin
1 tsp. Sugar
Juice of 1 Lemon
Club Soda

Shake first three ingredients with
ice and strain. Fill with Club Soda.

FABLES & LORE

Where'd the Gibson come from?

Some say this drink was named after
New York artist Charles Dana Gibson
by his bartender, Charles Connoly
of the Players Club in New York.
Another story credits Billie Gibson, a
fight promoter.

Gin Rickey

1½ oz. Gin
Club Soda

In a tall glass filled with ice, add Gin. Fill with Club Soda and stir. Garnish with a Lime Wedge.

Okay, it's just Gin and Club Soda.

Ginger Colada

1½ oz. Coco Lopez Cream of Coconut
1 oz. Canton Delicate Ginger Liqueur
½ oz. Rum

Blend with ice.

Ginger Gale

1¾ oz. Gosling's Gold Bermuda Rum
4 oz. Ginger Ale

Mix in a tall glass with ice. Garnish with Lime.

Ginger Mist

2 oz. Irish Mist
3 oz. Ginger Ale

Combine in a tall glass and serve with a Lime Wedge.

Ginolans

2 parts Carolans Irish Cream
1 part Gordon's Gin

Stir well and serve over ice.

Girl Scout Cookie #1

¾ oz. Peppermint Schnapps
½ oz. Coffee Liqueur
3 oz. Half & Half

Shake with ice and serve over ice.

You can also serve this drink in a shot glass (but strain the ice).

Girl Scout Cookie #2

1 oz. Green Crème de Menthe
1 oz. White or Dark Crème de Cacao
¼ oz. Cream

Shake with ice and strain into a shot glass.

You can also serve this drink over ice in a highball glass.

Glenbeigh Fizz

1½ oz. Irish Whiskey
1 oz. Medium Sherry
½ oz. Crème de Noyaux
½ oz. Lemon Juice
Club Soda

Pour all ingredients except Club Soda in a chilled highball glass with several ice cubes and stir. Fill with Club Soda.

Godfather

1½ oz. Scotch
½ oz. Amaretto

Combine in a rocks glass over ice.

A drink you can't refuse.

Godmother

1 oz. Vodka
¼ oz. Amaretto

Combine in a rocks glass over ice.

A woman you can't refuse.

Gold Digger Martini

1½ oz. Finlandia Pineapple Vodka
½ oz. Cointreau

Stir with ice; serve straight up or over ice.

For millionaire-chasing maids.

Gold Furnace

2 oz. Goldschläger
2 dashes Tabasco

Combine in a shot glass.

This is hot.

Gold Rush

1 oz. Goldschläger
1 oz. Cuervo Gold

Shake with ice and strain into a
shot glass.

This is not.

Golden Boy

1½ oz. Bourbon
½ oz. Rum
2 oz. Orange Juice
1 tsp. Lemon Juice
1 tsp. Sugar Syrup
1 scoop Crushed Ice
dash Grenadine

Mix all ingredients, except the
Grenadine, in a shaker. Strain
mixture into a chilled glass. Top
with a dash of Grenadine.

Golden Cadillac

¼ oz. Liquore Galliano
1 oz. White Crème de Cacao
1 oz. Cream

Mix in a blender with a little ice at
a low speed for a short time. Strain
into a champagne glass. A scoop of
Vanilla Ice Cream can be substituted
for Cream.

G

Golden Day

¾ oz. Vodka
½ oz. Liquore Galliano

Serve in a rocks glass over ice.

Golden Dream

1 oz. Liquore Galliano
¼ oz. Triple Sec
½ oz. Orange Juice
½ oz. Cream

Shake with cracked ice. Strain into a
cocktail glass.

You can also serve this one over ice in a highball glass.

Golden Girl Martini

1¾ oz. Dry Gin
¾ oz. Dry Sherry
1 dash Angostura bitters

Stir gently with ice. Serve straight
up or over ice.

Golden Martini

2½ oz. Seagram's Extra Dry
    Gin
¼ oz. French Vermouth

Stir gently with ice. Serve straight
up or over ice. Garnish with a
Lemon Peel Twist.

Good and Plenty

1 oz. Anisette
1 oz. Blackberry Brandy

Shake with ice and strain into a
shot glass.

Gorilla Sweat

1½ oz. Tequila
Hot Water
½ tsp. Sugar
1 pat Butter

Pour Tequila into a rocks glass
and fill with Hot Water. Add Sugar
and stir in Butter. Garnish with a
Cinnamon Stick and a sprinkle of
Nutmeg.

A great name?

Gotham

2 oz. Smirnoff Vodka
¼ oz. Campari

Shake with ice and strain into a
chilled martini glass. Serve straight up
or on the rocks. Garnish with Olives.

Grafton Street Sour

1½ oz. Irish Whiskey
½ oz. Triple Sec
1 oz. Lime Juice
¼ oz. Raspberry Liqueur

Mix all ingredients except the
Raspberry Liqueur with cracked ice
in a shaker or blender and strain
into a chilled cocktail glass. Top
with Raspberry Liqueur.

You can also serve this one on ice.

Grand Am

1 oz. Grand Marnier
1 oz. Di Saronno Amaretto

Shake with ice and strain into a
shot glass.

Grand Melon Mojito

12 Mint Leaves
½ tsp. Sugar
½ Lime
2 oz. Bacardi Grand Melon Rum
3 oz. Club Soda

Place Mint Leaves, Sugar, and Lime in a glass. Crush well with a pestle. Add Bacardi Grand Melon Rum. Top off with Club Soda. Stir well, and garnish with sprigs of Mint and a Lime Wheel or a Watermelon Slice.

Grand Ohranj

1½ oz. Stoli Ohranj Vodka
dash Extra Dry Vermouth
splash Grand Marnier

Stir gently with ice; serve straight up or over ice. Garnish with a slice of Orange Peel.

Grand Royale

1½ oz. Grand Marnier
6 oz. Pineapple Juice

Pour Grand Marnier into a tall glass with ice. Add Pineapple Juice and serve.

Granny Goose

2 oz. Grey Goose Vodka
¼ oz. Grand Marnier

Shake with ice and strain into a chilled martini glass. Serve straight up or on the rocks. Add an Orange Twist for garnish.

Grape Crush

1 oz. Vodka
1 oz. Black Raspberry Liqueur
2 oz. Sour Mix
1 oz. 7-Up

Serve over ice in a Collins glass. Garnish with an Orange Slice or Cherry.

Grape Punch

1¼ oz. Bacardi Light Rum
Grape Juice

Pour Rum into a tall glass filled with ice. Fill with Grape Juice and add a squeeze of Lime or Lemon.

Grasshopper

½ oz. Green Crème de Menthe
½ oz. White Crème de Cacao
½ oz. Cream

Combine in a blender with ice and blend until smooth. Strain into a margarita glass.

A grasshopper walks into a bar. Bartender says, "We have a drink named after you." The grasshopper replies, "You have a drink named Bruce?"

The Great White

1¼ oz. Jameson Irish Whiskey
2 oz. Apple Juice
1 oz. White Curaçao

Combine over ice in a tall glass and garnish with a Mint Sprig.

Green Chili

1 part Hiram Walker Peach
    Schnapps
1 part Midori
dash Tabasco Sauce

Shake with ice and strain into a shot glass.

Green Devil

1 oz. Bombay Gin
½ oz. Crème de Menthe
½ oz. Rose's Lime Juice

Shake with ice and strain into a shot glass.

Green Hornet

½ oz. Vodka
¼ oz. Midori
½ oz. Sweet & Sour Mix

Shake with ice; serve straight up or over ice.

Green Lizard

1 oz. Chartreuse (Green)
1 oz. Bacardi 151 Rum
¼ oz. Rose's Lime Juice

Layer this drink by pouring Chartreuse first, then the Rum, and then the Lime Juice.

Green Parrot

1½ oz. Appleton Estate Rum
4 oz. Orange Juice
1 oz. Blue Curaçao

Pour ingredients, one at a time in the order listed into large stemmed glass over ice. Do not mix. Garnish with an Orange Slice.

Green Sneaker

1 oz. Vodka
½ oz. Midori
½ oz. Triple Sec
2 oz. Orange Juice

Stir with ice, strain, and serve straight up.

Gremlin

½ oz. Vodka
¾ oz. Blue Curaçao
¾ oz. Rum
½ oz. Orange Juice

Shake with ice, strain, and serve straight up.

Greyhound

1½ oz. Vodka
Grapefruit Juice

Pour Vodka over crushed ice in a tall glass. Fill with Grapefruit Juice.

Most people order this drink by saying, "Give me a vodka and grapefruit juice."

Grit Cocktail

2½ oz. Irish Whiskey
¼ oz. Red Vermouth

Shake and then strain.

Gunga Din Martini

3 parts Dry Gin
1 part Dry Vermouth
Juice of ¼ Orange

Shake with ice. Garnish with a Pineapple Slice.

Gypsy Martini

1½ oz. Vodka or Gin
dash Martini & Rossi Extra Dry
Vermouth

Shake with ice; serve straight up
or on ice. Garnish with a Cherry.

Gypsy's Kiss

2½ oz. Irish Mist
½ oz. Orange Juice
½ oz. Lemon Juice or Sour Mix

Combine in a highball glass.

You can also add a dash of Grenadine.

Half & Half Martini

3 parts Gin
3 parts Vodka
1 part Dry Vermouth

Shake with ice; serve straight up or
on ice. Garnish with a Lemon Twist.

Harbor Breeze

1¼ oz. Lemon-Flavored Puerto
Rican Rum
½ oz. Fresh Kiwi Purée
2 oz. Pear Nectar

Add ingredients in a shaker. Shake
with ice and strain into a martini
glass. Garnish with a Kiwi Wheel
and a Lemon Twist.

Harbor Lights #1

1 oz. Galliano
1 oz. Remy Martin Cognac

Shake with ice and strain into a
shot glass.

Harbor Lights #2

1 oz. Chambord
1 oz. Puerto Rican Rum
1 oz. Orange Juice

Shake with ice and strain into a
shot glass.

Hard Hat

1¼ oz. Bacardi Silver Rum
1¼ oz. Fresh Lime Juice
1 tsp. Sugar
¼ oz. Rose's Grenadine
Club Soda

In a shaker with ice, combine all
but the Club Soda. Stir and strain
into a glass with ice. Fill with
Club Soda.

H

Harry's Martini

1¾ oz. Dry Gin
¾ oz. Sweet Vermouth
¼ oz. Pernod

Stir gently with ice; serve straight
up or on ice. Garnish with Mint
Sprigs.

Harvard Cocktail

1½ oz. Brandy
¾ oz. Sweet Vermouth
2 tsp. Fresh Lemon Juice
1 tsp. Grenadine
dash Angostura Bitters

Shake ingredients and serve over
ice in a rocks glass.

Harvey Wallbanger

1 oz. Vodka
Orange Juice
¼ oz. Liquore Galliano

In a tall glass with ice, add Vodka
and fill the glass ¾ full with Orange
Juice. Float the Galliano on top.

Havana Sidecar

1½ oz. Puerto Rican Golden
    Rum
¾ oz. Lemon Juice
¾ oz. Triple Sec

Mix with ice and serve on ice.

H

Hawaii Five-0

1½ oz. Finlandia Pineapple
    Vodka
¼ oz. Blue Curaçao

Shake. Serve in a glass with ice.
Garnish with a Pineapple Spear,
Cherry, and umbrella.

Hawaiian

1 part Cork Dry Gin
1 part Orange Juice
dash Orange Curaçao

Shake with ice. Serve on ice.

Hawaiian Highball

2½ oz. Irish Whiskey
2 tsp. Pineapple Juice
1 tsp. Lemon Juice
Club Soda

Combine the Whiskey with the
Juices. Add ice and fill with Soda.
Stir gently.

Hawaiian Night

1 oz. Light Rum
Pineapple Juice
¼ oz. Cherry-Flavored Brandy

Pour Rum into a tall glass half-filled
with ice. Fill with Pineapple Juice
and float Cherry-Flavored Brandy
on top.

Hawaiian Pipeline

1½ oz. Pineapple Vodka,
    chilled
2 oz. Orange Juice
1 oz. Cranberry Juice

Shake. Serve over ice in a tall glass.

Hawaiian Punch

½ oz. Southern Comfort
½ oz. Sloe Gin
½ oz. Cointreau
½ oz. Orange Juice

Shake with ice and strain into a
shot glass.

Hazelnut Martini

2 oz. Absolut Vodka
splash Frangelico

Stir with ice and serve straight up.
Garnish with an Orange Slice.

Invented at the Martini Bar at the Chianti Restaurant in Houston, Texas.

Heartthrob

1¼ oz. Finlandia Cranberry
    Vodka, chilled
¼ oz. Peach Schnapps
¼ oz. Grapefruit Juice

Shake. Serve in a tall glass with ice.

Heat Wave

1 oz. Myers's Dark Rum
½ oz. Peach Schnapps
Pineapple Juice
splash Grenadine

Add Rum and Schnapps to a highball glass with ice. Fill with Pineapple Juice. Add a splash of Grenadine.

Hendrick's Floradora

1½ oz. Hendrick's Gin
½ oz. Lime Juice
½ oz. Raspberry Syrup
½ oz. Spicy Ginger Beer

Assemble ingredients and shake well. Serve over ice in a Collins glass. Garnish with two Raspberries and a Lime Wheel.

The Hennessy Martini

1½ oz. Hennessy V.S. Cognac
dash Lemon Juice

Shake with ice and strain or serve straight up.

Invented at Harry Denton's in San Francisco, California.

Highball

1½ oz. American Whiskey
3 oz. Ginger Ale

Combine and stir.

H

Hollywood #1

1 oz. Vodka
1 oz. Black Raspberry Liqueur
Cranberry Juice

Combine ingredients in a tall glass with ice. Fill with Cranberry Juice.

Hollywood #2

1 oz. Stolichnaya Vodka
1 oz. Chambord
1 oz. Pineapple Juice

Shake with ice and strain into a shot glass.

Home Run

1 oz. Bourbon
1 oz. Light Rum
1 oz. Brandy
2 tsp. Lemon Juice

Shake with ice and serve over ice.

Take a swig at this one.

Honey Nut Cocktail

1½ oz. Celtic Crossing
1½ oz. Frangelico
1½ oz. Half & Half

Shake ingredients and serve over ice in a rocks glass.

The Honeymooner

2 oz. Bunratty Meade
½ oz. Amaretto
½ oz. Cream

Shake ingredients and pour over ice. Garnish with Cinnamon.

Honolulu Hurricane Martini

2 oz. Dry Gin
¼ oz. French Vermouth
¼ oz. Italian Vermouth
⅛ oz. Pineapple Juice

Shake with ice and strain.

H

Horny Bull

1¼ oz. Tequila
Orange Juice

Add Tequila to a chilled highball glass filled with ice. Fill with Orange Juice.

Hot Bomb

¾ oz. Two Fingers Tequila
¼ oz. Cinnamon Schnapps

Shake with ice; strain into a shot glass.

Hot Irish

½ slice Fresh Lemon
4 Cloves
2 tsp. Sugar (brown if available)
pinch Cinnamon
Boiling Water
1½ oz. Jameson Irish Whiskey

Stud the Lemon Slice with Cloves. Put Lemon, Sugar, and Cinnamon into a warm glass. Add Boiling Water and Irish Whiskey. Stir well and serve.

Hot Irish and Port

1½ oz. Bushmills Irish Whiskey
2 oz. Red or Tawny Port
2 oz. Water

Pour ingredients into a saucepan. Heat to boiling point but do not boil. Pour into a mug. Add a Cinnamon Stick and an Orange Slice.

Hot Irish Monk

2 oz. Bushmills Irish Whiskey
1 oz. Frangelico Hazelnut
    Liqueur
4 oz. Hot Chocolate

Stir thoroughly and then add a thick cap of Whipped Cream; sprinkle with chopped, toasted Hazelnuts.

Hot Lips

1½ oz. Finlandia Cranberry
    Vodka
¼ oz. Goldschläger

Shake with ice and strain into a shot glass.

Not to kiss and tell.

Hot Mist

2½ oz. Irish Mist
2 oz. Boiling Water

Combine in the glass and garnish with a slice of Lemon and some Cloves.

Hot Pants

¼ oz. Absolut Peppar Vodka
1 oz. Peach Schnapps

Combine over ice.

Bottoms up.

Hot Toddy

1½ oz. Seagram's V.O. Whisky
Hot Water
1 lump Sugar
2 Cloves

Pour Seagram's into Hot Water.
Add Sugar and Cloves. Stir.

Hula-Hoop

1½ oz. Vodka
2 oz. Pineapple Juice
½ oz. Orange Juice

Combine over ice.

Hurricane

1¼ oz. Myers's Dark Rum
4 oz. Pineapple Juice
2 oz. Orange Juice
splash Grenadine

Combine over ice.

Iceberg Martini

2 oz. Beefeater Gin
splash White Crème de
  Menthe

Stir with ice and strain. Garnish
with Mint.

Created at the Martini Bar at the Chianti Restaurant in Houston, Texas.

Iguana

½ oz. Tequila
¾ oz. Vodka
¾ oz. Coffee Liqueur

Combine over ice.

Imperial

1¼ oz. Bourbon
1¼ oz. Orange Liqueur
splash Simple Syrup
1 scoop Crushed Ice
splash Club Soda

Mix together all the ingredients
except the Club Soda in a shaker.
Strain the mixture into a rocks glass
over ice. Top off the glass with Club
Soda.

Incredible Hulk

1 oz. Hpnotiq
1 oz. Cognac

Layer over ice and then stir for transformation.

Indifferent Miss

¾ oz. Captain Morgan Original Spiced Rum
¾ oz. Lime Juice
1 tsp. Bar Syrup
3 oz. Club Soda

Pour the Rum, Juice, and Syrup over ice in a glass. Stir. Add the Soda and stir gently.

Ink Drop

1½ oz. Tattoo (chilled)
3 oz. Energy Drink

Mix ingredients in a rocks glass.

Inoculation Shot

1 oz. Jose Cuervo Gold Tequila
¼ oz. Blue Curaçao

Shake with ice and strain into a shot glass.

International Coffee

½ oz. Devonshire Irish Cream
½ oz. Chambord
5 oz. Coffee

Pour Devonshire and Chambord into a cup of hot Coffee.

One of many international coffees.

Irish Angel

1 oz. Bushmills Irish Whiskey
¼ oz. Crème de Cacao
¼ oz. White Crème de Menthe
½ oz. Cream

Mix with ice in a cocktail shaker or blender. Strain into a cocktail glass.

Irish Apple

1 oz. Carolans Irish Cream
1 oz. Laird's Applejack

Stir well with ice.

Irish Buck

1½ oz. Jameson Irish Whiskey
Ginger Ale

Pour Irish Whiskey into chilled
highball glass with cracked ice.
Twist a Lemon Peel over the drink
and drop it in. Fill with Ginger Ale.

Irish Canadian

½ oz. Irish Mist
1½ oz. Canadian Whisky

In a mixing glass half-filled
with ice, combine both of the
ingredients. Stir well. Strain into
a cocktail glass.

Irish-Canadian Sangaree

2 tsp. Irish Mist
1¼ oz. Canadian Whisky
1 tsp. Orange Juice
1 tsp. Lemon Juice

Combine and stir well. Add ice
and dust with Nutmeg.

Irish Candy

1½ oz. Baileys Irish Cream
½ oz. Chocolate Raspberry
Liqueur
½ oz. White Crème de Cacao

Build over ice. Stir and serve.

Candy is dandy, but liquor is quicker.

Irish Celebration

1¼ oz. Bushmills Irish Whiskey
¼ oz. Green Crème de Menthe
splash Champagne

Shake the first two ingredients
well with ice and strain. Top with
Champagne.

Irish Charlie

1 oz. Irish Cream
1 oz. White Crème de Menthe

Shake with ice and strain into a
shot glass.

You can also layer the Irish Cream over the Crème de Menthe.

Irish Coffee

1¼ oz. Irish Whiskey
Hot Coffee
Cream
Sugar

Pour Irish Whiskey in a warm
glass or mug. Fill with Coffee.
Stir in Cream and Sugar to taste.

Irish Collins

2 oz. Irish Whiskey
1 tsp. Powdered Sugar
Juice of a Small Lemon
Club Soda

Combine the first three ingredients
in a tall glass filled with ice. Fill
with Club Soda and stir.

A variation on the Tom Collins and Whiskey Collins.

Irish Cooler

2 oz. Irish Whiskey
6 oz. Club Soda

Pour Whiskey into a highball
glass over ice cubes. Top with
Soda and stir. Garnish with a
Lemon Peel Spiral.

Irish Cow

6 oz. Hot Milk
1 tsp. Sugar
1½ oz. Irish Whiskey

Pour the Milk into a glass. Add the
Sugar and Whiskey. Stir well.

Irish Cowboy

1 oz. Baileys Irish Cream
1½ oz. Bourbon

Shake or stir over ice.

Irish Cream Stinger

2½ oz. Carolans Irish Cream
½ oz. White Crème de Menthe

Stir well over ice.

Irish Dream

½ oz. Irish Cream Liqueur
½ oz. Hazelnut Liqueur
½ oz. Dark Crème de Cacao
1 scoop Vanilla Ice Cream

Combine ingredients in a blender with ice. Blend thoroughly. Pour into a Collins or parfait glass. Serve with a straw.

Irish Eyes

1 oz. Irish Whiskey
¼ oz. Green Crème de Menthe
2 oz. Heavy Cream

Shake well with crushed ice. Strain into a chilled cocktail glass. Garnish with Maraschino Cherry.

This will make you smile.

Irish Fix

2 oz. Irish Whiskey
½ oz. Irish Mist
1 oz. Pineapple Juice
½ oz. Lemon Juice
½ tsp. Sugar Syrup

Fill glass with ice. Combine ingredients and stir.

Irish Fizz

2½ oz. Irish Whiskey
1½ tsp. Lemon Juice
1 tsp. Triple Sec
½ tsp. Sugar
Club Soda

Combine all ingredients except the Soda with ice in a shaker and shake. Strain into a Collins glass. Add ice and Club Soda.

Irish Flag

⅓ shot Green Crème de Menthe
⅓ shot Irish Cream
⅓ shot Grand Marnier

Layer this drink in the order listed. Start with Crème de Menthe on the bottom and finish with Grand Marnier on top.

Irish Frog

¾ oz. Midori
¾ oz. Baileys Irish Cream, chilled

Layer this drink by pouring the Midori first and then adding the Irish Cream.

Irish Frost Shooter

1 shot Baileys Irish Cream
1 splash Coco Lopez Cream of Coconut
1 splash Half & Half

Shake and strain. Garnish with Cinnamon.

Irish Headlock

¼ oz. Brandy
¼ oz. Amaretto
¼ oz. Irish Whiskey
¼ oz. Irish Cream

Layer this drink by pouring the Brandy first, then the Amaretto, and so on.

Irish Horseman

1¼ oz. Bushmills Irish Whiskey
¼ oz. Triple Sec
½ oz. Lime Juice
1–2 dashes Raspberry Liqueur or Chambord

Combine the first three ingredients in a cordial glass with crushed ice and stir. Add one to two dashes of Raspberry Liqueur on top.

Irish Kiss

¾ oz. Irish Whiskey
½ oz. Peach Schnapps
4 oz. Ginger Ale
2 oz. Orange Juice

Combine ingredients in an ice cube–filled Collins glass. Garnish with a Lime Wheel.

Irish Knight

2 oz. Bushmills Irish Whiskey
2 dashes Noilly Prat Dry Vermouth
2 dashes Benedictine

Combine in a rocks glass with ice. Add a twist of Orange Peel.

Irish Lace

1 shot Irish Mist
2 splashes Coco Lopez
Cream of Coconut
2 splashes Half & Half
3 splashes Pineapple Juice
2 scoops Ice

Blend and serve in a margarita glass.
Garnish with an Orange Flag.

Irish Magic

1 oz. Tullamore Dew Irish Whiskey
¼ oz. White Crème de Cacao
5 oz. Orange Juice

Pour all ingredients over ice in a
glass. Stir.

Irish Mist Alexander

1 oz. Irish Mist
1 oz. Light Cream
1 oz. Dark Crème de Cacao

Shake ingredients with cracked ice
and strain. Sprinkle with Nutmeg.

Irish Mist Kiss

2 oz. Irish Mist
dash Blue Curaçao
splash Soda

Serve in a rocks glass over ice.

Irish Mist Sour

2 oz. Irish Mist
1 oz. Lemon Juice or Sour Mix

Shake well over ice. Serve in a tall
glass.

Irish Mocha Cooler

2 oz. Bushmills Irish Whiskey
1 oz. Dark Crème de Cacao
Iced Coffee
Whipped Cream

Combine first two ingredients over
ice in a 14 oz. glass. Fill with Iced
Coffee. Top with Whipped Cream.

Irish Night Cap

4 oz. Hot Milk
1 tsp. Sugar
1½ oz. Bushmills Irish Whiskey

Pour Milk into the glass. Add Sugar and Irish Whiskey. Stir well.

Irish Penance

2½ oz. Carolans Irish Cream
½ oz. Cointreau

Shake slowly and serve over ice.

Irish Prince

1¼ oz. Bushmills Irish Whiskey
3 oz. Tonic Water

Combine in a rocks glass. Add ice cubes and stir gently. Drop in a Lemon Peel.

Irish Quaalude

½ oz. Vodka
½ oz. Irish Cream
½ oz. Coffee Liqueur
½ oz. Hazelnut Liqueur

Shake with ice and strain.

Irish Rainbow

1½ oz. Irish Whiskey
3–4 dashes Pernod
3–4 dashes Orange Curaçao
3–4 dashes Maraschino Liqueur
3–4 dashes Angostura Bitters

Mix all ingredients with cracked ice in a shaker or blender. Pour into a chilled rocks glass. Twist an Orange Peel over the drink and drop it in.

Irish Raspberry

1 oz. Devonshire Irish Cream
½ oz. Chambord
1 cup Ice

Blend with ice and serve.

Irish Rickey

1½ oz. Tullamore Dew
1 cube Ice
Juice of ½ Lime
Carbonated Water

Combine first three ingredients in a highball glass. Fill with Carbonated Water and stir. Add a Lime Wedge.

Irish Rose

1½ oz. Jameson Irish Whiskey
½ oz. Plymouth Sloe Gin
⅓ oz. St. Germain Elderflower
   Liqueur
3 drops Rose Water
3 Lime Squeezes
top with Ginger Ale

Add all ingredients except the Ginger Ale into a mixing glass. Shake and strain over fresh ice in a highball glass. Top with Ginger Ale. Garnish with a Lime Squeeze and optional Rose Petal.

Irish Rose Highball

2 oz. Tullamore Dew
⅛ oz. Grenadine
Club Soda

Combine first two ingredients in a glass and fill with Club Soda.

Irish Russian

1 oz. Carolans Irish Cream
1 oz. Vodka

Stir well over ice.

Irish Shillelagh

1½ oz. Irish Whiskey
½ oz. Sloe Gin
½ oz. Light Rum
1 oz. Lemon Juice
1 tsp. Sugar Syrup
2 Peach Slices, diced

Mix all ingredients with cracked ice in a shaker or blender. Pour into a chilled rocks glass. Garnish with Raspberries and a Cherry.

Irish Sling

1 lump Sugar
1 oz. Tullamore Dew
1 oz. Gin

Crush Sugar with ice in a glass. Add Tullamore Dew and Gin. Stir.

Irish Sour

1½ oz. Irish Whiskey
1 tsp. Sugar
Juice of ½ Lemon

Shake vigorously with ice until frothy. Stir into sour glass. Add a Maraschino Cherry and an Orange Slice.

Irish Spring

1 oz. Bushmills Irish Whiskey
½ oz. Peach Schnapps
1 oz. Orange Juice
1 oz. Sweet & Sour

Combine in a Collins glass with ice and stir well. Garnish with an Orange Slice and a Cherry.

Irish Sting

1½ oz. Bushmills Irish Whiskey
¼ oz. White Crème de Menthe

Shake. Serve straight up or over ice.

Put a bee in your bonnet.

Irish Summer Coffee

1 oz. Irish Whiskey
¼ oz. Irish Cream Liqueur
4 oz. Cold Coffee
Whipped Cream

Stir first three ingredients with ice and strain. Top with Whipped Cream if desired.

Irish Sunburn

1½ oz. Ke Ke Beach
½ oz. 360 Vodka
splash Grenadine

Shake with ice and strain into a shot glass.

Irish Surfer

1¼ oz. Irish Mist
3 oz. Orange Juice
Sugar
Club Soda

Shake Irish Mist, Orange Juice, and Sugar. Pour into a glass and fill it with Club Soda.

Irish Whiskey Cooler

2 oz. Irish Whiskey
3 oz. Club Soda
dash Angostura Bitters

Combine in a tall glass with ice. Garnish with Lemon.

Iron Cross

1 part Apricot Brandy 1 part Rumple Minze	Layer Brandy over Rumple Minze in a shot glass.

Isla Grande Iced Tea

1½ oz. Puerto Rican Dark Rum 3 oz. Pineapple Juice Unsweetened, Brewed Iced Tea	Combine the first two ingredients in a tall glass with ice. Fill with Iced Tea.

Island Tea

1½ oz. Vodka 1 oz. Grenadine 1 tsp. Lemon Juice	Combine with ice and shake. Strain over ice in a rocks glass and garnish with a Mint Sprig.

Italian Colada

¼ oz. Coco Lopez Cream of Coconut 1½ oz. Puerto Rican White Rum ¼ oz. Amaretto ¾ oz. Sweet Cream 2 oz. Pineapple Juice	Blend with crushed ice.

Italian Martini

1½ oz. Vodka or Gin dash Amaretto	Stir with ice. Serve on ice or strain.

Very similar to a Godmother.

Italian Russian

½ oz. Sambuca 1 oz. Vodka	Pour over ice cubes in small rocks glass. Stir well. Twist an Orange Peel over the glass and drop it in.

Italian Stallion

1½ oz. Dewar's White Label
    Scotch
2 oz. Galliano

Stir ingredients in an ice-filled rocks glass. Serve on the rocks.

J.J.'s Shamrock

1 oz. Irish Whiskey
½ oz. White Crème de Cacao
½ oz. Green Crème de Menthe
1 oz. Milk

Mix in a shaker or blender with cracked ice and serve in a chilled glass.

Jack Daniel's & Coca-Cola or Jack & Coke

1¾ oz. Jack Daniel's Whiskey
3 oz. Coca-Cola

Combine over ice and stir.

Jack Rose

1½ oz. Laird's Applejack
¾ oz. Sour Mix
tsp. Grenadine

Shake with ice. Serve with ice or strain.

A very special New Jersey drink.

Jackson Martini

1½ oz. Absolut Vodka
dash Dubonnet
dash Angostura Bitters

Stir with ice. Serve with ice or strain.

J

Jade

1½ oz. Puerto Rican White Rum
¾ oz. Lime Juice
1 bar spoon Sugar
dash Triple Sec
dash Green Crème de Menthe

Shake with ice. Serve over ice.

Jäger Bomb

1½ oz. Jägermeister
1 can Red Bull

Serve in a tall glass with ice or as a shot.

Some people drop a shot glass of Jäger into a pint glass holding a can's worth of Red Bull. Then they chug the whole thing boilermaker-style. Whatever floats your boat.

Jamaican Dust

1 oz. Mount Gay Rum
½ oz. Tia Maria
½ oz. Pineapple Juice

Shake with ice and strain into a shot glass.

James Bond Martini #1

2 oz. Gordon's Gin
1 oz. Vodka
½ oz. Kina Lillet

Shake ingredients with ice until very cold. Pour into a chilled glass. Then add a large, thin slice of Lemon Peel.

From the 1967 movie Casino Royale.

James Bond Martini #2

½ oz. Martini & Rossi Extra Dry Vermouth
1½ oz. Smirnoff Vodka
1½ oz. Tanqueray Gin
½ oz. Lillet Blanc

Stir with ice and strain. Garnish with a Lemon Twist.

James Joyce

1½ oz. Jameson Irish Whiskey
¾ oz. Sweet Red Vermouth
¾ oz. Cointreau
½ oz. Freshly-Squeezed Lime Juice

Shake ingredients and strain into a chilled cocktail glass. Garnish with a Maraschino Cherry.

Created by Gary Regan.

Jamie's Highland Special

½ oz. Green Crème de Menthe
½ oz. Galliano
½ oz. Blackberry Liqueur
½ oz. Kirschwasser

Layer this drink in the order listed. Start with Crème de Menthe on the bottom and finish with Kirschwasser on top.

See Chapter 18 for more info on this type of Pousse-Café drink.

Jelly Bean

1 oz. Anisette
1 oz. Blackberry-Flavored Brandy

Combine in a rocks glass over ice.

You can also strain this one into a shot glass.

Jellyfish

1 oz. Irish Cream
1 oz. White Crème de Cacao
1 oz. Amaretto
1 oz. Grenadine

Pour first three ingredients directly into the glass. Pour Grenadine in the center of the glass.

Jersey Devil

1½ oz. Laird's Applejack
½ oz. Cointreau
½ tsp. Sugar
½ oz. Rose's Lime Juice
½ oz. Cranberry Juice

Shake ingredients and serve over ice.

Jewel Martini

2 oz. Ultimat Vodka
1 oz. Sunkist Orange Juice
¼ oz. Cointreau
dash Blue Curaçao

Shake over ice and strain into a chilled martini glass.

J

John Collins

Lemon Juice
½ oz. Sugar Syrup
1 oz. Bourbon or Whiskey
Juice of ½ Lime
Club Soda

Pour Lemon Juice, Syrup, and Whiskey in a highball glass filled with ice. Squeeze in the Juice from ½ Lime and save the shell. Fill the glass with Club Soda. Stir. Decorate with the used Lime.

This is Tom's brother.

Jolly Rancher #1

¾ oz. Peach Schnapps
¾ oz. Apple Schnapps
2½ oz. Cranberry Juice

Combine in a tall glass with ice.

Jolly Rancher #2

¾ oz. Midori
¾ oz. Peach Schnapps
¾ oz. Cranberry Juice

Shake with ice and strain into a shot glass.

Journalist Martini

1½ oz. Dry Gin
¼ oz. Sweet Vermouth
¼ oz. Dry Vermouth
1 dash Angostura bitters
1 dash Lemon Juice
1 dash Orange Curaçao

Stir with ice. Serve over ice or strain.

Juicy Fruit

1 oz. Absolut Vodka
½ oz. Peach Schnapps
½ oz. Midori
½ oz. Pineapple Juice

Shake with ice and strain into a shot glass.

J

Jump Up and Kiss Me

1¼ oz. Myers's Dark Rum
4 oz. Pineapple Juice
½ oz. Rose's Lime Juice
dash Angostura Bitters

Shake with ice and serve over ice.

Kahlúa & Cream

2 oz. Kahlúa
1 oz. Cream/Milk

Combine in a highball glass and stir.

The Kahlúa Colada

1 oz. Coco Lopez Cream of
    Coconut
2 oz. Pineapple Juice
1 oz. Kahlúa
½ oz. Rum
1 cup Ice

Blend with ice and serve in a
margarita glass.

Kahlúa Hummer

1 oz. Kahlúa
1 oz. Light Rum
2 scoops Vanilla or Chocolate
    Ice Cream

Blend with ice.

Kahlúa Iced Cappuccino

1½ oz. Kahlúa
1 oz. Carolans Irish Cream
    Liqueur
4 oz. Cold Coffee
dash Cinnamon

Pour Kahlúa and Irish Cream into
Coffee and sprinkle with Cinnamon.

K

Kahlúa Sunset

1 oz. Kahlúa
2½ oz. Cranberry Juice
3 oz. Pineapple Juice

Combine in a tall glass with ice.

Kamikazi

1 oz. Vodka
½ oz. Cointreau
¼ oz. Rose's Lime Juice

Shake with ice and strain into a
shot glass.

Kandy Kane

1 oz. Hiram Walker Crème de
   Noya
1 oz. Rumple Minze

Layer Crème de Noya over Rumple
Minze.

No, you will not find this under "Candy Cane."

Kentucky Cocktail

2 oz. Bourbon
2½ oz. Pineapple Juice

Shake with ice and serve over ice
or strain.

Kentucky Colonel

1½ oz. Jim Beam Bourbon
½ oz. Benedictine

Shake with ice. Strain into chilled
cocktail glass. Add a Lemon Twist.

Kentucky Martini

1½ oz. Maker's Mark Bourbon
½ oz. Amaretto
2 oz. Orange Slice Soda

Stir with ice; strain.

*Invented at the Martini Bar at the Chianti Restaurant in Houston, Texas.
A Kentucky Martini from a bar in Texas — only in America.*

Kerry Cooler

2 oz. Irish Whiskey
1½ oz. Sherry
1¼ tbsp. Crème de Almond
1¼ tbsp. Lemon Juice
Club Soda

Combine (except the Soda) with ice
and shake well. Strain into a glass
with ice and add Soda. Top with a
Lemon Slice.

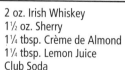

Key Largo

2 oz. Mount Gay Rum
½ oz. Coco Lopez Real Cream of
Coconut
scoop orange Sherbet

Blend ingredients slowly. Garnish
with an Orange Slice.

Key Lime Pie

2 oz. Licor 43
1 oz. Stolichnaya Vodka
splash Lime Juice

Shake over ice and strain.

Killer Colada

2 oz. Whaler's Coconut Rum
3 tbsp. Coconut Milk
3 tbsp. Pineapple (crushed)
2 cups Crushed Ice

Blend at high speed. Serve with a
Pineapple Wedge.

Killer Kool-Aid

¼ oz. Chambord
¼ oz. Vodka
¼ oz. Gin
¼ oz. Rum
2 oz. Cranberry Juice
1 oz. Sour Mix

Combine in a tall glass over ice.

King Alphonse

1 oz. Dark Crème de Cacao
1 oz. Cream

Layer the Cream on top of the Crème
de Cacao.

Add a cherry and it's called an Angel Tit.

Kinsale Cooler

1½ oz. Irish Whiskey
1 oz. Irish Mist
1 oz. Lemon Juice
Club Soda
Ginger Ale

Mix the first three ingredients with
cracked ice in a shaker or blender.
Pour into a chilled Collins glass with
equal parts of Club Soda and Ginger
Ale. Stir gently. Twist a Lemon Peel
over the drink and drop it in.

Kir or Kir Royale

3 oz. Champagne
splash Crème de Cassis

Fill the glass with Champagne and
add a splash of Crème de Cassis.

Kiss Me Kate

1 oz. Saint Brendan's Superior
Irish Cream
½ oz. Crème de Cacao
½ oz. Raspberry Liqueur

Shake with ice and strain into a
shot glass.

Koala Hug

1¼ oz. Jameson Irish Whiskey
2 oz. Lemon Juice
1 oz. Cointreau
dash Pernod

Shake with ice. Serve in a tall glass
with ice cubes. Garnish with an
Orange Slice and straws.

Kool-Aid

1 oz. Vodka
1 oz. Melon Liqueur
2 oz. Cranberry Juice

Combine ingredients over ice in a
rocks glass.

Krazy Kangaroo

1¼ oz. Jameson Irish Whiskey
dash Pernod
2 oz. Orange Juice

Pour into a mixing glass with ice.
Stir and strain into a glass or serve
over ice. Decorate with Orange
Rind.

The Irish created civilization and Australia.

Kretchma

1 oz. Vodka
1 oz. Crème de Cacao
½ oz. Lemon Juice
½ tsp. Grenadine

Mix all ingredients with cracked ice
in a shaker or blender. Strain into a
chilled glass.

Kurant Affair

1¼ oz. Absolut Kurant Vodka
Cranberry Juice
splash Club Soda

Pour Vodka over ice in a tall glass. Fill most of the way with Cranberry Juice. Top with a splash of Soda. Garnish with a Lime Wedge.

Kurant Bon Bon

1 oz. Absolut Kurant Vodka
½ oz. Godiva Liqueur

Combine Vodka and Godiva in a brandy snifter.

Kurant Cosmopolitan

1¼ oz. Absolut Kurant Vodka,
     chilled
splash Cranberry Juice
splash Lime Juice

Pour chilled Vodka into a glass. Add a splash of Cranberry Juice and a splash of Lime Juice.

Kurant Martini

1¼ oz. Absolut Kurant Vodka
dash Extra Dry Vermouth

Pour Vodka and Vermouth over ice. Shake or stir well. Strain and serve in a cocktail glass. Garnish with a Twist or an Olive.

You can also serve this one with ice.

La Bomba

1¼ oz. 1800 Tequila
¾ oz. Cointreau
1½ oz. Pineapple Juice
1½ oz. Orange Juice
2 dashes Grenadine

Shake all ingredients except Grenadine. Pour into glass and add Grenadine. Garnish with a Lime Wheel.

Lady Hamilton

L

2 oz. Pusser's Rum
⅛ oz. Fresh Lime Juice
1 oz. Passion Fruit Juice
1 oz. Orange Juice
1 oz. Ginger Ale

Combine ingredients in a tall glass. Garnish with a Maraschino Cherry and a Pineapple Slice.

La Jollarita

1½ oz. Jose Cuervo Traditional
Tequila
½ oz. Cointreau
½ oz. Chambord

Shake, strain, and serve.

Latin Lover

1 oz. Herradura Tequila
½ oz. Amaretto

Combine in a rocks glass over ice.

You can also serve this one as a shot (without the ice).

Lazer Beam

1 oz. Bourbon
1 oz. Rumple Minze
½ oz. Drambuie

Shake with ice and strain into a shot
glass.

Lemon Chiffon

1½ oz. Vodka
¼ oz. Triple Sec
1 oz. Sweet & Sour Mix

Shake ingredients with ice and serve
over ice. Squeeze and drop in a fresh
Lemon Wedge.

Lemon Drop #1

2 oz. Absolut Citron Vodka
1 oz. Lemon Juice
Sugar

Shake. Serve in a sugar-coated chilled
cocktail glass with a squeeze of
Lemon.

Lemon Drop #2

1½ oz. Absolut Citron Vodka
½ oz. 7-Up
½ oz. Lemon Juice

Serve in shot glass whose rim is
sugar-coated.

Lemon Ice

¼ oz. Lemon
2 tsp. Sugar
2 oz. Absolut Vanilia
Ginger Ale

Mull fresh Lemon with Sugar and
place in a Collins glass. Add ice and
Absolut Vanilia. Fill with Ginger Ale.

Lemongrad

1½ oz. Stoli Limonnaya Vodka
3–4 oz. Cranberry Juice

Serve over ice.

Lemontini

Cointreau
2 oz. Stoli Limonnaya Vodka
½ oz. Dry Vermouth

Line a cocktail glass with Cointreau
and pour out excess. Combine Vodka
and Vermouth over ice in a mixing
glass. Strain into the cocktail glass.

Leprechaun

1½ oz. Irish Whiskey
3 oz. Tonic Water
3–4 Ice Cubes

Put Whiskey and Tonic Water in a
rocks glass. Add Ice Cubes and stir
gently. Drop in a slice of Lemon Peel.

Leprechaun's Choice

1¼ oz. Baileys Irish Cream
¾ oz. Smirnoff Vodka
Club Soda

Combine in a tall glass. Top with
Club Soda.

Leprechaun's Libation

3½ oz. Cracked Ice
½ oz. Green Crème de Menthe
½ oz. Bushmills Irish Whiskey

Fill blender with Cracked Ice. Add
Crème de Menthe and Bushmills Irish
Whiskey. Blend. Pour into a goblet or
large wine glass.

Courtesy of Beach Grill in Westminster, Colorado.

Liar's Martini

1½ oz. Dry Gin
½ oz. Martini & Rossi Extra Dry
    Vermouth
¼ oz. Orange Curaçao
¼ oz. Sweet Vermouth

Stir gently with ice and strain.

Who lies after a couple of chilled Martinis?

Licorice Stick

1 oz. Stolichnaya Vodka
1 oz. Anisette
½ oz. Triple Sec

Shake with ice and strain into a shot glass.

Lillet Spritzer

2 oz. Lillet Blanc
¼ oz. Bols Triple Sec
Brut Champagne

Build cocktail over ice, top with Champagne, and garnish with an Orange Slice.

You can substitute Club Soda for the Champagne.

Li'l Orphan Annie

1½ oz. Irish Whiskey
1 oz. Baileys Irish Cream
2 tbsp. Chocolate-flavored Ovaltine powder (or 1 tbsp. Chocolate Syrup)
1 tsp. Shaved Chocolate

Combine all ingredients except the Shaved Chocolate in a shaker and shake vigorously. Strain into a glass. Garnish with Shaved Chocolate.

Lime Light Martini

2 oz. Finlandia Vodka
½ oz. Grapefruit Juice
½ oz. Midori

Stir gently with ice and strain into a chilled glass. Garnish with thinly sliced Lemon and Lime Twists.

Limp Moose

1 oz. Irish Cream
1 oz. Canadian Whisky

Shake with ice and strain into a shot glass.

Lizard Slime

1½ oz. Jose Cuervo Mistico Tequila
Midori

In a shot glass, float the Midori on top of the Tequila.

What twisted genius created Long Island Iced Tea?

This drink does hail from Long Island, specifically the Oak Beach Inn in Hampton Bays. Spirits writer John Mariani credits bartender Robert (Rosebud) Butt as the inventor, whose original recipe called for an ounce each of clear liquors (vodka, gin, tequila, light rum), a half ounce of triple sec, some lemon juice, and a splash of cola.

This drink comes in many forms and is still popular with young drinkers, though not with those who have to get up early the next day.

Loca Pasion (Crazy Passion)

1½ oz. Agavero Tequila
2 oz. Pomegranate Juice
2 oz. Chilled Champagne
splash of Grenadine
1 Fresh Strawberry

Pour Tequila, Pomegranate Juice, and Champagne into a glass flute. Top with Grenadine and a Whole Strawberry.

Long Island Iced Tea

½ oz. Vodka
½ oz. Rum
½ oz. Gin
½ oz. Triple Sec
½ oz. Tequila
½ oz. Sour Mix
Cola

Shake the first five ingredients over ice and strain into a glass. Fill with Cola.

There are many variations on this popular drink.

Long Island Sweet Tea

½ oz. Seagram's Sweet Tea
½ oz. Bafferts Gin
½ oz. Zaya Gran Reserva Rum
½ oz. Tequila Corralejo Anejo
½ oz. Triple Sec
1 oz. Sweet & Sour
3 oz. cola

Combine ingredients in a tall glass with ice.

L

Lovers' Margarita

1 oz. Agavero
1 oz. 1800 Reposado
splash Fresh Lime Juice

Pour over ice. Garnish with a Lime Wedge. Salt the rim beforehand if you prefer.

Double the recipe and serve with two straws per couple.

Low Tide Martini

3 oz. Grey Goose Vodka
½ oz. Martini & Rossi Dry Vermouth
1 tsp. Clam Juice

Shake ingredients with ice and strain into a chilled martini glass. Garnish with a Smoked Clam.

Loyal Martini

2 oz. Ketel One Vodka
3 drops Expensive Balsamic Vinegar

Stir gently with ice; strain.

From the Bar D'O in New York, New York.

Lucky Lady

¾ oz. Bacardi Light Rum
¼ oz. Hiram Walker Anisette
¼ oz. Hiram Walker White Crème de Cacao
¾ oz. Cream

Blend with crushed ice and serve in a margarita glass.

M & M

1 part Kahlúa
1 part Di Saronno Amaretto

Layer the Amaretto over the Kahlúa.

Madras

1¼ oz. Vodka
2 oz. Orange Juice
2 oz. Cranberry Juice

Pour Vodka over ice in a tall glass. Fill halfway with Orange Juice and top it off with Cranberry Juice.

M

Magellan Straits

2½ oz. Magellan Gin

Shake with ice; strain. Add Twist of Lime.

Magical Mojito

8–10 Mint Leaves
2 oz. Bacardi Limon Rum
¾ oz. Fresh Lime Juice
2 dashes Angostura Bitters
1 fist-sized ball Pink Cotton Candy
1 sprig Fresh Mint for garnish

In a mixing glass, gently muddle the Mint Leaves. Add Bacardi Limon, Lime Juice, and Bitters with ice and shake vigorously. Place Cotton Candy atop a chilled cocktail glass and carefully strain the drink over the Cotton Candy, allowing it to melt into the drink. Garnish with a sprig of Fresh Mint.

Mai Tai

¾ oz. Bacardi Light Rum
¼ oz. Bacardi 151 Rum
½ oz. Orange Curaçao
½ oz. Rose's Lime Juice
¼ oz. Orgeat Syrup
¼ oz. Simple Syrup

Stir with ice. Garnish with Mint, Cherry, and Pineapple.

FABLES & LORE

Mai Tai: Out of this world

Vic Bergeron invented the Mai Tai in 1944 at his Polynesian-style Oakland bar. He didn't want fruit juices detracting from the two ounces of J. Wray Nephew Jamaican rum he poured as the base for his creation. He merely added a half ounce of French orgeat (an almond-flavored syrup), a half ounce of orange Curaçao, a quarter ounce of rock candy syrup, and the juice of one lime. Customer Carrie Wright of Tahiti, the first to taste the concoction, responded, "Mai tai . . . roe ae!" (Tahitian for "Out of this world . . . the best!")

The Mai Tai became famous, and conflicting stories about its origins aggravated Bergeron so much that he elicited a sworn statement from Mrs. Wright in 1970, testifying to his authorship of the cocktail.

M

Maiden's Prayer

2 oz. Cork Dry Gin
½ oz. Cointreau
½ oz. Orange Juice
½ oz. Lemon Juice

Shake with ice and strain into a glass.

Main Squeeze

1½ oz. Hiram Walker Crème de
   Strawberry Liqueur
2 oz. Cranberry Juice
2 oz. Orange Juice
Club Soda

Combine first three ingredients in a
tall glass and top with Club Soda.

Maker's Mist

¾ oz. Irish Mist
¾ oz. Maker's Mark
¾ oz. Stoli Ohranj

Shake with ice. Serve on the rocks
with an orange slice.

Malibu Bay Breeze

1½ oz. Malibu Rum
2 oz. Cranberry Juice
2 oz. Pineapple Juice

Combine over ice.

Malibu Beach

1½ oz. Malibu Rum
1 oz. Smirnoff Vodka
4 oz. Orange Juice

Combine over ice.

Malibu Cove

½ oz. Malibu Rum
½ oz. Myers's Dark Rum
½ oz. White Rum
2 oz. Pineapple Juice
2 oz. Sweet and Sour Mix

Shake all ingredients with ice and
serve over ice.

M

Malibu Orange Colada

1½ oz. Malibu Rum
1 oz. Triple Sec
4 oz. Coco Lopez Cream of
Coconut

Blend with crushed ice.

Malibu Rain

1 oz. Vodka
1½ oz. Pineapple Juice
½ oz. Malibu Rum
splash Orange Juice

Shake with ice and serve over ice.

Malibu Suntan

1½ oz. Malibu Rum
5 oz. Iced Tea

Combine over ice. Add a squeeze of
Lemon.

Mandarin Martini

1½ oz. Godiva Liqueur
1½ oz. Absolut Vodka
splash Cointreau or Orange
Juice

Combine with ice and shake well.
Strain. Garnish with an Orange Slice.

Manhattan

2 oz. American or Canadian
Whisky
splash Sweet or Dry Vermouth
dash Angostura Bitters

Stir. Garnish with a Cherry.

Manhattan

The Manhattan recipe was created around 1874 at the Manhattan
Club, New York, for Lady Randolph
Churchill, Winston's mother. She
was attending a banquet in honor of
the lawyer and politician Samuel J.
Tilden.

M

The Margarita: Behind every great drink is . . .

Using her two favorite spirits, cointreau and tequila, Margarita Sames invented this classic drink in 1948 in Acapulco, Mexico. Presenting his wife with glassware etched with Margarita!, her husband gave the drink its name.

Margarita

1 oz. Tequila
1 oz. Cointreau or Triple Sec
1 oz. Sweet & Sour Mix or Lime Juice

Blend with crushed ice. Serve in a salt-rimmed glass. Garnish with a Lime Wheel.

Margarita Madres

1¼ oz. Jose Cuervo Gold Tequila
½ oz. Cointreau
½ oz. Sweet & Sour Mix
1½ oz. Orange Juice
1½ oz. Cranberry Juice

Blend with crushed ice. Garnish with a Lime.

Margavero

3 oz. Agavero Liqueur
1 oz. Fresh Lime Juice
1 dash Stolichnaya Ohranj
Coarse Salt

Shake with ice or blend and strain into a chilled cocktail glass, the rim of which has been moistened with Lime Juice and dipped in Salt. Garnish with a Lime Wedge.

Martini

2 oz. Gin
dash Extra Dry Vermouth

Shake or stir Gin and Vermouth over ice. Strain and serve in a cocktail glass straight up or over ice. Garnish with a Twist or an Olive.

From the Gallery Lounge Sheraton in Seattle, Washington.

Martini mythology

You're likely to hear several stories about the creation of the Martini, such as the few that follow:

- ✓ A stranger on his way to Martinez, California, told bartender Jerry Thomas of San Francisco, California, about this drink made with gin, vermouth, bitters, and dash of maraschino.

- ✓ A bartender in Martinez, California, created it for a gold-miner who struck it rich: The miner ordered champagne for the house, but none was available. The bartender offered something better — a Martinez Special — some sauterne and gin. The rich miner spread the word throughout California about this Martinez Special.

- ✓ The drink is named after Martini & Rossi vermouth because it was first used in the drink Gin and It, which contains Gin and Martini & Rossi vermouth.

- ✓ The drink is named after the British army rifle, the Martini and Henry. The rifle was known for its kick, like the first sip of Gin and It.

- ✓ At the Knickerbocker Hotel in the early 1900s, a bartender named Martini di Arma Tiggia mixed a Martini using only a dry gin and dry vermouth.

Martini Bellini

2 oz. Vodka or Gin
¼ oz. Peach Schnapps

Shake or stir Vodka or Gin and Schnapps over ice. Strain and serve in a cocktail glass straight up or over ice. Garnish with a Twist.

From the Gallery Lounge Sheraton in Seattle, Washington.

Martini Picante

2 oz. Absolut Peppar Vodka
Jalapeño
Olive

Stir with ice and strain. Add a Jalapeño and an Olive.

From the Gallery Lounge Sheraton in Seattle, Washington.

M

Mary Pickford

1½ oz. Puerto Rican White Rum
1½ oz. Pineapple Juice
1 splash Grenadine

Shake with crushed ice. Serve over ice or strain.

Named after the actress.

Melon Ball

¾ oz. Midori
1 oz. Vodka
4 oz. Orange Juice

Combine in a glass and stir.

Metropolitan

1 oz. Sweet Vermouth
1½–2 oz. Brandy
½ tsp. Sugar Syrup
2 dashes Angostura Bitters
4–5 Ice Cubes

Combine all ingredients except one or two Ice Cubes in a shaker and shake vigorously. Put one or two Ice Cubes in a chilled cocktail glass. Strain the drink into the glass.

Mets Manhattan

1¼ oz. Whiskey
¼ oz. Extra Dry Vermouth
¼ oz. Strawberry Schnapps

Mix all ingredients with ice and stir well. Strain into a chilled cocktail glass.

Mexican Banana

1½ oz. Sauza Tequila
¾ oz. Crème de Banana

Pour ingredients into a rocks glass filled with ice.

Mexican Berry

1 oz. Chambord
1 oz. Cuervo Tequila

Shake with ice and strain into a shot glass.

Mexican Gold

1½ oz. Sauza Tequila
¾ oz. Galliano

In a rocks glass filled with ice, pour Sauza Tequila and float the Galliano on top.

M

Mexican Margarita

2 oz. Agavero Tequila Liqueur
2 oz. Tequila
splash Fresh Lime Juice

Combine in a shaker and pour over rocks.

Mexicarolans

1 oz. Carolans Irish Cream
1 oz. Tequila

Shake well with ice and serve over ice.

Mexico Martini

1½ oz. Gran Centenario Plata
    Tequila
1 tbsp. Extra Dry Vermouth
2–3 drops Vanilla Extract

Shake and strain into an iced glass.

Mexico Rose

½ oz. Sauza Tequila
1 oz. Lime Juice
½ oz. Grenadine (or Crème de
    Cassis)

Combine in a rocks glass filled with ice.

Miami Shades

1 oz. Stoli Ohranj Vodka
¼ oz. Peach Schnapps
2 oz. Grapefruit Juice

Combine over ice.

Miami Special

1 oz. Bacardi Light Rum
¼ oz. Hiram Walker White
    Crème de Menthe
¾ oz. Lemon or Rose's Lime
    Juice

Blend with ice.

Mickey Finn Martini

1½ oz. Absolut Vodka
dash Martini & Rossi Extra Dry
  Vermouth
splash Hiram Walker White
  Crème de Menthe

Stir with ice and strain. Garnish
with Mint.

Midnight Martini

1½ oz. Vodka
½ oz. Chambord

Stir with ice and strain. Garnish
with a Lemon Twist.

From the Gallery Lounge Sheraton in Seattle, Washington.

Midnight Orchid

1½ oz. Finlandia Cranberry
  Vodka, chilled
¼ oz. Chambord
2 oz. Pineapple Juice
½ oz. Half & Half

Shake. Serve over crushed ice or
blend with ice.

Midnight Sun Martini

2 oz. Finlandia Cranberry Vodka
½ oz. Classic Finlandia Vodka
½ oz. Kahlúa

Stir with ice and strain.

Midori Cheap Shades

¾ oz. Midori
¾ oz. Peach Schnapps
3 oz. Orange Juice
3 oz. Pineapple Juice
1½ oz. Margarita Mix

Shake with ice and serve over ice
in a tall glass.

Midori Green Iguana Margarita

½ oz. Midori
1 oz. Tequila
2 oz. Sweet & Sour Mix

Blend and pour into a salted glass.

M

Midori Skinny Dipper

2 oz. Midori
3 oz. Cranberry Juice

Combine over ice in a tall glass.

Midori Sun of a Beach

1 oz. Midori
1 oz. Beefeater Gin
6 oz. Orange Juice

Combine over ice in a tall glass.

Milagro Freshest Margarita

2 oz. Milagro Tequila
½ oz. Agave Nectar
¼ oz. Lime Juice
¼ oz. Chilled Water

Combine ingredients with ice and shake. Strain over fresh ice in a rocks glass and garnish with a Lime Wheel.

Optional: Rim the rocks glass with Salt.

Milk & Honey

1 oz. Irish Mist
1 oz. Carolans Irish Cream

Combine in a rocks glass on ice.

Mimosa

3 oz. Champagne
2 oz. Orange Juice

Combine in a champagne flute and stir.

A great brunch drink.

Mind Eraser

1½ oz. Vodka
1½ oz. Kahlúa
splash of Tonic Water

Shake the Vodka and Kahlúa with ice and strain into a shot glass. Top with Tonic Water.

M

The Mimosa: A French creation

The Mimosa was created around 1925 at the Ritz Hotel Bar in Paris, France. It took its name from the mimosa flowering plant, whose color it resembles.

Mingling of the Clans

1¼ oz. Bushmills Irish Whiskey
½ oz. Scotch Whisky
2 tsp. Lemon Juice
3 dashes Orange Bitters

Combine in a mixing glass with ice. Strain into a cocktail glass.

Mint Cooler

1 oz. Bombay Gin
¼ oz. Peppermint Schnapps
Club Soda

In a tall glass with ice, combine the first two ingredients. Fill the glass with Club Soda.

Mint Julep

5 Mint Leaves
¼ oz. Sugar Syrup
2 oz. Maker's Mark Bourbon

In a silver cup, mash four Mint Leaves with Sugar Syrup. Fill the cup with crushed ice. Add Bourbon and garnish with a Mint Leaf.

A favorite at the Kentucky Derby. Don't forget that it's served in a silver cup.

Mint Martini

1½ oz. Godiva Liqueur
1½ oz. Absolut Vodka
splash White Crème de Menthe

Combine with ice and shake well. Serve straight up. Garnish with a Mint Leaf.

M

Mintini or Gin Stinger

2 oz. Bombay Gin
¼ oz. White Crème de Menthe

Stir gently with ice and strain.

Mist Old Fashioned

Orange Slice
Angostura Bitters
Sugar
2 oz. Irish Mist
Club Soda or Water

Muddle the Orange, Cherry Bitters, and Sugar. Add Irish Mist. Top with Club Soda or Water.

Mist Opportunity

2 oz. Stoli Ohranj
½ oz. Irish Mist

Shake with ice; garnish with Orange Slice.

Mister Murphy

1 oz. Irish Mist
1 oz. White Rum
1 oz. Orange Juice
dash Angostura Bitters

Combine in a rocks glass over ice with a dash of Angostura Bitters.

Misty Mist

1¼ oz. Irish Mist

Serve on shaved ice.

Misty-Eyed Irishman

¾ oz. Bushmills Irish Whiskey
1 oz. Peppermint Schnapps
1 pkg. Hot Chocolate Mix
Hot Coffee
Whipped Cream

Combine first three ingredients in the glass. Fill with Coffee and stir well. Top with Whipped Cream.

Optional: Sprinkle with Candy Mint Shavings.

M

Mocha Melt

1 oz. Jose Cuervo Gold Tequila
5 oz. Freshly Brewed Strong,
  Hot Coffee
1 pkg. Hot Cocoa Mix (single-
  serving envelope)
½ oz. Coffee Brandy
Whipped Cream

Combine ingredients in a glass and
stir. Top with Whipped Cream.

Mocha Mint

¾ oz. Coffee-Flavored Brandy
¾ oz. White Crème de Menthe
¾ oz. White Crème de Cacao

Combine ingredients in a glass and
stir. Strain into a cocktail glass.

Mockingbird

1¼ oz. Tequila
2 tsp. White Crème de Menthe
1 oz. Fresh Lime Juice

Combine in a shaker and shake
vigorously. Strain into a chilled cocktail
glass with ice.

Mojito

¾ oz. Simple Syrup
½ Lime, cut into wedges
8–10 Mint Leaves
2 oz. Bacardi Superior Rum
¼ oz. Club Soda

Combine Simple Syrup, Lime, and Mint.
Muddle ingredients to extract the juice
of the Limes. Fill glass halfway with
crushed ice. Add Bacardi Superior and
stir to combine. Top with more crushed
ice and Club Soda. Garnish with a Lime
Wedge and a sprig of Fresh Mint.

Mojito (Bee)

12 Mint Leaves
Juice of ½ Lime
1 tsp. Honey
2 oz. Bacardi Rum
1 oz. Club Soda

Place Mint Leaves and crushed ice in a
glass. Muddle well with a pestle. Add
Lime Juice, Honey, and Bacardi. Stir well.
Top off with Club Soda. Stir. Garnish
with Mint Sprigs or a Lime Wheel.

M

Monkey See Monkey Do

1 oz. Baileys Irish Cream
1 oz. Rhum Barbancourt
1 oz. Banana Liqueur
1 oz. Orange Juice

Shake with ice and strain.

Monsoon

¼ oz. Vodka
¼ oz. Coffee Liqueur
¼ oz. Amaretto
¼ oz. Irish Cream
¼ oz. Hazelnut Liqueur

Shake with ice; serve over ice.

Montego Margarita

1½ oz. Appleton Estate Rum
½ oz. Triple Sec
1 oz. Lemon or Lime Juice
1 scoop Crushed Ice

Blend with Crushed Ice and serve.

Moonlight Margarita

1½ oz. Jose Cuervo Gold Tequila
1 oz. Blue Curaçao
1 oz. Lime Juice
Salt

Rub the rim of a margarita glass with Lime Rind and dip it into Salt. Blend ingredients and serve in the prepared glass. Garnish with a Lime Slice.

Moonraker

1½ oz. Jose Cuervo Especial
4 oz. Pineapple Juice
½ oz. Blue Curaçao

Pour the Jose Cuervo Especial and Pineapple Juice into a glass almost filled with ice cubes. Stir well. Drop the Curaçao into the center of the drink.

Morgan's Madras

1¼ oz. Captain Morgan Spiced Rum
5 oz. Orange Juice
splash Cranberry Juice

Combine over ice in a tall glass.

M

Morgan's Red Rouge

1 oz. Captain Morgan Spiced
 Rum
½ oz. Blackberry Brandy
2 oz. Pineapple Juice
½ oz. Lemon Juice

Stir with ice and serve over ice.

Morgan's Spiced Rum Alexander

1 oz. Captain Morgan Spiced
 Rum
½ oz. Crème de Cacao
1 oz. Heavy Cream

Shake and strain. Dust with Nutmeg.

Morgan's Wench

¾ oz. Captain Morgan Spiced
 Rum
¾ oz. Amaretto
¾ oz. Dark Crème de Cacao

Shake Rum and Amaretto with ice
and strain into a shot glass. Float
Crème de Cacao on top.

Moscow Chill

1½ oz. Vodka
4 oz. Dr. Pepper

Pour Vodka over shaved ice in
a champagne glass. Fill with Dr.
Pepper. Garnish with a Lime Wedge.

Moscow Mule

1½ oz. Smirnoff Vodka
4 oz. Ginger Beer

Stir with ice. Garnish with a Lime
Wedge.

Should be served in a bronze cup or mug.

The Mount Gay Grinder

1½ oz. Mount Gay Rum
2 oz. Cranberry Juice
splash 7-Up

Combine in a tall glass.

M

The Mr. President

2 oz. Templeton Rye Whiskey
1 oz. Ginger Liqueur
splash Champagne

Combine Templeton Rye Whiskey
and Ginger Liqueur in a shaker.
Shake well and strain. Serve in
a martini glass and float the
Champagne on top.

Ms. Tea

1¼ oz. Irish Mist
3 oz. Iced Tea

Mix with ice; serve over ice.

Mudslide

¼ oz. Coffee Liqueur
1 oz. Vodka
¼ oz. Irish Cream
Cola

Combine first three ingredients in
a glass with ice and fill with Cola.

Murphy's Dream

1 oz. Irish Mist
1 oz. Gin
½ oz. Lemon Juice
Sugar

Shake. Serve straight up or over ice.

My BFF

2 oz. Branca (Fernet)
2 oz. Fresca

Serve in a tall glass with ice and
garnish with an Orange Slice.

Myers's Heatwave

¾ oz. Myers's Dark Rum
½ oz. Peach Schnapps
6 oz. Pineapple Juice
1 splash Grenadine

Pour Rum and Schnapps over ice.
Fill with Pineapple Juice and add a
splash of Grenadine.

M

Myers's Madras

1¼ oz. Myers's Dark Rum
1½ oz. Orange Juice
1½ oz. Cranberry Juice

Serve in a tall glass over ice.

Myers's Sharkbite

1¼ oz. Myers's Dark Rum
Orange Juice
splash Grenadine

Add Rum to a tall glass with ice. Fill
with Orange Juice. Add a splash of
Grenadine.

Myers's Sunset

1¼ oz. Myers's Dark Rum
4 oz. Pineapple Juice
2 oz. Orange Juice
2 oz. Cranberry Juice
dash Rose's Grenadine
(optional)

Combine over ice and stir.

Naked Martini

2 oz. Vodka or Gin

Serve over ice or chill and strain
into glass.

Nation Cocktail

1½ oz. Jose Cuervo Gold Tequila
1½ oz. Pineapple Juice
1½ oz. Orange Juice
¼ oz. Blue Curaçao

Combine first three ingredients over
ice. Float Blue Curaçao.

You can also serve this one without ice.

Negroni

½ oz. Dry Vermouth
½ oz. Bombay Gin
½ oz. Campari

Combine in a rocks glass over ice.
Garnish with a Lemon Twist.

Nellie Janez

½ oz. Grand Marnier
1 oz. Stoli Vanil
1 oz. Stoli Ohranj
½ oz. Marie Brizard Parfait Amour
splash Fresh Lime Juice

Combine ingredients in an ice-filled glass. Stir and strain. Garnish with an Orange Peel.

Nervous Breakdown

1½ oz. Vodka
½ oz. Chambord
splash Cranberry Juice
Soda

Combine the first three ingredients in a tall glass. Fill with Soda.

Neva

1½ oz. Vodka
½ oz. Tomato Juice
½ oz. Orange Juice

In a shaker, mix all ingredients. Pour over ice into a stemmed glass.

New Life

1 lump Sugar
3 dashes Angostura Bitters
1½ oz. Sauza Tequila

Muddle Sugar and Bitters in a rocks glass and fill with crushed ice. Add Tequila. Garnish with a Lemon Twist.

1951 Martini

splash Cointreau
2 oz. Gordon's Gin
Anchovy-Stuffed Olive

Rinse glass with Cointreau. Add the Gin and Olive.

The return to another classic with a rinse.

Nut House

1½ oz. Finlandia Cranberry
        Vodka
¼ oz. Amaretto

Combine over ice.

Nut 'n' Holli

½ oz. Irish Mist
½ oz. Amaretto
½ oz. Carolans Irish Cream
½ oz. Frangelico

Shake. Serve straight up in a shot glass.

Nuts & Berrys

½ oz. Vodka
½ oz. Hazelnut Liqueur
½ oz. Coffee Liqueur
¼ oz. Cream

Combine with ice and shake. Strain and serve straight up in a rocks glass.

Nutty Irishman

1 part Irish Cream
1 part Hazelnut Liqueur
  (Frangelico)

Layer Irish Cream over Hazelnut Liqueur in a shot glass.

Nutty Professor

1 oz. Irish Cream
1 oz. Hazelnut Liqueur
½ oz. Grand Marnier

Combine over ice.

You can also serve this one straight up in a shot glass.

O'Casey's Scotch Terrier

1 oz. Baileys Irish Cream
1½ oz. J&B Scotch

Stir well over ice.

O.J. Mist

1½ oz. Irish Mist
3 oz. Orange Juice

Combine in a tall glass over ice.

O.J. Morgan

1½ oz. Captain Morgan Spiced
Rum
5 oz. Orange Juice

Combine in a tall glass over ice.

Oatmeal Cookie #1

½ oz. Butterscotch Schnapps
½ oz. Goldschläger
½ oz. Baileys Irish Cream

Layer with Schnapps on the
bottom, then the Goldschläger,
and then the Irish Cream.

Oatmeal Cookie #2

¾ oz. Baileys Irish Cream
¾ oz. Butterscotch Schnapps
½ oz. Jägermeister
¼ oz. Cinnamon Schnapps

Shake with ice and serve over ice.

You can also strain this one into a shot glass.

Ohranj Juice

1½ oz. Stoli Ohranj Vodka
¼ oz. Hiram Walker Peach
Schnapps
¼ oz. Cranberry Juice

Mix all ingredients over ice. For
uptown, upscale parties only.

Ohranj Julius

1 oz. Stoli Ohranj Vodka
1 oz. Cointreau
1 oz. Sour Mix
1 oz. Orange Juice

Combine in a tall glass with ice.
Garnish with an Orange Slice.

Ohranj Martini

1½ oz. Stoli Ohranj Vodka
splash Triple Sec

Shake with ice. Serve straight up or
over ice. Garnish with an Orange Peel.

Oil Slick

1 oz. Rumple Minze
1 oz. Bourbon

Shake with ice and strain into a shot glass.

Old Fashioned

Cherry and Orange Slice
¼ tsp. Superfine Sugar
splash Club Soda
1½ oz. American or Canadian Whisk(e)y
2 dashes Angostura Bitters

Muddle the Cherry (without stem), Orange Slice, Sugar, and a splash of Club Soda. Add the remaining ingredients and stir.

You can also use Scotch, Brandy, or just about any other spirit in this drink.

Old San Juan

1½ oz. Gold Rum
½ oz. Cranberry Juice
1 oz. Fresh Lime Juice
Lime Wedge

Rim a chilled martini glass with the Lime Wedge. Combine other ingredients in cocktail shaker with ice. Shake well and strain into the glass. Squeeze Lime Wedge into the drink and drop it in.

Opening Cocktail

½ oz. Canadian Club Whisky
½ oz. Sweet Vermouth
½ oz. Grenadine

Mix all ingredients in a shaker with crushed ice. Strain the mixture into a chilled cocktail glass.

Orange Blossom

1¼ oz. Absolut Vodka
3 oz. Orange Juice
1 tsp. Superfine Sugar

Stir with ice in a tall glass.

Orange Crush

1¼ oz. Vodka
¾ oz. Triple Sec
2 oz. Orange Juice

Shake with ice. Strain or serve over ice.

Orange Margarita

1½ oz. Jose Cuervo Gold Tequila
½ oz. Triple Sec
3 oz. Orange Juice
½ oz. Sweet & Sour Mix

Blend. Garnish with Strawberries.

Orange Sunset

1 oz. Bombay Gin
¼ oz. Banana Liqueur
1 oz. Sweetened Lemon Mix
1 oz. Orange Juice

Combine over ice.

Orangesicle

1½ oz. Bacardi O
1½ oz. Cream
2½ oz. Orange Juice

Combine ingredients in a shot glass
or mix over ice in a rocks glass.

Orangetini

1½ oz. Absolut Vodka
dash Martini & Rossi Extra Dry
    Vermouth
splash Hiram Walker Triple Sec

Stir gently and strain over ice.
Garnish with an Orange Peel.

Orgasm #1

1 oz. Irish Cream
1 oz. Amaretto
½ oz. Kahlúa

Shake with ice and strain into a shot
glass.

Orgasm #2

½ oz. Di Saronno Amaretto
½ oz. Kahlúa
½ oz. Baileys
½ oz. Cream

Shake with ice and strain into a shot
glass.

Outrigger

1 oz. Vodka
½ oz. Peach Schnapps
1 dash Lime Juice
2 oz. Pineapple Juice

Combine with ice in a shaker and shake. Strain over ice into a rocks glass.

Oyster Shooter

1 oz. Vodka
1 Raw Oyster
1 tsp. Cocktail Sauce

Pour Vodka over the Oyster and Sauce in a small rocks glass and stir. Add a squeeze of Lemon.

You can also add a dash of Horseradish if you dare.

Paddy Cocktail

1½ oz. Irish Whiskey
¾ oz. Sweet Vermouth
3–4 dashes Angostura Bitters

Mix all ingredients with cracked ice in a shaker or blender. Serve in a chilled glass.

Paddy O'Rocco

1½ oz. Irish Mist
3 oz. Orange Juice
splash Amaretto

Mix Irish Mist and Orange Juice. Top with a splash of Amaretto.

Paddy Patrón

2½ oz. Patrón Tequila
½ oz. Green Crème de Menthe

Shake and serve on the rocks.

Paddy's Wagon

1½ oz. Irish Whiskey
1½ oz. Sweet Vermouth
1–2 dashes Angostura Bitters
1–2 dashes Southern Comfort

Combine all ingredients in a shaker and shake. Serve straight up or over ice in a chilled glass.

Painkiller

½ oz. Jose Cuervo Especial
½ oz. Vodka
½ oz. Light Rum
1 oz. Pineapple Juice
½ oz. Orange Juice
2 tbsp. Coco Lopez Real Cream
of Coconut

Blend all ingredients with ice until smooth and pour into a chilled rocks glass. Garnish with freshly ground Nutmeg.

Pama Martini

1¾ oz. Belvedere Vodka
1 oz. PAMA Pomegranate
Liqueur
½ oz. Triple Sec
splash Cranberry Juice

Combine all ingredients in a shaker over ice. Shake and strain into a chilled martini glass.

Parisian Pousse-Café

1 oz. Orange Curaçao
1 oz. Kirschwasser
½ oz. Green Chartreuse

Layer this drink in the order listed. Start with Curaçao on the bottom and finish with Chartreuse on top.

Park Avenue Princess

½ Lemon
1½ oz. SKYY Infusions Grape
3 oz. 7-Up
¼ oz. Fresh Lemon Juice
¼ oz. Red Wine

Squeeze and drop half a Lemon into a cocktail shaker. Add SKYY Infusions Grape, 7-Up, and Lemon Juice with ice and shake. Strain into a tall Collins glass with fresh ice, and float Red Wine over the top of the drink.

Parknasilla Peg Leg

1½ oz. Irish Whiskey
1 oz. Coconut Syrup
3 oz. Pineapple Juice
1 tsp. Lemon Juice
Club Soda

Mix Whiskey, Coconut Syrup, and Fruit Juices in a shaker or blender with cracked ice and pour into a chilled highball glass along with several ice cubes. Fill with Club Soda. Stir gently.

Parrot Bay Mango Madras

1½ oz. Captain Morgan's Parrot
Bay Mango Flavored Rum
2 oz. Cranberry Juice
2 oz. Orange Juice

Shake with ice and strain into a tall glass.

A Rum version of the classic Madras.

Patio Punch

1 oz. Cruzan Citrus
1 oz. Cruzan Pineapple Rum
splash Raspberry Liqueur

Mix with ice. Top with Orange Juice.

Patrón Grapefruit

1 oz. Patrón Silver
¼ oz. Patrón Citronge
2 oz. Fresh Grapefruit Juice
splash Club Soda

Pour Patrón Silver and Patrón Citronge over ice. Add Grapefruit Juice. Top off with splash of Club Soda. Garnish with Grapefruit Peel and a Lime Slice.

Patrón Perfect Martini

2 oz. Patrón Silver Tequila
½ oz. Patrón Citronage
½ oz. Sour Mix

Combine ingredients in a shaker with ice. Shake. Serve in a salt-rimmed glass.

Created at Gatsby's in Boca Raton, Florida.

Patrón Pineapple

1 oz. Patrón Silver
¼ oz. Patrón Citronge
2 oz. Fresh Pineapple Juice
squeeze of Lime Juice

Pour Patrón Silver and Patrón Citronge over ice. Add Pineapple Juice. Finish with a squeeze of Lime. Garnish with Pineapple and a Lime Slice.

Patrón Pomegranate

1 oz. Patrón Silver
¼ oz. Patrón Citronge
2 oz. Fresh Pomegranate Juice
Squeeze of Lemon Juice

Pour Patrón Silver and Patrón Citronge over ice. Add Pomegranate Juice. Finish with a squeeze of Lemon. Garnish with an Orange Twist.

Patty's Pride

1¼ oz. Bushmills Irish Whiskey
¼ oz. Peppermint Schnapps

Combine in a shot glass.

You can also serve this one with Club Soda in a highball glass.

Peach Banana Daiquiri

1½ oz. Puerto Rican Light Rum
½ Medium Banana, diced
1 oz. Fresh Lime Juice
¼ cup Sliced Peaches (fresh, frozen, or canned)

Blend with crushed ice.

Peach Irish

1½ oz. Irish Whiskey
1 Ripe Peach (peeled, pitted, and sliced)
½ cup Fresh Lime Juice
1 oz. Apricot Brandy
1 tbsp. Superfine Sugar
dash Vanilla Extract

Blend with crushed ice.

Peach Margarita

1½ oz. Jose Cuervo Gold Tequila
1 oz. Triple Sec
1 oz. Lime Juice
½ cup Peaches (canned)

Blend. Garnish with Peach Slices.

Peach Melba

½ oz. Captain Morgan Spiced Rum
¾ oz. Raspberry Liqueur
2 oz. Peach Cocktail Mix
1 oz. Heavy Cream
2 Peach Halves
Raspberry Syrup

Blend with crushed ice. Top with Raspberry Syrup.

P

Peach Prayer

1½ oz. DeKuyper Peach Schnapps
½ oz. Cointreau
¼ oz. Champagne
splash of Sunkist Orange Juice

Combine ingredients over ice.

Peaches & Cream

3 oz. Coco Lopez Cream of Coconut
2 oz. Pineapple Juice
1 oz. Coffee Liqueur
½ oz. Rum

Blend with crushed ice.

Pearl Diver

1½ oz. Midori
½ oz. Coconut Rum
4 oz. Orange Juice

Combine in a tall glass over ice.

Pecan Pie Martini

2 oz. Templeton Rye Whiskey
1 oz. Dark Crème de Cocoa
1 oz. Frangelico
½ oz. Irish Cream Liqueur

Shake all ingredients with ice. Strain. Serve up in a martini glass.

Peppar Manhattan

1½ oz. Absolut Peppar Vodka
½ oz. Sweet Vermouth

Mix Vodka and Sweet Vermouth in a cocktail shaker over ice and stir. Strain into a stemmed glass. Add a Cherry for garnish.

Peppar Martini

2 oz. Absolut Peppar Vodka
dash Dry Vermouth

Stir gently with ice and strain. Garnish with a Jalapeño-Stuffed Olive.

Peppar Salty Dog

1¼ oz. Absolut Peppar Vodka
Grapefruit Juice

Salt the rim of a rocks glass. Fill with ice. Pour in Vodka and fill with Grapefruit Juice.

Peppermint Kiss

1 oz. Godiva Chocolate Liqueur
1 oz. Peppermint Schnapps
1 sprig Mint

Add Chocolate Liqueur and Peppermint Schnapps to an ice-filled rocks glass and stir. Garnish with Mint Sprig.

Peppermint Patti

¾ oz. Peppermint Schnapps
½ oz. Green Crème de Menthe

Combine over ice in a rocks glass.

Peppertini

1½ oz. Absolut Peppar Vodka
½ oz. Dry Vermouth

Mix Vodka and Dry Vermouth in a cocktail shaker over ice. Stir and pour into a rocks glass. Add an Olive for garnish.

Perfect Patrón

1½ oz. Patrón Silver
½ oz. Patrón Citronge
Juice of ½ Lime

Shake well, strain, and serve on the rocks with a Lime Wedge.

Phoebe Snow

1¼ oz. Brandy
1 oz. Dubonnet
¾ oz. Pernod

Shake in a cocktail mixer with ice. Strain into a chilled martini glass.

Picadilly

2 oz. Cork Dry Gin
¼ oz. Dry Vermouth
dash Pernod
dash Grenadine

Mix with ice. Serve over ice.

Pickle Back

1½ oz. Jameson Irish Whiskey
1 oz. Chilled Pickle Juice

Pour the Jameson (room
temperature) in one shot glass
and the Pickle Juice in another.
Shoot the Jameson and chase with
the Pickle Juice.

Pickle Tickle

1 oz. Cuervo Gold Tequila
1 oz. Pickle Juice

Pour the Tequila in one shot glass
and the Pickle Juice in another. Shoot
the Cuervo and chase with the Pickle
Juice.

Piña Colada

1¼ oz. Light or Dark Rum
2 oz. Unsweetened Pineapple
Juice
2 oz. Coco Lopez Cream of
Coconut

Mix in a shaker and serve over ice, or
blend with crushed ice.

Piñata

1½ oz. Jose Cuervo Gold Tequila
5 oz. Pineapple Juice

Combine in a Collins glass. Garnish
with Fresh Pineapple.

Pineapple Bomb

½ oz. Malibu Rum
½ oz. Bacardi Black
½ oz. Pineapple Juice

Shake with ice and strain into a shot
glass.

Pineapple Pie

1¼ oz. Finlandia Pineapple
  Vodka, chilled
¼ oz. White Crème de Cacao
Whipped Cream

Shake with ice. Strain into a rocks glass and add a dollop of Whipped Cream.

Pineapple Twist

1½ oz. Appleton Estate Rum
6 oz. Pineapple Juice
splash Lemon Juice

Shake and pour into a tall glass over ice.

Pineapple Upside-Down Cake

1 oz. Stoli Vanil Vodka
½ oz. Butterscotch Schnapps
¾ oz. Pineapple Juice
splash Grenadine

Combine the Vanil Vodka, Butterscotch Schnapps, and Pineapple Juice in a shaker. Shake and strain into a shot glass. Carefully pour the Grenadine down the inside of the glass.

Pink Cadillac with Hawaiian Plates

1¼ oz. 1800 Tequila
2 oz. Pineapple Juice
2 oz. Cranberry Juice
½ oz. Sweet & Sour Mix

Combine in a rocks glass. Garnish with a Lime Wedge.

Pink Gin (aka Gin & Bitters)

dash Angostura Bitters
1¾ oz. Gin

Rinse a chilled glass with Bitters. Add Gin.

Pink Lady

1¼ oz. Tanqueray Gin
2 tsp. Grenadine
3 oz. Half & Half

Shake with ice and strain into a cocktail glass or serve over ice.

The ori-gins of Pink Gin

In 1824, Dr. Johann G. B. Siegert created Angostura bitters as a remedy for stomach complaints suffered by the Venezuelan army. He named this concoction after the town on the Orinoco River where he had worked.

The British Navy added this product to its medicine chest but soon discovered that it added a whole new dimension to Plymouth gin, and thus Pink Gin came to be.

Pink Lemonade

1¼ oz. Vodka
½ tsp. Sugar
1¼ oz. Sweet & Sour Mix
1 oz. Cranberry Juice
Club Soda

Combine Vodka, Sugar, Sweet & Sour Mix, and Cranberry Juice in a tall glass. Stir to dissolve Sugar. Add ice and top with Club Soda. Add a squeeze of Lime.

Pink Mustang

1 oz. Finlandia Cranberry Vodka
1 oz. Rumple Minze

Serve on ice.

Pink Panther #1

1½ oz. Sauza Tequila
½ oz. Grenadine
2 oz. Cream or Half & Half

Blend with crushed ice and strain into a chilled glass.

Pink Panther #2

1¼ oz. Bacardi Light Rum
¾ oz. Lemon Juice
¾ oz. Cream
½ oz. Rose's Grenadine

Blend with crushed ice and strain.

Pink Snowball

³/₄ oz. Amaretto
³/₄ oz. Malibu Rum
³/₄ oz. Grenadine
Whipped Cream

Combine the first three ingredients with one good squirt of Whipped Cream in a shaker with ice. Shake vigorously and strain over ice in a rocks glass. Garnish with a Cherry and more Whipped Cream.

Pink Squirrel

1 oz. Crème de Almond
1 oz. Crème de Cacao
4 oz. Cream

Shake all ingredients over cracked ice. Strain.

Pirate's Punch

1³/₄ oz. Rhum Barbancourt
¹/₄ oz. Sweet Vermouth
dash Angostura Bitters

Shake with ice and serve over ice.

Planter's Punch

1³/₄ oz. Rum
2 tsp. Sugar
2 oz. Orange Juice
dash Rose's Grenadine
splash Myers's Dark Rum

Shake or blend all ingredients except the Dark Rum and pour into a glass. Top with Dark Rum.

The Player

¹/₄ oz. Fresh Lime Juice
¹/₄ oz. Ginger Liqueur
3 oz. Moët Impérial

Pour the Fresh Lime Juice and Ginger Liqueur into a champagne flute. Fill with Moët Impérial. Stir gently with a long spoon. Add Lime Peel garnish.

Pomtree Cocktail

2 oz. DeKuyper Peachtree
  Schnapps
2¹/₂ oz. POM Wonderful
  Pomegranate Juice

Shake with ice. Strain and serve in a martini glass or pour over the rocks in a rocks glass. Stir.

Created by Ray Foley.

FABLES & LORE

Planter's Punch

In 1879, Fred L. Myers founded the Myers's Rum distillery in Jamaica and celebrated by creating what he named a Planter's Punch. This concoction became the house specialty at Kelly's Bar in Sugar Wharf, Jamaica, and its popularity spread soon after.

P

Port Royal

1½ oz. Appleton Estate Rum
½ oz. Sweet Vermouth
Juice of ¼ Orange
Juice of ¼ Lime

Shake with ice and strain into a large rocks glass over ice cubes. Garnish with Orange or Lime Wedge.

Pot o' Gold

1 oz. Goldschläger
1 oz. Baileys Irish Cream

Combine in a shot glass.

Pousse-Café #1

¼ oz. Grenadine
¼ oz. Yellow Chartreuse
¼ oz. White Crème de Menthe
¼ oz. Sloe Gin
¼ oz. Green Chartreuse
¼ oz. Brandy

Layer this drink in the order listed. Start with Grenadine on the bottom and finish with Brandy on top.

Pousse-Café #2

½ oz. Benedictine
½ oz. White Crème de Cacao
½ oz. Remy Martin Cognac

Layer this drink by pouring the Benedictine first, then the Crème de Cacao, and then Cognac.

Pousse-Café Standish

½ oz. Grenadine
½ oz. White Crème de Menthe
½ oz. Galliano
½ oz. Kummel
½ oz. Brandy

Layer this drink in the order listed. Start with Grenadine on the bottom and finish with Brandy on top.

Prairie Fire

1½ oz. Tequila
2 or 3 drops Tabasco

Combine in a shot glass.

Presbyterian

2–3 oz. Bourbon or American
    Whiskey
Ginger Ale
Club Soda

Pour the Bourbon into a chilled highball glass. Add ice cubes. Top off the glass with equal parts of Ginger Ale and Soda.

Presidente

6–8 Ice Cubes
¼ oz. Dry Vermouth
¾ oz. Sweet Vermouth
1½ oz. Puerto Rican White Rum
splash Grenadine

Mix with ice and serve.

Princess Mary

2 oz. Cork Dry Gin
½ oz. Crème de Cacao
½ oz. Fresh Cream

Shake with ice and serve in a margarita glass.

Puerto Rican Rum Cappuccino

1½ oz. Puerto Rican Dark Rum
1 tsp. Sugar
Hot Coffee
Steamed Milk
Whipped Cream
Ground Cinnamon

Combine the Rum and Sugar in a glass. Add equal parts Coffee and Milk. Top with Cream and Cinnamon.

Pulco

2 oz. Jose Cuervo 1800 Tequila
½ oz. Cointreau
1½ oz. Lime Juice

Combine over ice.

Purple Goose Martini

3 oz. Grey Goose Vodka
1 oz. Chambord

Shake with ice.

Purple Haze

1 oz. Chambord
1 oz. Vodka
½ oz. Cranberry Juice or Sour Mix

Combine in a shot glass.

Purple Haze Martini Cocktail

2 oz. Bacardi O
2 oz. Lemonade
½ oz. Grenadine
½ oz. Blue Curaçao
Orange Slice

Shake with ice. Strain into a martini glass.

Purple Hooter

½ oz. Vodka
½ oz. Black Raspberry Liqueur
½ oz. Cranberry Juice
splash Club Soda

Shake and strain Vodka, Black Raspberry Liqueur, and Cranberry Juice. Top with a splash of Club Soda.

Purple Orchid

1 oz. White Crème de Cacao
1 oz. Blackberry Brandy
½ oz. Cream

Combine in a shot glass.

Purple Passion

1¼ oz. Vodka
2 oz. Grapefruit Juice
2 oz. Grape Juice
Sugar

Combine ingredients and stir. Chill and add Sugar to taste. Serve in a Collins glass.

Pyrat Ginger Tea

1½ oz. Pyrat Rum
¾ oz. Patrón Citronge Orange
  Liqueur
¾ oz. Canton Ginger Liqueur
squeeze of Lemon Juice
2 oz. Club Soda

Shake with ice and serve in a rocks glass. Top with Club Soda.

Queen Elizabeth Martini

1½ oz. Absolut Vodka
dash Martini & Rossi Extra Dry
  Vermouth
splash Benedictine

Stir gently with ice and strain.

R

R & B

1¼ oz. Captain Morgan Original
  Spiced Rum
2 oz. Orange Juice
2 oz. Pineapple Juice
splash Grenadine

Pour ingredients over ice.

Racer's Edge

1½ oz. Bacardi Light Rum
Grapefruit Juice
¼ oz. Green Crème de Menthe

Pour Rum into a glass half-filled with ice. Fill with Grapefruit Juice and float Crème de Menthe.

Raffles Bar Sling

¾ oz. Gin
2 dashes Bitters
½ tsp. Lime Juice
¼ oz. Cherry-Flavored Brandy
Ginger Beer
¼ oz. Benedictine

Combine Gin, Bitters, Lime Juice, and Cherry-Flavored Brandy with ice in a highball glass. Stir in Ginger Beer. Float Benedictine on top. Garnish with Mint.

Rainbow Pousse-Café

½ oz. Dark Crème de Cacao
½ oz. Crème de Violette
½ oz. Yellow Chartreuse
½ oz. Maraschino Liqueur
½ oz. Benedictine
½ oz. Green Chartreuse
½ oz. Cognac

Layer this drink in the order listed.
Start with Crème de Cacao on the
bottom and finish with Cognac
on top.

Ramos Fizz

1½ oz. Gin
1 tbsp. Powdered Sugar
3–4 drops Orange-Flower Water
Juice of ½ Lime
Juice of ½ Lemon
1 Egg White
1½ oz. Cream
1 squirt Seltzer
2 drops Vanilla Extract (optional)

Mix ingredients in the order given.
Add crushed ice. Shake for a long
time, until the mixture acquires body.
Strain into a tall glass.

Check local laws about using egg whites.

Rasmopolitan

1¼ oz. VOX Raspberry
½ oz. Cointreau
1 oz. Cranberry Juice

Mix in a shaker half-filled with ice.
Pour into a chilled martini glass.
Garnish with Fresh Raspberries or a
Lime Peel.

Raspberry Bluetini

2 oz. VOX Vodka
1 oz. Blue Curaçao
¼ oz. Sour

Mix in a shaker half-filled with ice.
Pour into a chilled martini glass.
Garnish with a Maraschino Cherry.

Raspberry Martini

1 oz. Godiva Liqueur
1 oz. Absolut Vodka
½ oz. Chambord or Raspberry
Liqueur

Combine with ice and shake well.
Serve in a glass whose rim has been
dipped in Powdered Sugar.

A very sweet, sweet drink.

Raspberry Spritzer

1½ oz. VOX Raspberry
3 oz. Lemon-Lime Soda
¾ oz. Chambord

Combine VOX Raspberry and Lemon-Lime Soda in a tall glass filled with ice. Add Chambord, letting it gently sink to the bottom. Garnish with a Fresh Raspberry.

Raspberry Truffle

1½ oz. VOX Raspberry
½ oz. White Crème de Cacao
½ oz. Chambord
½ oz. Half & Half

Mix in a shaker half-filled with ice. Pour into a martini glass rimmed with Cocoa.

Razz-Ma-Tazz

1½ oz. Vodka
½ oz. Chambord
1½ oz. Club Soda

Serve over ice in a tall glass, chilled.

Razzputin

1½ oz. Stoli Razberi Vodka
3 oz. Cranberry Juice
2 oz. Grapefruit Juice
Lime Slice

Mix all ingredients, except Lime Slice, with cracked ice in a shaker or blender and serve in a chilled glass. Garnish with Lime Slice.

It's raspberry at its jazziest.

Real Gold

1 oz. Stolichnaya Vodka
1 oz. Goldschläger

Combine in a shot glass.

Red Devil

2 oz. Irish Whiskey
1½ oz. Clam Juice
1½ oz. Tomato Juice
1 tsp. Lime Juice
few drops Worcestershire Sauce
pinch Pepper

Combine with ice and shake gently. Strain straight up.

Red-Headed Slut

½ oz. Jägermeister
½ oz. Peach Schnapps
½ oz. Cranberry Juice

Shake over ice and strain into a shot glass.

A relative of the Surfer on Acid.

Red Hook

2 oz. Rye Whiskey
½ oz. Punt y Mes
¼ oz. Maraschino

Stir with ice and strain into a chilled cocktail glass.

Red Hot Mama

1¼ oz. Bacardi Silver Rum
4 oz. Cranberry Juice
2 oz. Club Soda

Combine ingredients over ice in a tall glass.

R

For a less tart version, substitute 7-Up for Club Soda.

Red Lion

1½ oz. Grand Marnier
1 tbsp. Tanqueray Gin
2 tsp. Orange Juice
2 tsp. Lemon Juice

Combine in a shaker with ice. Shake and strain into a martini glass.

Red Over Heels

2 oz. SKYY Infusions Ginger
1 oz. Honey Syrup
¾ oz. Fresh Lemon Juice

To make Honey Syrup, combine ½ oz. of Water with ½ oz. of Honey. Combine all ingredients in a cocktail shaker with ice. Shake vigorously and strain into a chilled martini glass. Lay Lemon Peel Twirl across the rim of the glass with cocktail pick.

Red Snapper

1 oz. Crown Royal Canadian
    Whisky
¼ oz. Amaretto
¾ oz. Cranberry Juice

Combine ingredients with ice in a shaker and shake well. Strain into a shot glass.

You can also serve this drink in a rocks glass with ice.

Red Tide Martini

2 oz. Grey Goose Vodka
1 oz. Martini & Rossi Rosso
　 Vermouth
dash Crème de Cassis
dash Luxardo Maraschino Liqueur

Shake ingredients with ice and strain into a chilled martini glass.

Ring of Kerry

1½ oz. Irish Whiskey
1 oz. Baileys Irish Cream
½ oz. Kahlúa or Crème de Cacao
1 tsp. Shaved Chocolate

Mix all ingredients except Shaved Chocolate with cracked ice in a shaker or blender. Strain into a chilled glass. Sprinkle with Shaved Chocolate.

Road Kill

1 oz. Irish Whiskey
1 oz. Wild Turkey Bourbon
½ oz. 151-proof Rum

Combine in a shot glass.

Rob Roy

2 oz. Scotch
dash Sweet or Dry Vermouth

Stir over ice and strain. Garnish with a Cherry.

You can also serve it with ice.

Rocket Fuel

1 oz. Rumple Minze
1 oz. Bacardi 151 Rum

Combine in a shot glass.

Root Beer

½ oz. Kahlúa
½ oz. Galliano
½ oz. Cola
½ oz. Beer

Combine in a shot glass.

Rosalind Russell Martini

2½ oz. Absolut Vodka
dash Aquavit

Stir gently with ice and strain.

Named after actress Rosalind Russell. You can also serve this drink over ice.

Royal Cape

1¾ oz. Crown Royal Whisky
1 oz. Cranberry Juice
½ oz. Lime Juice

Combine over ice.

Royal Stretch

1½ oz. Crown Royal
3 oz. Sparkling Water or Club
    Soda
splash Cherry Juice or Grenadine

Serve over ice in a tall glass with a
Mint Leaf garnish.

Created by Ray Foley.

Ruby Slippers

1 oz. Finlandia Cranberry Vodka
1 oz. Goldschläger

Shake and pour over ice.

Ruddy McDowell

1½ oz. Irish Whiskey
2 oz. Tomato Juice
1 dash Tabasco Sauce
6–8 Ice Cubes
dash Freshly Ground Pepper

Combine all ingredients in a shaker
and shake vigorously. Strain into a
glass with ice.

Rum & Coke

1½ oz. Rum
3 oz. Cola

Stir ingredients with ice.

Rum Apple Martini

1½ oz. Bacardi Big Apple Puerto
   Rican Rum
2½ oz. Sour Apple Mix
splash Club Soda

Chill a martini glass in ice or in the
freezer. In a shaker, add ice, Bacardi
Big Apple, and Sour Apple Mix.
Shake well and strain into the chilled
martini glass. Add Club Soda and
garnish with thin Apple Slices.

Rum Sangria

1 oz. Light Puerto Rican Rum
½ oz. Gold Puerto Rican Rum
½ oz. Triple Sec
1 oz. Orange Juice
½ oz. Pineapple Juice
½ oz. Grape Juice
½ oz. Passion Fruit Juice
½ oz. Guava Juice
½ oz. Cranberry Juice
splash Grenadine

Combine all ingredients in a Collins
glass. Garnish with a Lemon Twist.

Rum Yum

1 oz. Baileys Irish Cream
1 oz. Malibu Rum
1 oz. Cream or Milk

Blend with ice and serve.

This drink also looks nice in a margarita glass.

Runaway Bride

2 oz. Coffee Liqueur
½ oz. Raspberry Flavored Vodka
½ oz. Heavy Cream, Milk, or Ice
   Cream

Shake with ice. Serve straight up in a
chilled martini glass or over ice.

Created by Ray Foley.

Rusty Nail (aka Nail Drive)

1 oz. Scotch
1 oz. Drambuie

Combine in a rocks glass, add ice,
and stir.

Sailor Jerry Perfect Storm

2 oz. Sailor Jerry Rum
splash Fresh Lime Juice
2 dashes Angostura Bitters
3 oz. Ginger Beer

Serve over ice in a rocks glass.

Sakitini

1½ oz. Absolut Vodka
dash Sake

Gently stir with ice and strain.

Salt Lick

1¼ oz. Vodka
2 oz. Bitter Lemon Soda
2 oz. Grapefruit Juice

Pour ingredients over ice in a
salt-rimmed wine glass.

Salty Dog

1½ oz. Gin or Vodka
3 oz. Grapefruit Juice

Mix with ice and pour into a
salt-rimmed glass.

San Juan Irishman

1 oz. Baileys Irish Cream
1 oz. Puerto Rican Rum

Shake with ice and serve over ice.

Santa Fe Maggie

1¼ oz. Jose Cuervo
  Gold Tequila
½ oz. Triple Sec
2 oz. Sweet & Sour Mix
2 oz. Cranberry Juice

Combine ingredients over ice and
garnish with a Lime Wedge.

Savoy Hotel

½ oz. White Crème de Cacao
½ oz. Benedictine
½ oz. Brandy

Layer this drink in the order listed.
Start with Crème de Cacao on the
bottom and finish with Brandy on top.

Sazerac Cocktail

2 oz. Bourbon
1 tsp. Ricard/Pernod
½ tsp. Superfine Sugar
2 dashes Orange Bitters
1 tsp. Water

Shake ingredients with ice. Garnish with a Lemon Twist.

Scarlett O'Hara

1½ oz. Southern Comfort
3 oz. Cranberry Juice

Combine with ice and stir.

Gone with the Cranberry Juice.

Schnappy Shillelagh

2 oz. Carolans Irish Cream
1 oz. Peppermint Schnapps

Stir well over ice.

Scooby Snack

¾ oz. Malibu Rum
¾ oz. Midori Melon Liqueur
1½ oz. Pineapple Juice
splash Milk

Combine ingredients in a shaker with ice. Shake and strain over ice in a rocks glass or serve as a shot.

Don't know why it's called Scooby Snack because it's way too tasty to serve to a dog.

Scorpion

1½ oz. Vodka
¼ oz. Blackberry Brandy
⅛ oz. Rose's Grenadine

Combine in a shot glass.

Scorpion's Sting

1¾ oz. Absolut Peppar Vodka
¼ oz. White Crème de Menthe

Combine in a glass over ice.

Scotch & Soda

1½ oz. Scotch
3 oz. Club Soda

Stir with ice.

Scotch & Water

1½ oz. Scotch
3 oz. Water

Stir with ice.

Scotch Irish

1 oz. Baileys Irish Cream
1 oz. J&B Scotch

Shake or stir over ice.

Scotch Smoothie

1 oz. Coco Lopez Cream of
   Coconut
1¼ oz. Scotch
½ oz. Baileys Irish Cream
½ oz. Almond Liqueur
2 scoops Vanilla Ice Cream

Blend with crushed ice.

Scotch Sour

1¼ oz. Scotch
1 oz. Lemon Juice
1 tsp. Sugar

Stir ingredients in a mixing glass
and pour into a rocks glass with ice.
Garnish with a Cherry and an Orange
Slice.

You can also shake this drink with cracked ice.

Scotch Swizzle

1¾ oz. Chivas Regal Scotch
¼ oz. Lime Juice
dash Angostura Bitters
Club Soda

Combine first three ingredients in
a glass and fill with Club Soda.

Scotty Dog

1¼ oz. Scotch
1½ oz. Lime Juice

Shake with ice and strain into a glass. Garnish with a Lime Slice.

Screaming Banana Banshee

½ oz. Banana Liqueur
½ oz. Vodka
½ oz. White Crème de Cacao
1½ oz. Light Cream
1 Maraschino Cherry

Shake first four ingredients well with ice. Strain into a chilled martini glass. Drop in a Maraschino Cherry.

Screaming Orgasm

½ oz. Irish Cream
½ oz. Kahlúa
½ oz. Vodka
½ oz. Amaretto

Combine in a shot glass.

Screwdriver

2 oz. Vodka
4 oz. Orange Juice

Add Vodka to a tall glass with ice and fill with Orange Juice.

Sea Dipper

1½ oz. Puerto Rican Rum
1 oz. Pineapple Juice
¼ oz. Rose's Lime Juice
1 tsp. Powdered Sugar

Shake with ice and serve over ice.

Seagram's Sweet Georgia Brown

2 oz. Seagram's Sweet Tea
  Vodka
¼ oz. Coffee Liqueur

Shake and serve on the rocks.

Seabreeze

2 oz. Vodka
Grapefruit Juice
Cranberry Juice

Pour Vodka over ice. Fill halfway with Grapefruit Juice and top it off with Cranberry Juice.

Secret Place

1½ oz. Puerto Rican Dark Rum
½ oz. Cherry Brandy
2 tsp. Dark Crème de Cacao
4 oz. Cold Coffee

Stir with crushed ice and serve.

Serpent's Smile

¾ oz. Irish Whiskey
1½ oz. Sweet Vermouth
¾ oz. Lemon Juice
1 tbsp. Kummel
2 dashes Angostura Bitters
5–7 Ice Cubes
1 strip Lemon Peel

Combine all ingredients except
two to three Ice Cubes and the
Lemon Peel in a shaker and shake
vigorously. Place remaining Ice Cubes
in a glass and strain drink into the
glass. Twist the Lemon Peel over the
drink to release oil and drop it in.

Serpent's Tooth

1 oz. Irish Whiskey
2 oz. Sweet Vermouth
½ oz. Kummel
1 oz. Lemon Juice
dash Angostura Bitters

Stir well and strain into a small wine
glass.

7 & 7

1½ oz. Seagram's 7 Whiskey
3 oz. 7-Up

Combine over ice.

Sex on the Beach (The Original)

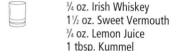

½ oz. Vodka
¼ oz. Peach Schnapps
½ oz. Cranberry Juice
½ oz. Grapefruit Juice

Combine in a mixing glass. Shake
or stir. Pour into a shot glass.

For Lori from Brewster, NY.

Sex on the Beach #1

¾ oz. Chambord
¾ oz. Midori
2 oz. Pineapple Juice
splash Cranberry Juice

Combine in a mixing glass. Shake
or stir. Pour in a shot glass.

You can also serve this one over ice in a rocks glass.

Shady Lady

1 oz. Two Fingers Tequila
1 oz. Melon Liqueur
3 oz. Grapefruit Juice

Combine all ingredients in a
shaker and shake. Serve over ice.

Shamrock Cocktail #1

1½ oz. Irish Whiskey
½ oz. French Vermouth
¼ oz. Green Crème de Menthe

Stir well with cracked ice and
strain or serve over ice. Garnish
with an Olive.

Shamrock Cocktail #2

1½ oz. Irish Whiskey
¾ oz. Green Crème de Menthe
4 oz. Vanilla Ice Cream

Mix all ingredients in a blender at
high speed until smooth. Pour into
a chilled wine goblet.

Shamrocked

2 oz. Midori Melon Liqueur
½ oz. Tullamore Dew Irish
   Whiskey
½ oz. Carolans Cream Liqueur

Combine ingredients and shake
thoroughly. Serve in a 3-oz. shot
glass.

This drink is a hot bar shot in New York these days.

Shetland Pony

1½ oz. Scotch
¾ oz. Irish Mist
dash Orange Bitters (optional)

Mix all ingredients with cracked
ice in a mixing glass and strain
into a chilled cocktail glass.

You can also serve this drink over ice.

Shore Breeze

1½ oz. Puerto Rican Light Rum
3 oz. Pineapple Juice
2 oz. Cranberry Juice
2 dashes Angostura Bitters

Shake with ice and serve in a
rocks glass.

Siberian Sunrise

1½ oz. Vodka
4 oz. Grapefruit Juice
½ oz. Triple Sec

Mix all ingredients with cracked
ice in a shaker or blender.

Sicilian Kiss

1 oz. Southern Comfort
1 oz. Di Saronno Amaretto

Shake with ice and strain into a
shot glass.

Sidecar

½ oz. Cointreau
½ tsp. Fresh Lemon Juice
1 oz. Remy Martin Cognac
3–4 Ice Cubes

Combine all ingredients in a shaker
and shake vigorously. Strain into a
chilled cocktail glass.

Siesta

1½ oz. Sauza Tequila
¾ oz. Lime Juice
½ oz. Sloe Gin

Blend or shake with ice and strain
into a chilled cocktail glass.

Silk Panties

1 oz. Stolichnaya Vodka
1 oz. Peach Schnapps

Combine in a shot glass.

Created by Sandra Gutierrez of Chicago, Illinois.

Silver Bullet

2 oz. Gin or Vodka
splash Scotch

Float Scotch on top.

Silver Bullet Martini

2 oz. Vodka
dash Extra Dry Vermouth
splash Scotch

Stir the first two ingredients gently
over ice and strain. Float Scotch
on top.

Silver Shamrock

2 oz. Bunratty Meade
1 oz. Vodka

Stir with ice.

Silver Splinter

½ oz. Sambuca
1 oz. Dark Rum
2 oz. Heavy Cream

Combine over crushed ice.

Simply Bonkers

1 oz. Chambord
1 oz. Puerto Rican Rum
½ oz. Cream

Combine in a shot glass.

Singapore Sling

1½ oz. Gin
½ oz. Cherry-Flavored Brandy
3 dashes Benedictine
dash Rose's Grenadine
dash Sweetened Lime Mix
Club Soda

Shake first five ingredients and pour
into a tall glass. Top with Club Soda.

Sling this . . .

Ngiam Tong Boon, a bartender at
the Long Bar in Singapore's Raffles
Hotel, invented the Singapore Sling
around 1915. The Raffles Bar Sling, a
variation of the Singapore Sling, gets
its name from the very same Raffles
Hotel.

Sixty-Ninth Regiment Punch

1 oz. Irish Whiskey
1 oz. Scotch Whisky
3 oz. Hot Water
1 tsp. Sugar
2–3 dashes Lemon Juice

Pour the Whiskeys into Hot Water.
Add Sugar and Lemon Juice and stir.

Should be served in a warm glass.

SKYY Berry-Sprite

1 oz. SKYY Berry
6 oz. Sprite

Pour SKYY Berry over ice in a
highball glass. Fill with Sprite.

SKYY Citrus Combo

2 oz. SKYY Citrus
1 oz. Triple Sec
splash Cranberry Juice
1 squeeze Fresh Lime
Lemon Twist

Pour ingredients into a shaker with
ice and shake well. Strain into a
martini glass and garnish with a
Lemon Twist.

SKYY White Monk

3 oz. SKYY Vanilla
1 oz. Frangelico
splash Cream

Shake vigorously and serve with
ice in a rocks glass.

Slainte Sobieski

2 oz. Sobieski Vodka
½ oz. Irish Cream
¼ oz. Marie Brizard Green
   Crème de Menthe

Shake all ingredients and serve on
the rocks.

Slim Gin

1¼ oz. Gin
Diet Soda

Pour Gin in a glass filled with ice.
Fill with your favorite Diet Soda.

Slippery Elf

1 oz. Baileys Irish Cream
1 oz. Smirnoff Vodka

Combine in a shot glass.

Slippery Nipple

1 oz. Sambuca Romana
1 oz. Baileys Irish Cream

Shake with ice and strain into a shot glass.

Slippery Nut

1½ oz. Saint Brendan's Irish Cream
2 oz. Roncoco Rum Liqueur

Combine in a shot glass.

Sloe Gin Fizz

1½ oz. Sloe Gin
3 oz. Sweetened Lemon Mix
Club Soda

Shake Gin and Lemon Mix and pour into a glass. Top with Club Soda.

A popular drink of the '60s.

Slow Comfortable Screw

1 oz. Sloe Gin
½ oz. Southern Comfort
Orange Juice

Pour Sloe Gin and Southern Comfort into a highball glass over the rocks. Top with Orange Juice. Stir.

Snobieski

2½ oz. Sobieski Citron Vodka
½ oz. Cointreau
½ oz. Cream or Irish Cream

Shake and serve over crushed ice shaped like a ball in a rocks glass.

Snowshoe

1 oz. Rumple Minze
1 oz. Brandy

Shake with ice and strain into a shot glass.

SoCo Lime

2 oz. Southern Comfort
squeeze of Lime Juice

Serve as a shot or on the rocks.

Sol-a-Rita

1¼ oz. Jose Cuervo Gold Tequila
¾ oz. Cointreau
1½ oz. Orange Juice
2 dashes Grenadine

Combine over ice.

Sombrero

1½ oz. Coffee Liqueur
½ oz. Half & Half

Combine in a snifter with ice.

This drink is also known as a Muddy River.

S.O.S.

1 oz. Stoli Ohranj Vodka
1 oz. Sambuca

Combine over ice.

Southern Frost

1½ oz. Southern Comfort
2 oz. Cranberry Juice
2 oz. Ginger Ale

Combine in a tall glass with ice.

Southern Lady

1 oz. Knob Creek Bourbon
¼ oz. Southern Comfort
¼ oz. DeKuyper Crème de
   Almond
1½ oz. Pineapple Juice
1 oz. Lemon-Lime Soda
1 oz. Lime Juice

In a tall glass with ice, combine the
first four ingredients. Add the Soda
and top with Lime Juice.

Southern Sour

¼ oz. Bourbon
¾ oz. Southern Comfort
3 oz. Sweetened Lemon Mix

Shake with ice and strain or serve over ice. Garnish with a Cherry and an Orange Slice.

Southern Traditional Margarita

1½ oz. Jose Cuervo Gold Tequila
⅝ oz. Southern Comfort
5 oz. Sweet & Sour Mix
½ oz. Fresh Lime Juice

Combine in a tall glass over ice. Garnish with a Lime Wedge.

Soviet Cocktail

1½ oz. Vodka
½ oz. Dry Vermouth
½ oz. Dry Sherry

Shake or blend all ingredients with cracked ice in a shaker or blender and strain into a chilled glass. Twist a Lemon Peel over the drink and drop it in.

Spanish Moss

½ oz. Herradura Tequila
¾ oz. Kahlúa
½ oz. Green Crème de Menthe

Shake ingredients with ice and strain or serve over ice.

Spanish Town Cocktail

2 oz. Rhum Barbancourt
1 tsp. Triple Sec

Stir ingredients and serve straight up or over ice in a cocktail glass.

Sparks

1 oz. Absolut Peppar Vodka
3 oz. Champagne

Combine in a champagne glass.

Spearamisty

1 oz. Irish Mist
¼ oz. Spearmint Schnapps

Stir ingredients and serve straight up or over ice.

Spike

1½ oz. Jose Cuervo Gold Tequila
4 oz. Grapefruit Juice

Combine in a highball glass.

Spinner

1½ oz. Bourbon
1 oz. Orange Juice
1 tbsp. Lime Juice
1 tsp. Superfine Sugar
1 scoop Crushed Ice

Combine all ingredients in a shaker.
Shake briskly and strain the mixture
into a cocktail glass. Garnish with an
Orange Slice.

You can also serve this one over ice in a rocks glass.

Spritzer

3 oz. Dry White Wine
Club Soda

Pour Wine in a glass and fill with
Soda. Garnish with a Lemon Twist.

Spyglass

1 oz. Captain Morgan Spiced
   Rum
2 scoops Vanilla Ice Cream
1 tbsp. Honey
dash Milk

Blend until smooth.

St. Patrick's Day Cocktail

¾ oz. Irish Whiskey
¾ oz. Green Crème
   de Menthe
¾ oz. Green Chartreuse
1 dash Angostura Bitters

Stir well with cracked ice and strain
into a cocktail glass.

St. Petersburg

2 oz. Vodka
¼ tsp. Angostura Bitters

Stir with ice. Garnish with an Orange
Peel.

Starry Night

¾ oz. Jägermeister
¾ oz. Goldschläger

Combine ingredients in a shot glass.

Jägermeister and Goldschläger should be stored in the fridge. If they aren't ice cold, shake with ice and strain to make this shot.

Stinger

1¾ oz. Cognac/Brandy
¼ oz. White Crème de Menthe

Shake well with ice.

Stoli Blue-Tini Martini

1½ oz. Stoli Blueberi Vodka
1½ oz. Stoli Vanil Vodka

Stir with ice. Strain into a martini glass. Garnish with Blueberries.

Stoli Butterfly

1 oz. Stoli Vanil
1 oz. Stoli Razberi
1 oz. Hiram Walker Crème de Banana
splash Soda

Serve over ice and garnish with a Cherry.

Stoli O Rouge

2 oz. Stoli Ohranj
½ oz. Cranberry Juice
Club Soda

Shake first two ingredients and serve over ice in a Collins glass. Fill with Club Soda. Garnish with an Orange Slice.

Stoli Power Martini

1½ oz. Stoli Ohranj Vodka
½ oz. Lemon Juice
3 oz. Orange Juice
1 oz. Raspberry Syrup

Pour ingredients into a mixing glass, add ice, and shake well. Strain into a chilled glass and garnish with an Orange Peel.

Stoli Sunset

1½ oz. Stoli Limonnaya Vodka
4 oz. Cranberry Juice
1–2 oz. Grapefruit Juice

Combine in a tall glass with ice.

Stolichnaya Lemonade

1¼ oz. Stoli Limonnaya Vodka
¼ oz. Grand Marnier
½ oz. Sweet & Sour Mix
½ oz. Lemon Soda

Combine in a tall glass with ice.

Stolichnaya Paradise Martini

2 parts Stoli Ohranj Vodka
1 part Orange Juice

Shake ingredients with ice. Pour into a martini glass. Garnish with an Orange Slice.

Strasberi Lemonade

2 oz. Stoli Strasberi
2 oz. Lemonade

Serve on the rocks. Garnish with Lemon or Strawberry.

Sunsplash

¾ oz. Coco Lopez Cream of Coconut
1¼ oz. Frangelico Liqueur
¾ oz. Captain Morgan Spiced Rum
5 oz. Orange Juice

Shake with ice and serve.

Sunstroke

1½ oz. Vodka
3 oz. Grapefruit Juice
splash Triple Sec

Pour Vodka and Grapefruit Juice into a rocks glass filled with ice. Add a little Triple Sec and stir.

Super Sempe Stinger

2½ oz. Sempe Armagnac
½ oz. Marie Brizard White Crème de Menthe

Shake with ice and pour into a sugar-rimmed martini glass.

Surfer on Acid

½ oz. Jägermeister
½ oz. Peach Schnapps
½ oz. Pineapple Juice

Shake over ice and strain into a shot glass.

It looks all brown and not very palatable, but the young folks seem to like it.

Swedish Bear

¾ oz. Absolut Vodka
½ oz. Dark Crème de Cacao
1 tbsp. Heavy Cream

Pour ingredients over ice in a chilled rocks glass and stir.

Sweet Ginger

1½ oz. Seagram's Sweet Tea
3 oz. Ginger Ale

Mix together in a cocktail glass and garnish with a Lemon Wedge.

Sweet Irish Storm

1½ oz. Bushmills Irish Whiskey
¾ oz. Noilly Prat Sweet French Vermouth
3–4 dashes Angostura Bitters
3–4 dashes Southern Comfort

Mix ingredients with cracked ice in a shaker or blender. Pour into a chilled rocks glass.

Sweet Tart

1 oz. Absolut Vodka
¼ oz. Chambord
¼ oz. Rose's Lime Juice
¼ oz. Pineapple Juice

Shake with ice and strain into a shot glass.

Sweet Tea Palmetto

1½ oz. Seagram's Sweet Tea
3 oz. Lemonade

Mix together in a cocktail glass and garnish with a Lemon Wedge.

Szarburst

2 oz. Stoli Strasberi Vodka
½ oz. Cranberry Juice
splash Lime Juice

Shake with ice. Strain into a shot
glass.

Taboo

1½ oz. Finlandia Pineapple
Vodka, chilled
½ oz. Cranberry Juice
½ oz. Sour Mix
splash Triple Sec

Blend with crushed ice. Serve in a
tall glass. Garnish with a Pineapple
Wedge and a Cherry.

Tailgate

1½ oz. Don Q Cristal Rum
½ oz. Grenadine
½ oz. Fresh Lime Juice
Coca-Cola

Combine the first three ingredients in
a tall glass with ice. Fill with Cola.

Tangerine

1¼ oz. Stoli Ohranj Vodka
2 oz. Orange Juice
dash Grenadine

Shake with ice and serve.

Tango

2 oz. Cork Dry Gin
1 oz. Sweet Vermouth
1 oz. Dry Vermouth
2 dashes Orange Curaçao
dash Orange Juice

Shake with ice and serve.

You'll dance all night.

Tanqueray & Tonic

1½ oz. Tanqueray Gin
3 oz. Tonic Water

Pour Gin in a glass with ice. Fill with
Tonic. Garnish with a Lime Wedge.

Tarzan O'Reilly

1 oz. Baileys Irish Cream
½ oz. Smirnoff Vodka
½ oz. Crème de Banana

Build in a shot glass over ice. Stir.

You'll swing from trees.

Taxi

1 oz. Stoli Ohranj Vodka
1 oz. Coffee Liqueur

Combine in a shot glass.

You can also serve this drink over ice in a highball glass.

Tear Drop

1¼ oz. Absolut Peppar Vodka
¼ oz. Orange Liqueur or
    Triple Sec

Combine in a shot glass. Drop in
a Cherry.

Not on your head.

Tequador

1½ oz. Tequila
2 oz. Pineapple Juice
1 dash Rose's Lime Juice
Grenadine

Shake the first three ingredients with
crushed ice. Strain. Add a few drops
of Grenadine.

Tequila Gimlet

1½ oz. Tequila
1½ oz. Rose's Lime Juice

Blend Tequila and Lime Juice with
crushed ice and pour into a glass.
Garnish with a Lime Wheel or Green
Cherry.

Tequila Julep

2 sprigs Fresh Mint
1 tsp. Superfine Sugar
1¼ oz. Tequila
Club Soda

Crush three Mint Leaves with Sugar
in a chilled highball glass and fill
with ice. Add Tequila and top with
Club Soda. Garnish with a Mint Sprig.

Tequila Sunrise

½ oz. Grenadine
1½ oz. Tequila
Orange Juice

Pour Grenadine into a tall glass first. Then add Tequila and fill with ice and Orange Juice. Garnish with an Orange Slice.

Tequila Teaser

1½ oz. Tequila
½ oz. Cointreau
1½ oz. Orange Juice
½ oz. Grapefruit Juice

Pour ingredients into a tall glass filled with ice.

Tequina

2 oz. Tequila
½ oz. Dry Vermouth

Stir Tequila and Vermouth with ice in a mixing glass until chilled. Strain into a chilled cocktail glass and garnish with a Lemon Twist.

Terminator #1

½ oz. Bacardi 151 Rum
½ oz. Hiram Walker Blackberry
  Brandy
½ oz. Cranberry Juice

Combine in a shot glass.

I'm back.

Terminator #2

⅓ oz. Vodka
⅓ oz. Grand Marnier
⅓ oz. Sambuca
⅓ oz. Coffee-Flavored Liqueur
⅓ oz. Irish Cream

Layer. Pour the Vodka first, then the Grand Marnier, and so on.

I'm back again.

Three Barrels of Monkeys

1 oz. Myers's Dark Rum
¼ oz. Banana Liqueur
¼ oz. Irish Cream

Combine over ice and stir.

Three-Leaf Shamrock Shaker

1 oz. Bushmills Irish Whiskey
1 oz. Light Rum
1 oz. Brandy
1 tsp. Lemon Juice
dash Sugar Syrup

Shake ingredients with cracked ice. Strain into a chilled glass.

Thunder and Lightning

1 oz. Rumple Minze
1 oz. Bacardi 151 Rum

Combine in a shot glass.

Thunderbolt

2 oz. Herradura Tequila
1 oz. Dr. McGillicuddy's
    Mentholmint Schnapps

Stir over ice in a rocks glass.

Tic Tac

1½ oz. Absolut Mandarin Vodka
4 oz. Red Bull Energy Drink

Pour ingredients over ice in a rocks glass.

Tidal Wave

1½ oz. Laird's Applejack
4 oz. Orange Juice
splash Cranberry Juice

Pour Applejack over ice in a tall glass. Add Orange Juice and Cranberry Juice. Garnish with slice of Orange.

Tidy Bowl

1½ oz. Ouzo
splash Blue Curaçao

Combine in a shot glass.

It's blue.

Tijuana Tea

¾ oz. 1800 Tequila
¾ oz. Jose Cuervo Gold Tequila
½ oz. Triple Sec
1 oz. Sweet & Sour Mix
3 oz. Cola

Combine ingredients in the glass and stir. Garnish with a Lime Slice and a Maraschino Cherry.

Tinker's Tea

1½ oz. Baileys Irish Cream
Hot Tea

Pour Irish Cream in a glass and fill
with Hot Tea.

Tipperary Cocktail

¾ oz. Irish Whiskey
¾ oz. Green Chartreuse
¾ oz. Italian Vermouth

Stir well with cracked ice and strain
into a cocktail glass.

Toasted Almond

1 oz. Kahlúa
½ oz. Amaretto
1 oz. Cream or Milk

Pour over ice and stir.

Tom Collins

1½ oz. Gin
Juice of ½ Lemon
1 tsp. SugarClub Soda

Shake first three ingredients and
pour over ice. Top with Club Soda.

Tootsie Roll #1

1 oz. Kahlúa
1 oz. Vodka
1 oz. Orange Juice

Combine in a shot glass.

Tootsie Roll #2

1 oz. Root Beer Schnapps
½ oz. Baileys Irish Cream

Top Root Beer Schnapps with Irish
Cream in a shot glass.

John or Tom Collins?

John Collins, a waiter at Lipmmer's
Old House on Coduit Street in
Hanover Square, England, invented
this drink. The name Tom was used
instead of John because the drink
was made with Old Tom Gin. Today,
a John Collins is made with whiskey.

Topaz Martini

1¾ oz. Bacardi Limón
¼ oz. Martini & Rossi Extra Dry
   Vermouth
splash Blue Curaçao

Combine in a cocktail glass.

Invented at the Heart and Soul in San Francisco, California.

Traffic Light

⅓ oz. Green Crème de Menthe
⅓ oz. Crème de Banana
⅓ oz. Sloe Gin

Layer this drink in the order listed. Start with Crème de Menthe on the bottom and finish with Sloe Gin on top.

Transfusion

1½ oz. Stolichnaya Vodka
3 oz. Grape Juice

Combine over ice and stir.

Tres Martini

splash Cointreau
1½ oz. Tres Generaciones

Rinse a chilled martini glass with a splash of Cointreau and discard. Place Tres Generaciones in a shaker. Fill with ice, shake, and strain into the prepared glass. Garnish with Orange Zest.

Trilby

¾ oz. Scotch
¾ oz. Sweet Vermouth
¾ oz. Parfait Amour
3–4 dashes Pernod
3–4 dashes Angostura Bitters

Mix all ingredients with cracked ice in a shaker or blender. Pour into a chilled rocks glass.

Trip to the Beach

½ oz. Malibu
½ oz. Peach Schnapps
½ oz. Smirnoff Vodka
3 oz. Orange Juice

Combine over ice.

Tropical Breeze

1 oz. Coco Lopez Cream
  of Coconut
2 oz. Orange Juice
1 oz. Rum
½ oz. Crème de Banana

Blend with crushed ice. Garnish
with a Pineapple Slice.

Tropical Iceberg

1½ oz. Finlandia Pineapple
  Vodka, chilled
½ oz. Banana Liqueur or
½ Banana
½ oz. Cream of Coconut
dash Cream or Half & Half

Blend ingredients and serve in a
margarita glass.

Tropico 2000 Cocktail

2 oz. Bacardi 151 Rum
4 oz. Tropico
1 drop Martini & Rosso Sweet
  Vermouth

Mix all ingredients and pour.

Tuaca Frizzante

1½ oz. Tuaca
splash Mineral Water

Pour Tuaca over ice in a rocks glass.
Stir in a splash of Mineral Water to
taste. Garnish with a Lemon Peel.

Tuaca Rocca

1 oz. Tuaca
1 oz. Peach Schnapps
1 oz. Vodka

Combine with ice in a rocks glass.

Tullamore Toddy

2 oz. Tullamore Dew Irish
  Whiskey
1 Lemon, sliced
2 lumps Sugar
Hot Water

Combine all ingredients in a glass
mug and stir well. Fill to the top with
Hot Water. Garnish with a Cinnamon
Stick.

The Tully-Tini

1½ oz. Tullamore Dew Irish
   Whiskey
1½ oz. Sour Apple Schnapps
1½ oz. Cranberry Juice

Combine Tullamore Dew and Sour
Apple Schnapps into a shaker with
ice. Shake and strain into a chilled
martini glass. Top with Cranberry
Juice.

Turbo

¼ oz. Vodka
¼ oz. Peach Schnapps
¼ oz. Apple Schnapps
¼ oz. Cranberry Juice

Combine in a shot glass.

You can also combine the ingredients with ice in a rocks glass.

Turkey Shooter

¾ oz. Bourbon
¼ oz. White Crème de Menthe

Shake in cocktail shaker. Strain into a
brandy snifter.

This drink is also known as a Bourbon Stinger.

24 Karat Nightmare

1 oz. Goldschläger
1 oz. Rumple Minze

Combine in a shot glass.

Twilight Zone

1½ oz. Puerto Rican Light Rum
½ oz. Myers's Rum
splash Rose's Grenadine

Shake with ice and strain into a shot
glass.

The Ultimate Tea

1½ oz. Irish Mist
Hot Tea

Pour Irish Mist in a warm glass. Fill
with Hot Tea. Garnish with a Lemon
Slice.

Ultimate White Russian

1½ oz. Absolut Vanilla Vodka
1½ oz. Starbucks Coffee Liqueur
1½ oz. Half & Half

Combine in a shaker with ice and strain over ice in a Collins glass.

A drink fit for the Big Lebowski. Careful, man! There's a beverage here!

Under the Volcano Martini

2 oz. Mezcal
½ oz. Martini & Rossi Vermouth

Stir over ice in a cocktail glass. Garnish with a Jalapeño-Stuffed Olive.

Invented at Harry Denton's in San Francisco, California.

U-Z

¾ oz. Irish Mist
¾ oz. Baileys Irish Cream
¾ oz. Kahlúa

Shake ingredients and strain into a shot glass.

Vanilia Martini

2½ oz. Absolut Vanilia
½ oz. Godiva White Chocolate
  Liqueur

Shake with ice; strain.

Vanilia Pop

1 part Absolut Vanilia
3 parts Cola

Serve over ice in a tall glass.

Vanilia Valentine

2 oz. Absolut Vanilia
1½ oz. Chambord
Champagne
1 Strawberry

Mix Absolut Vanilia and Chambord. Top with chilled Champagne. Garnish with a Fanned Strawberry.

Vanilla Cosmo

2 oz. Mount Gay Vanilla Rum
1 oz. Cointreau
Juice of ½ a Lime
splash Cranberry Juice

Combine ingredients in a shaker
with ice. Stir and strain into a martini
glass.

Vanilla Koke

1½ oz. Stoli Vanil Vodka
3 oz. Cola

Combine in a Collins glass and stir.

Vesper Martini

1½ oz. Gin
dash Blonde Lillet

Stir gently with ice and strain into a
cocktail glass.

Vicious Sid

1½ oz. Puerto Rican Light Rum
½ oz. Southern Comfort
½ oz. Cointreau or Triple Sec
1 oz. Lemon Juice
dash Bitters

Shake ingredients with ice and serve
over ice.

Victoria's Secret

1½ oz. Magellan Gin
¾ oz. Apricot Brandy
1½ oz. Fresh Sour Mix
¼ oz. Campari

Shake ingredients with ice until cold.
Strain into a chilled cocktail glass.

Created by Ray Srp, Bar Manager, Bellagio Hotel, Las Vegas, NV.

Viking

1 oz. Liquore Galliano
¼ oz. Akvavit (ice cold)

Float Akvavit on top of the Galliano
in a shot glass.

Violetta Martini

2 oz. Classic Finlandia Vodka
2 oz. Cranberry Juice Cocktail
splash Blue Curaçao

Stir gently over ice and strain.

You can also serve this drink over ice.

Vodka & Tonic

1½ oz. Vodka
3 oz. Tonic

Stir ingredients with ice in a glass.
Garnish with a Lime Wheel.

Vodka Martini

2 oz. Vodka
dash Dry Vermouth

Stir ingredients with ice and strain.
Garnish with a Lemon Twist or an
Olive.

You can also serve a Vodka Martini on ice.

Vulcan Mind Probe #1

1 oz. Ouzo
1 oz. Bacardi 151 Rum

Shake with ice and strain into a shot
glass.

Vulcan Mind Probe #2

½ oz. 151-proof Rum
½ oz. Peppermint Schnapps
½ oz. Irish Cream

Layer in a shot glass by first pouring the Rum, then the Schnapps,
and then the Irish Cream. Serve
with a large straw.

*You drink this one by sucking the drink down through the straw in
one gulp.*

Ward Eight

2 oz. Whiskey
4 dashes Grenadine
Juice of ½ Lemon

Shake ingredients with cracked ice
and strain into a glass with finely
cracked ice.

W

The origins of the Ward Eight

This drink is named after Boston's Ward Eight, known years ago for its bloody political elections. The drink is basically a Whiskey Sour with a splash of grenadine. Locke-O-Ber's in Boston is a great place to try one.

Watermelon

1 oz. Vodka
1 oz. Midori
2 oz. Orange Juice
2 oz. Cranberry Juice

Combine ingredients in a glass over ice.

Wavecutter

2 oz. Bacardi Rum
2 oz. Cranberry Juice
2 oz. Orange Juice

Pour Rum into a glass with ice. Add Cranberry Juice and Orange Juice. Decorate with Cranberries.

You probably don't have Cranberries lying around. An Orange Slice makes a fine garnish too.

Wet & Wild

1½ oz. Absolut Vanilia
¾ oz. Cointreau
½ oz. Lime Juice
½ oz. Watermelon Juice

Shake ingredients with ice and strain.

Wet Spot

1 oz. Cuervo Tequila
1 oz. Baileys Irish Cream

Shake with ice and strain into a shot glass.

Whiskey Collins

1¼ oz. Whiskey
Juice of ½ lemon
1 tsp. Sugar
Club Soda

Shake the first three ingredients with cracked ice and strain in a glass over ice. Fill with Club Soda and stir. Decorate with a Cherry and an Orange Slice.

Whiskey Sour

1½ oz. Whiskey
¾ oz. Sweetened Lemon Juice
1 tsp. Superfine Sugar

Shake with ice. Serve straight up or over ice.

White Chocolate Martini

1½ oz. Vodka
½ oz. White Crème de Cacao

Stir gently with ice and strain into a chocolate-rimmed cocktail glass.

Invented at the Continental Cafe in Philadelphia, Pennsylvania.

White Lady

1½ oz. Gin
½ oz. Cointreau
1½ oz. Lemon Juice

Shake and strain into a frosted glass.

White Russian

1½ oz. Vodka
½ oz. Kahlúa
½ oz. Cream

Shake and serve over ice.

The Dude calls this drink a Caucasian in The Big Lebowski.

White Spider

1 oz. Stolichnaya Vodka
1 oz. Rumple Minze

Combine in a shot glass.

FABLES & LORE

W

The lowdown on the White Lady

Harry MacElhone created the White Lady in 1919 at Ciro's Club in London, England. In 1923, he took over a bar in Rue Daunou, Paris, renaming it Harry's New York Bar. In 1929, using gin in place of white crème de menthe, he altered the original White Lady recipe, and this concoction became a worldwide favorite.

Wild Irish Rose

1½ oz. Irish Whiskey
1½ tsp. Grenadine
½ oz. Lime Juice
Club Soda

Fill a highball glass with ice. Add Irish Whiskey, Grenadine, and Lime Juice. Stir well. Fill with Club Soda.

Wild Thanksgiving

1 oz. Wild Turkey
1 oz. Apple Brandy
splash Lime Juice
Cranberry Juice

Serve over ice with a Mint garnish.

Wolfhound

1 oz. Bushmills Irish Whiskey
¾ oz. Dark Crème de Cacao
½ oz. Half & Half
splash Club Soda

Stir ingredients with ice and serve over ice.

Woo Woo #1

¾ oz. Vodka
¾ oz. Peppermint Schnapps

Combine in a glass with ice.

Woo Woo #2

1 oz. Vodka
½ oz. Peach Schnapps
2 oz. Cranberry Juice

Combine ingredients over ice.

Yellow Bird

¾ oz. Bacardi Rum
¼ oz. Liquore Galliano
¼ oz. Hiram Walker Crème de Banana
2 oz. Pineapple Juice
2 oz. Orange Juice

Shake with ice. Serve over ice.

Y

Yellow Morning

1 oz. Crème de Banana
1 oz. Cherry Herring
1 oz. Cognac

Layer this drink in the order listed. Start with Crème de Banana on the bottom and finish with Cognac on top.

Zipperhead

1 oz. Stolichnaya Vodka
1 oz. Chambord
½ oz. Club Soda

Combine in a shot glass with the Club Soda on top.

Zombie

¾ oz. Bacardi Light Rum
¼ oz. Bacardi Dark Rum
1 oz. Pineapple Juice
1 oz. Orange Juice
1 oz. Lemon or Rose's Lime Juice
¼ tsp. Bacardi 151 Rum (optional)
1 tsp. Powdered Sugar (optional)

Mix the first two Rums and all Juices with ice in a shaker or blender and pour into a tall glass. Garnish with a Pineapple Spear and a Red Cherry. If desired, float ¼ tsp. Bacardi 151 on top with 1 tsp. Powdered Sugar.

Zorbatini

1½ oz. Stolichnaya Vodka
¼ oz. Metaxa Ouzo

Stir gently with ice and strain. Garnish with a Green Olive.

Chapter 18

"Martini" Madness

In This Chapter

▶ Following the latest trend

▶ Mixing a few Martinis

*W*hat's with all the Martinis these days? I get new recipes submitted to me all the time, and every day I hear about these trendy new Martinis that look like nothing more than pink Kool-Aid in a dressed-up cocktail glass.

The truth of the matter is that a real Martini is simply a couple ounces of ice-cold gin (or vodka if gin isn't your thing) with a dash of vermouth. Some people like more or less vermouth than others (or none at all), and some people prefer an olive or a twist of lemon or even a pearl onion for a garnish. But that's really about it when it comes to Martini variations as far as I'm concerned.

Ultimately, the Martinis in this chapter are just cocktails like any other, but they're called Martinis because they're served in a martini glass. It's trendy. In a few years, something else will be trendy. At one time, people drank cocktails with raw eggs in them because they were popular. Tab and Fresca used to be popular. In five years, something else will be popular. What are you gonna do?

So anyway, I tried to pick out around 30 interesting or trendy "Martinis" that actually taste good and are worth drinking. Enjoy.

The All-American Martini

2½ oz. Glacier Vodka
dash Dry Vermouth

Stir with ice. Strain into a
martini glass. Garnish with
two Olives skewered by an
American Flag toothpick.

Angel Martini

2½ oz. Ketel One Vodka
½ oz. Frangelico

Shake with ice. Strain into a
chilled martini glass.

*A little Italy and a littler Netherlands. (This one was invented at the
Bowery Bar of New York, New York.)*

Apeach Cosmopolitan

2 oz. Absolut Apeach
½ oz. Triple Sec
½ oz. Lime Juice
1 oz. Cranberry Juice
Lime Wedge

Shake with ice and strain
into a chilled cocktail glass.
Garnish with a Lime Wedge.

Apple Martini

2 oz. Glacier Vodka
½ oz. Schönauer Apfel
    Schnapps
dash Cinnamon

Shake with ice. Strain into a
chilled martini glass. Garnish
with a slice of Apple.

Apricot Martini

1 oz. Godiva Liqueur
1 oz. Absolut Vodka
1 oz. Apricot Brandy

Combine with ice; shake well.
Serve chilled with a Cherry.

It's not the pits.

Bacardi Sweet Martini

2 oz. Bacardi Light Rum
½ oz. Martini & Rossi Rosso
    Vermouth

Stir gently with ice in a
cocktail glass.

Black Magic

1½ oz. Jägermeister
1½ oz. Vodka

Shake with ice and strain into
a chilled martini glass.

Black Tie Martini

1½ oz. SKYY Vodka
splash Campari
splash Chivas
2 Cocktail Onions
1 Black Olive

Shake with ice and strain into
a chilled martini glass.

Blue Beast

2 oz. Magellan Gin
1 oz. Hpnotiq
splash of Chambord

Shake Magellan and Hpnotiq
until cold and pour into a
martini glass. Add a splash
of Chambord. Garnish with a
Maraschino Cherry.

Blue Goose Martini

2 oz. Hpnotiq
1 oz. Grey Goose Vodka
splash Pineapple Juice

Shake well. Garnish with a
Pineapple Wedge.

Blue Hawaiian Martini

1 oz. Stoli Blueberi
1 oz. Malibu Rum
¼ oz. Grenadine
1 oz. Pineapple Juice

Shake with ice. Strain into a
chilled martini glass. Garnish
with Lemon.

Blue SKYY Martini

2½ oz. SKYY Vodka
splash Blue Curaçao

Stir with ice and strain into a
chilled martini glass.

Blues Martini

1½ oz. Ketel One Vodka
1½ oz. Bombay Sapphire Gin
few drops Blue Curaçao

Stir gently with ice. Serve
straight up or over ice.

Bootlegger Martini

2 oz. Bombay Gin
¼ oz. Southern Comfort

Stir gently with ice; serve
straight up or over ice. Garnish
with a Lemon Twist.

*Created at the Martini Bar at the Chianti Restaurant in Houston,
Texas.*

Dry Victoria Martini

3 oz. Bombay Sapphire Gin
1 oz. Martini & Rossi Extra
   Dry Vermouth
1 or 2 dashes Angostura
   Bitters

Shake or stir. Serve in a classic
martini glass. Garnish with 1
Cocktail Olive and a Twist of
Lemon.

The Engaging Martini

2 oz. Finlandia Vodka
dash Dry Vermouth
2 Olives
Diamond Ring

Stir Vodka and Vermouth with
ice and strain into a chilled
martini glass. Garnish with a
pair of Olives and a One-Carat
Diamond Engagement Ring.

*Also known as The Most Expensive Martini, the Oak Bar in Boston
has a version that includes dinner for two and a hotel suite stocked
with champagne, chocolates, and flowers for just $12,750. The
chunk of ice in her drink will seal the deal.*

Godiva Naked Martini

1½ oz. Godiva Liqueur
1½ oz. Absolut Vodka

Combine with ice; shake well.
Serve in a chilled martini glass.
Garnish with a Lemon Peel or
a Strawberry.

Grand Obsession

2 oz. Absolut Kurant Vodka
½ oz. Grand Marnier
½ oz. Cranberry Juice

Shake with ice. Strain into a
chilled martini glass.

"In and Out" Martini

¼ oz. Dry Vermouth
2 oz. Gin or Vodka
Garnish with Lemon Twist or
　an Olive.

Fill shaker glass with ice and
add Vermouth. Swirl ice around
in glass and pour out. Add
Gin/Vodka and shake vigorously.
Pour into a cocktail glass.

From Patrick Ford, Smith & Wollensky, New York, NY

Jersey Lightning Martini

2 oz. Laird's Applejack Brandy
1 oz. Sweet Vermouth
¾ oz. Fresh Lime Juice

Shake with ice. Strain into a
chilled martini glass.

Kremlin Martini

2 oz. Smirnoff Vodka
1½ oz. Crème de Cacao
1½ oz. Half & Half

Shake well with ice. Strain into
a chilled martini glass.

Lavender Orchid

1 oz. Tanqueray No. Ten
¼ oz. Chambord
1 oz. Sour Mix
splash Ginger Ale
1 Orchid

In a shaker with ice, add
Tanqueray, Chambord, and
Sour Mix. Shake gently and
strain into a martini glass and
top with Ginger Ale. Decorate
with a floating Orchid.

Limón Martini

2 oz. Bacardi Limón
¾ oz. Martini & Rossi
　Extra Dry Vermouth
splash Cranberry Juice

Shake with ice and strain into
a chilled martini glass. Garnish
with a Lemon Twist.

Limontini

1 oz. Vanilla Vodka
½ oz. Caravella Limoncello
1½ oz. Pomegranate Juice
squeeze of Lime

Shake vigorously, strain into a
martini glass, and serve
immediately. Garnish with a
Lemon Twist.

You can substitute Orange-Flavored Vodka for the Vanilla Vodka.

Martini avec Moi

2 oz. Absente
1½ oz. Remy Martin Grand Cru
VS Cognac
¾ oz. Lillet Blanc
splash Crème de Cassis

Shake ingredients until
freezing cold and pour into a
martini glass. Garnish with a
Lemon Twist.

Mayflower Martini

2 oz. Plymouth Gin
1 oz. French Vermouth
dash Angostura Bitters
Orange or Lemon Twist

Shake with ice and strain into
a chilled martini glass.

*This drink is based on Thomas Stuart's original recipe. Modern
tastes may prefer a drier version with less Vermouth; an Orange
rather than a Lemon Twist is also good.*

Midnite Martini

1¼ oz. Glacier Vodka
¾ oz. Echte Kroatzbeere
Blackberry Liqueur

Stir ingredients with ice. Strain
into a chilled martini glass.

Mystique Martini

2 oz. Smirnoff Vodka
dash Green Chartreuse

Chill, strain, and garnish with
a Lemon or Lime Twist.

Orange Mochantini

2 oz. Stoli Kafya Vodka
1 oz. Stoli Vanil Vodka
splash Chocolate Liqueur
splash Orange Liqueur

Stir ingredients with ice. Strain into a chilled martini glass. Garnish with 3 Coffee Beans or an Orange Twist.

Purple Hooter Martini

1¼ oz. Chambord
1¼ oz. Vodka
¼ oz. Sour Mix
¼ oz. Lemon-Lime Soda

Combine ingredients, except Soda, into a shaker filled with ice. Shake thoroughly and pour into a martini glass. Top with Lemon-Lime Soda.

It's not all that different from a Purple Hooter shot, but it looks classier in a martini glass.

Raschocolate Martini

1½ oz. Smirnoff Vodka
1 oz. White Crème de Cacao
dash Chambord
2 oz. Cranberry Juice

Combine ingredients into a shaker filled with ice. Shake thoroughly and pour into a martini glass.

Raspberripolitan

2 oz. Absolut Raspberri
½ oz. Cointreau
½ oz. Cranberry Juice
dash Lime Juice

Shake with ice and strain into a well-chilled cocktail glass. Garnish with a Lime Wedge.

A variation of the popular Cosmopolitan. I suppose we'll be seeing Applepolitans, Strawberripolitans, Lemonpolitans, and maybe Chocopolitans soon enough.

Ruby Slipper Martini

2 oz. Bombay Sapphire
¼ oz. Grand Marnier
1 or 2 splashes Grenadine
dash Peppermint Schnapps

Shake with ice and strain into a well-chilled cocktail glass. Garnish with a Mint Leaf (set it on the edge of the drink and let it stick out).

Stoli Blue-Tini

1½ oz. Stoli Blueberi
1½ oz. Stoli Vanil

Stir with ice. Strain into a
martini glass. Garnish with
Blueberries.

Tanqueray "Perfect Ten" Martini

2 oz. Tanqueray No. Ten
1 oz. Grand Marnier
½ oz. Sour Mix

Shake with ice. Strain into a
martini glass. Garnish with
Lemon.

Thrilla in Vanilla

2 oz. Sobieski Vanilla Vodka
½ oz. DeKuyper Peach
    Schnapps

Shake with ice and strain into
a martini glass.

Created by L. Saccone, Basking Ridge, NJ.

Topaz Martini

1¾ oz. Bacardi Limón
¼ oz. Martini & Rossi
    Extra Dry Vermouth
splash Blue Curaçao

Stir in a cocktail glass. Strain
and serve straight up or on the
rocks. Add a Lemon Twist or
Olives.

Trinity Martini

1 oz. Bombay Gin
½ oz. Sweet Vermouth
½ oz. Dry Vermouth

Stir in a cocktail glass. Strain
and serve straight up or on the
rocks. Add a Lemon Twist or
Olives.

This cocktail is also known as the Trio Plaza Martini.

Warden Martini

1½ oz. Bombay Gin
dash Martini & Rossi
    Extra Dry Vermouth
dash Pernod

Stir in a cocktail glass. Strain
and serve straight up or on the
rocks. Add a Lemon Twist or
Olives.

Chapter 19

Drinks for Special Occasions

● ●

In This Chapter

▶ Preparing punches for parties

▶ Serving special holiday drinks

● ●

*Y*ou're bound to have a few parties throughout the year, and some of those parties will probably fall on holidays. I start the chapter with a few pages of punch recipes. They'll be a hit at any gathering. The chapter ends with a sampling of holiday drinks. Try them with your friends throughout the year.

Punches

Punch may have come from the word *puncheon,* a cast made to hold liquids, such as beer. The word may also have come from the Hindu word *pantsh,* which means *five.* What does five have to do with anything? British expatriates in India in the 17th century made a beverage consisting of five ingredients: tea, water, sugar, lemon juice, and a fermented sap called *arrack.*

Regardless of the history or origin, punches of all kinds are an expected beverage at many of today's social gatherings. Whether you're an aspiring bartender or just someone who wants to be a good host (and the life of the party), you need to have at least a few of the following punches in your repertoire.

Ambrosia Punch

20 oz. can Crushed Pineapple,
   undrained
15 oz. Coco Lopez Cream of
   Coconut
2 cups Apricot Nectar, chilled
2 cups Orange Juice, chilled
1½ cups Light Rum, optional
1 liter Club Soda, chilled

In a blender, purée the Pineapple and Cream of Coconut until smooth. In a punch bowl, combine the pureed mixture, Nectar, Orange Juice, and Rum (if desired). Mix well. Just before serving, add Club Soda and serve over ice.

This recipe serves about 24.

Bacardi Confetti Punch

750 ml. Bacardi Light Rum
6 oz. can Frozen Lemonade
   Concentrate
6 oz. can Frozen Grapefruit
   Juice Concentrate
6 oz. can Fruit Cocktail,
   drained
2 liters Club Soda, chilled

Combine the first four ingredients in a large container and chill for two hours, stirring occasionally. To serve, pour the mixture over ice in a punch bowl and add two liters of chilled Club Soda. Stir gently.

This recipe makes 8 servings.

Champagne Punch Royale

1 cup Sliced Strawberries
2 tbsp. Sugar
1 cup Orange Juice
⅓ cup Royale Montaine
   Cognac and Orange Liqueur
1 bottle Chantaine Sparkling
   Wine, chilled
1 small bottle Club Soda

Place Sliced Strawberries in large bowl and sprinkle with Sugar. Add Orange Juice and Royale Montaine Cognac and Orange Liqueur. Macerate for 1 hour. Add the chilled Sparkling Wine and Club Soda.

This recipe serves 8.

Citrus Serenade

8 oz. Ocean Spray Cranberry
    Juice Cocktail with Calcium
½ Banana, cut into slices
½ cup Low-Fat Vanilla Yogurt
¼ cup Red Grapefruit Sections,
    membranes removed
½ cup Crushed Ice

Put all ingredients in a blender. Blend for a few seconds on high speed or until ingredients are thoroughly combined. Pour into a large glass.

Makes 1 serving.

Cointreau Punch

1 bottle Cointreau
1 bottle Vodka
3 quarts Club Soda
6 oz. can Orange Juice
    Concentrate
6 oz. can Pineapple Juice
    Concentrate

Place a clear block of ice in a large punch bowl. Combine ingredients and stir. Garnish with Orange Slices decorated with Cranberries and studded with Cloves.

This recipe makes enough for 40 punch-cup drinks.

Coral Paradise

10 oz. Ocean Spray Ruby
    Mango Grapefruit Juice
    Cocktail
4 oz. Orange Juice
¼ cup Crushed Pineapple,
    drained
¼ cup Crushed Ice

Put all ingredients in a blender. Blend for a few seconds on high speed or until ingredients are thoroughly combined.

Makes 1 serving.

Variation: Substitute 1 scoop vanilla yogurt for crushed ice.

Double Berry Coco Punch

20 oz. Frozen Strawberries in
Syrup, thawed
15 oz. Coco Lopez Cream of
Coconut
48 oz. Cranberry Juice
Cocktail, chilled
2 cups Light Rum, optional
1 liter Club Soda, chilled

In a blender, purée the
Strawberries and Cream of
Coconut until smooth. In a
large punch bowl, combine
the pureed mixture, Cranberry
Juice, and Rum (if desired).
Just before serving, add Club
Soda and serve over ice.

This recipe serves about 32.

Formula #21

1 bottle Smirnoff Vodka
1 bottle White Wine
2 quarts Pineapple Juice
½ cup Lime Juice
2 quarts chilled Club Soda
Sugar to taste

Mix the ingredients in a punch
bowl.

This recipe serves 12–20.

Fruit Punch

4 oz. Pineapple Juice
6 oz. Orange Juice
6 oz. Lemon or Lime Juice
1 fifth Bacardi Light Rum
1 quart Ginger Ale or Club
Soda
Fine Sugar to taste

Mix ingredients in a large
container. Chill 2 hours. Pour
mixture over a block of ice in a
bowl. Add 1 quart cold Ginger
Ale or Club Soda. Decorate
with Fresh Fruit.

Serves 9 people twice.

Grapefruit Banana Shake

4 oz. Ocean Spray White
Grapefruit Premium 100%
Juice
2 oz. Pineapple Juice
¼ cup Fat-Free Vanilla Yogurt
½ Banana, cut into slices

Put all ingredients in a blender.
Blend for a few seconds on
high speed or until ingredients
are thoroughly combined. Pour
into a glass with crushed ice.

Makes 1 serving.

Malibu Party Punch

1 bottle Malibu Rum
48 oz. Cranberry Juice
6 oz. can Frozen Orange Juice
   Concentrate
6 oz. can Frozen Lemonade or
   Limeade Concentrate

Combine ingredients in a
punch bowl and stir. Garnish
with Lemon, Orange Slices,
and Cloves.

This recipe serves 12–20.

M&R Hot Spiced Wine Punch

1.5 liters Martini & Rossi Red
   Vermouth
2 dashes Angostura Bitters
6 Cloves
3 Cinnamon Sticks
3 tsp. Superfine Sugar
pinch Allspice
pinch Ground Clove
Orange Slices

Combine all ingredients except
Orange Slices in a heavy
saucepan and heat but don't
boil. Strain into a punch bowl.
For added effect, heat a poker
and dip it into the punch
before serving. Garnish with
Orange Slices.

This recipe serves 6–12.

Metaxa Fruit Punch

½ gallon Orange Sherbet
3 bottles 7-Up
16 oz. Metaxa Manto Liqueur
6–8 scoops Raspberry Sherbet
1 Orange, sliced thin

Mix all ingredients except the
Raspberry Sherbet and Orange
Slices. Chill for 1 hour. Place
scoops of Raspberry Sherbet
atop the punch. Add Orange
Slices.

This recipe serves 10–15.

Myers's Planter's Punch

3 oz. Orange Juice
Juice of ½ Lemon or Lime
1½ oz. Myers's Rum
1 tsp. Superfine Sugar
dash Grenadine

Shake or blend until frothy.
Serve over shaved ice in a
highball glass. If desired,
garnish with an Orange Slice
and a Cherry.

*This recipe makes only one drink, so you'll have to do some
multiplying to make enough to serve a bunch of people.*

Open House Punch

750 ml. Southern Comfort
6 oz. Lemon Juice
6 oz. can Frozen Lemonade
6 oz. can Frozen Orange Juice
3 liters 7-Up or Sprite
Red Food Coloring

Chill ingredients. Mix the first four ingredients in a punch bowl. Add 7-Up or Sprite. Add drops of Red Food Coloring as desired and stir. Float a block of ice and garnish with Orange and Lemon Slices. Note that the first four ingredients may be mixed in advance. Add 7-Up or Sprite and ice when ready to serve.

This recipes makes 32 4-oz. servings.

Orange Coconut Frost

15 oz. can Coco Lopez Cream of Coconut
12 oz. can Frozen Orange Juice Concentrate, thawed
1 tsp. Vanilla Extract
4 cups Ice Cubes
Mint Leaves and Orange Slices, optional

In a blender, combine Cream of Coconut, Juice Concentrate and Vanilla; blend well. Gradually add Ice, blending until smooth. Garnish with Mint and Orange if desired. Serve immediately. Refrigerate leftovers.

In case you hadn't noticed, this is a nonalcoholic punch. It makes about 5 servings.

Party Punch

16 oz. Orange Juice
16 oz. Pineapple Juice, unsweetened
16 oz. Club Soda
3 oz. Lime Juice
16 oz. White or Gold Puerto Rican Rum

Pour ingredients into a large punch bowl filled with ice. Add Sugar to taste.

This recipe serves 12.

Patio Punch

750 ml. Southern Comfort
16 oz. Grapefruit Juice
8 oz. Fresh Lime Juice
2 liters 7-Up or Ginger Ale

Mix ingredients and add ice. Serve from a punch bowl or pitcher. Note that the first three ingredients can be mixed in advance and refrigerated. Add the 7-Up or Ginger Ale and ice when ready to serve.

This recipe serves 15–20.

Peach-E-Vino Punch

⅓ cup Sugar
½ cup Fresh Lemon Juice
1 bottle Dry White Wine
¼ cup DeKuyper Peachtree
    Schnapps
¼ cup DeKuyper Apple Barrel
    Schnapps
1 quart Club Soda
Fresh Fruit
Ice Cubes

In a large pitcher, combine Sugar and Lemon Juice. Stir until dissolved. Add Wine and Schnapps. Just before serving, add Club Soda, Sliced Fruit (Apples, Peaches, Cherries, Limes, Oranges, Lemons), and Ice Cubes.

This recipe serves 15–20.

Shower Punch

2 quarts Orange Juice
2 quarts Grapefruit Juice
1 quart Bacardi Light Rum

Mix ingredients in a large container. Chill 2 hours. Pour mixture over a block of ice just before serving. Add 3 thinly sliced Oranges.

Serves 25 people twice.

Snow Blower

6 oz. Cran-Apple Cranberry
    Apple Juice Drink
1 tsp. Lemon Juice
pinch Cloves or Nutmeg
1 oz. Rum, optional
Lemon Slice, garnish

Heat Cranberry Apple Drink, Lemon Juice, and Cloves or Nutmeg in a small saucepan. Pour into a mug and stir in Rum, if desired. Garnish with a Lemon Slice.

Makes 1 serving.

Tropical Fruit Smoothie

15 oz. Coco Lopez Cream of
Coconut
1 medium Banana
8 oz. juice-pack Crushed
Pineapple, undrained
1 cup Orange Juice
1 tbsp. Real Lemon Juice from
Concentrate or ReaLime
Lime Juice from Concentrate
2 cups Ice Cubes

In a blender, combine all
ingredients, except Ice; blend
well. Gradually add Ice,
blending until smooth. Garnish
as desired. Serve immediately.
Refrigerate leftovers.

Makes about 5 servings.

Holiday Cocktails

Here are several drinks you can serve on holidays throughout the calendar year. Sure, you can have green beer on St.
Patrick's Day, but where's the fun in that? Sample something
different.

New Year's Eve: Midnight Cocktail

3 oz. Dry Champagne
½ oz. Goldschläger

Fill a champagne flute with
chilled Champagne, leaving
room at the top. Pour in the
Goldschläger, making sure to
include a few flakes of gold!

Valentine's Day: Valentine's Special

3½ oz. Fragoli
½ oz. Godiva Liqueur

Shake. Serve on the rocks with
Candy Kisses as a garnish.

St. Patrick's Day: Nutty Irishman

1 part Carolans Irish Cream
  Liqueur
1 part Frangelico

Shake all ingredients and serve
as a shot.

Easter: Bunny Hop

2 oz. Teton Glacier Potato
  Vodka
½ oz. Creme Yvette/Parfait
  Amour

Shake with ice and strain
into a chilled, sugar-rimmed
martini glass.

Cinco De Mayo: Iguana

½ oz. Tarantula Reposado
  Tequila
¾ oz. 360 Vodka
¾ oz. Coffee Liqueur

Combine ingredients over ice
and serve in a rocks glass.

Independence Day: Apple Pie

1 oz. Vodka
½ oz. Apple Schnapps
½ oz. Pineapple Juice
dash Powdered Cinnamon

Combine ingredients in a
shaker and serve straight up in
a shot glass.

Halloween: Bloody Brew

1½ oz. Sobieski Vodka
4 oz. Beer (your choice)
4 oz. Tomato Juice
dash Tabasco
Salt and Pepper

Combine ingredients in a
tall glass and garnish with a
Lemon Wedge or any of the
following: Pickle, Green Bean,
or Celery Spear.

Thanksgiving: Wild Thanksgiving

1 oz. Wild Turkey
1 oz. Apple Brandy
½ oz. Lime Juice
2 oz. Cranberry Juice

Combine over ice and garnish
with Mint.

Hanukkah: Israeli Sunrise

1½ oz. Sabra
1 oz. Vodka
2 tbsp. Softened Orange
    Sherbet

Combine Sabra and Vodka.
Stir into Softened Sherbet.
Serve in a rocks glass.

Christmas: Gingerbread Man

1½ oz. Vanilla-Flavored Vodka
4 oz. Ginger Beer

Pour Vodka over a couple of
ice cubes in a cocktail glass.
Add Ginger Beer, garnish with
a Cherry, and serve.

Chapter 20

Nonalcoholic Drinks

- -

In This Chapter

▶ Several recipes for nonalcoholic beverages

- -

A good number of your guests may choose not to drink alcohol, but this decision doesn't mean that they're stuck with boring soft drinks. Any of the following recipes are sure to impress.

Chocolate Banana Colada Shake

⅓ cup Coco Lopez Cream of Coconut
½ cup Milk
1 tbsp. Chocolate Syrup
1½ cups Chocolate or Vanilla Ice Cream
½ cup Sliced Banana

Mix in a blender until smooth. Serve immediately.

Chocolate Colada Shake

⅓ cup Coco Lopez Cream of Coconut
½ cup Milk
1 tbsp. Chocolate Syrup
1½ cups Chocolate or Vanilla Ice Cream

Mix in a blender until smooth. Serve immediately.

Clamato Cocktail

1 oz. Rose's Lime Juice
6 oz. Mott's Clamato Juice

Stir together in a highball glass filled with ice.

Coco Lopez Shake

2½ oz. Coco Lopez Cream of Coconut
1 scoop Vanilla Ice Cream
1 cup Ice

Mix in a blender until smooth.

Cranberry Collins

½ cup Ocean Spray Cranberry Juice Cocktail
½ tbsp. Lime Juice
1 cup Club Soda, chilled
Ice Cubes
Lime Slices

Mix Cranberry Juice Cocktail and Lime Juice. Stir in Club Soda. Add Ice Cubes and Lime Slices.

Dust Cutter

¾ oz. Rose's Lime Juice
6 oz. Schweppes Tonic Water

Combine over ice in a tall glass.

Fruit Bowl

1 oz. Orange Juice
1 oz. Pineapple Juice
1 oz. Grape Juice
1 oz. Grapefruit Juice

Shake with ice. Serve in a tall glass.

The Garnet

4 Sprigs Mint
2 oz. Pomegranate Juice
1 cube Frozen Orange Juice
6 oz. Perrier

Crush one Sprig of Mint in each of two rocks glasses. Add Pomegranate Juice and Orange Juice Cube. Top with Perrier and garnish with additional Sprig of Mint.

Grapefruit Cooler

8 oz. Grapefruit Juice
3 dashes Angostura Bitters

Pour Grapefruit Juice into a
tall glass filled with ice. Add
Bitters and stir.

Kona Coast

1 oz. Rose's Lime Juice
¼ oz. Rose's Grenadine
5 oz. Mott's Apple Juice
2 oz. Schweppes Ginger Ale

Stir together and serve over
ice in a tall glass.

Nada Colada

1 oz. Coco Lopez Cream of
Coconut
2 oz. Pineapple Juice
1 cup Ice

Mix in a blender until smooth.

New Orleans Day

2 oz. Coco Lopez Cream of
Coconut
1 oz. Butterscotch Topping
1 oz. Half & Half
1 cup Ice

Mix in a blender until smooth.

Orange Smoothie

2½ oz. Coco Lopez Cream of
Coconut
3 oz. Orange Juice
1 scoop Vanilla Ice Cream
1 cup Ice
Nutmeg

Mix first four ingredients in a
blender until smooth. Sprinkle
with Nutmeg.

Perrier Mimosa

⅓ cup Freshly Squeezed Orange
Juice, chilled
1½ cups Perrier, chilled
4 Raspberries or Grapes

Divide the Orange Juice
between two champagne
flutes and top with Perrier.
Garnish with two Raspberries
or Grapes in each glass.

Piña Colada Shake

½ cup Unsweetened Pineapple
Juice
⅓ cup Coco Lopez Cream of
Coconut
1½ cups Vanilla Ice Cream

Mix in a blender until smooth.
Serve immediately.

Red Racket

½ cup Ocean Spray Cranberry
Juice Cocktail, chilled
½ cup Ocean Spray Grapefruit
Juice, chilled
10 Ice Cubes

In a blender, combine
Cranberry and Grapefruit
Juice and Ice Cubes. Blend on
high speed till frothy. Pour
into a tall glass.

Ruby Cooler

1 cup Ocean Spray Cranapple
Drink
1 tsp. Instant Tea
Lemon Wedges

Mix together Cranapple Juice
and Tea. Pour over ice into
two tall glasses with Lemon
Wedge garnishes.

Shirley Temple

1 oz. Rose's Lime Juice
1 oz. Rose's Grenadine
6 oz. Schweppes Ginger Ale

Pour ingredients over ice in
a tall glass. Garnish with a
Cherry.

Virgin Mary

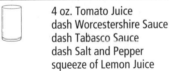

4 oz. Tomato Juice
dash Worcestershire Sauce
dash Tabasco Sauce
dash Salt and Pepper
squeeze of Lemon Juice

In a glass filled with ice, add
Tomato Juice. Add a dash or
two of Worcestershire Sauce,
Tabasco, Salt, Lemon Juice,
and Pepper. Garnish with a
celery stalk.

Part IV
The Part of Tens

The 5th Wave   By Rich Tennant

"Okay, we got one cherry lager with bitters and a pineapple slice, and one honey malt ale with cinnamon and an orange twist. You want these in steins or parfait glasses?"

In this part . . .

*I*n Chapter 21, I recommend ten drinks to try and ten drinks to decline if offered. Chapter 22 contains roughly ten cures for hiccups and hangovers.

Chapter 21

Ten Drinks to Try and Ten Drinks to Let Someone Else Try

* *

In This Chapter

▶ Fun cocktails you should imbibe

▶ Fun cocktails you may want to avoid

* *

This book is full of strange recipes. Some are strange and delightful; a few are strange and, honestly, awful. But cocktails get invented and catch on even though they offend the palates of most people. Maybe they have catchy names. Maybe they look neat when served. Who knows?

In this chapter, I give you a list of ten off-the-wall drinks that are worth sampling. I also offer you, for your own protection, a list of drinks that you may want to avoid unless you're really brave.

Crazy Cocktails You Really Ought to Try

Some of the following drinks look kind of gross when you make them. Some just don't sound right when you read the recipe. But I think you'll have an enjoyable experience giving any of these cocktails a try.

- **Anti-Freeze:** It's bright green, tastes like melon, and has a kick.

- **Between the Sheets:** I generally prefer cognac by itself, but this cocktail is an exception.

- **Cement Mixer:** Coagulation is cool.

- **Freddy Fudpucker:** You wouldn't think that tequila and Galliano really go together, but this one works.

- **Limp Moose:** Yes, you can mix Canadian whisky and Irish cream.

- **Meat & Potatoes:** You can't go wrong with a slice of salami.

- **Monkey See Monkey Do:** Fruity and creamy.

- **Pickleback:** Jameson and pickle juice? How can that be bad?

- **S.O.B.:** It looks nice in a martini glass.

- **Zipperhead:** Who doesn't like raspberry shots?

Cocktails That May Not Go Down So Easily

If someone places any of the following cocktails in front of you, I believe your response should be something like, "Please don't make me drink that!" But if you're out at a bar having fun and one of your friends says, "I want to try something different," then by all means suggest one of the following:

- **Gold Furnace:** Tabasco goes well in a Bloody Mary, but not in a shot of Goldschläger. This one must have been invented at a frat party.

- **Iguana:** This is one of those recipes where you have to assume that the person who invented it had three dusty bottles in his or her liquor cabinet and decided to mix all three to see what would happen.

- **Incredible Hulk:** Looks good? Yes. Tastes good? You can do better. How about a snifter of fine cognac all by itself instead?

- **Lizard Slime:** Melon and tequila? I'm not so sure.

✔ **Mind Eraser:** People generally order Mind Erasers so that they can drink them quickly through a straw in order to, well, get drunk quickly. Have a Black Russian instead and enjoy it by drinking slowly.

✔ **Neva:** Well, it's a good way to get your vitamin C.

✔ **Oil Slick:** Peppermint and bourbon? Let someone else be the guinea pig.

✔ **Scorpion:** There are better tropical cocktail options. Have a Hurricane or a Mai Tai.

✔ **Three Wise Men:** Three Wise Men isn't a cocktail recipe. When you order one at a bar, you'll be served a shot of Jim Beam, a shot of Jack Daniel's, and a shot of Johnnie Walker, and you're expected to shoot all three rather quickly. To say the least, that's not responsible drinking. Now if you have two pals and you're going to share the shots, that's a more reasonable proposition. And if you really enjoy these fine products, you may want to try sipping instead of shooting.

✔ **Wet Spot:** The name raises an eyebrow (ahem), but no part of me thinks that tequila and Irish cream go together.

Chapter 22

At Least Ten Cures and Lores

*P*art of being a bartender is settling arguments, mending broken hearts, and curing two primary medicinal problems: hiccups and hangovers.

Hiccups

The rapid closure of the vocal cords that follows the involuntary contraction of the diaphragm causes hiccups. (When you put it this way, hiccups don't seem nearly as embarrassing as most people consider them.) Here's a list of possible cures:

- ✔ Slice a lemon and remove the pits. Top the slices with sugar and Angostura bitters and eat the whole thing. This is the sure cure.

- ✔ Mix Angostura bitters and club soda and sip slowly.

- ✔ Drink a glass of water backward (from the opposite side of the glass). This can be a really wet cure!

- ✔ Hold your nose and breathe through your mouth. Then count to 10 or 20, or count to 100 to be certain.

- ✔ Blow into a paper bag.

Hangovers

Cause: Take a guess.

Cures: Only a few cures really work.

- ✔ A little prevention: Don't overindulge or let yourself be overserved. (Someone told me once that even in moderation, I am excessive.)
- ✔ Sleep. Drink plenty of fluids (water-based, not alcohol-based). Get some peace and quiet.

Consider a few more possible cures:

- ✔ Drink 2 ounces of Fernet-Branca or Branca Menta (Italian digestives) on the rocks.
- ✔ Drink one small bottle of Underberg (a German digestive).
- ✔ From my friends in Puerto Rico (Gere and Linda), rub half a lemon under each armpit!
- ✔ Drink a bottle of flat beer left out open overnight.
- ✔ Hair of the dog: one shot of whatever you were drinking!

Recipe Index

• *D* •

• *W–Z* •

Topics Index

• *T* •

Available wherever books are sold. For more information or to order direct: U.S. customers visit www.dummies.com or call 1-877-762-2974.
U.K. customers visit www.wileyeurope.com or call (0) 1243 843291. Canadian customers visit www.wiley.ca or call 1-800-567-4797.

Internet
Blogging For Dummies,
2nd Edition
978-0-470-23017-6

eBay For Dummies,
6th Edition
978-0-470-49741-8

Facebook For Dummies
978-0-470-26273-3

Google Blogger
For Dummies
978-0-470-40742-4

Web Marketing
For Dummies,
2nd Edition
978-0-470-37181-7

WordPress
For Dummies,
2nd Edition
978-0-470-40296-2

Language & Foreign Language
French For Dummies
978-0-7645-5193-2

Italian Phrases
For Dummies
978-0-7645-7203-6

Spanish For Dummies
978-0-7645-5194-9

Spanish For Dummies,
Audio Set
978-0-470-09585-0

Macintosh
Mac OS X Snow Leopard
For Dummies
978-0-470-43543-4

Math & Science
Algebra I For Dummies
978-0-7645-5325-7

Biology For Dummies
978-0-7645-5326-4

Calculus For Dummies
978-0-7645-2498-1

Chemistry For Dummies
978-0-7645-5430-8

Microsoft Office
Excel 2007 For Dummies
978-0-470-03737-9

Office 2007
All-in-One
Desk Reference
For Dummies
978-0-471-78279-7

Music
Guitar For Dummies,
2nd Edition
978-0-7645-9904-0

iPod & iTunes
For Dummies,
6th Edition
978-0-470-39062-7

Piano Exercises
For Dummies
978-0-470-38765-8

Parenting & Education
Parenting For Dummies,
2nd Edition
978-0-7645-5418-6

Type 1 Diabetes
For Dummies
978-0-470-17811-9

Pets
Cats For Dummies,
2nd Edition
978-0-7645-5275-5

Dog Training
For Dummies,
2nd Edition
978-0-7645-8418-3

Puppies For Dummies,
2nd Edition
978-0-470-03717-1

Religion & Inspiration
The Bible For Dummies
978-0-7645-5296-0

Catholicism
For Dummies
978-0-7645-5391-2

Women in the Bible
For Dummies
978-0-7645-8475-6

Self-Help & Relationship
Anger Management
For Dummies
978-0-470-03715-7

Overcoming Anxiety
For Dummies
978-0-7645-5447-6

Sports
Baseball For Dummies
3rd Edition
978-0-7645-7537-2

Basketball For
Dummies,
2nd Edition
978-0-7645-5248-9

Golf For Dummies,
3rd Edition
978-0-471-76871-5

Web Development
Web Design All-in-One
For Dummies
978-0-470-41796-6

Windows Vista
Windows Vista
For Dummies
978-0-471-75421-3

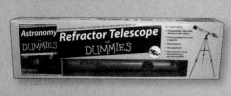

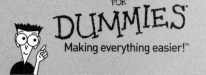